IN THE WORLD TODAY

3

IN THE WORLD TODAY

Essays by

Lloyd Geering

ALLEN & UNWIN/
PORT NICHOLSON PRESS

A&U
P N P

First published by Allen & Unwin/New Zealand Limited in association with the Port Nicholson Press, 60 Cambridge Terrace, Wellington, New Zealand

Allen & Unwin Australia Limited, NCR House, 8 Napier Street, North Sydney, NSW 2060, Australia

Unwin Hyman Limited, 15–17 Broadwick Street, Soho, London, England

Allen & Unwin Inc, 8 Winchester Place, Winchester, Mass. USA

© Lloyd Geering 1988

ISBN 0 86861 523 4

The first six essays in this book were originally published by the St Andrew's Trust for the Study of Religion and Society, Wellington.

Cover design by Lindsay Missen
Produced by SRM Production Services, Malaysia

Contents

Preface

The world is today engaged in a process of accelerating change. There have of course been many earlier periods when cultural change has speeded up but never before has it occurred on such a global scale. Before about 1800 civilisations and cultures of various orders existed in relative independence, clashing with or influencing one another only in confined areas. Today they are all caught up in a veritable maelstrom, where the traditional character of each is being increasingly undermined and reshaped by the consequences of the scientific and technological revolution so characteristic of the modern age.

Modernity consists of nothing less than a radical shift in human consciousness by which the perceived world in which we live has expanded into a vast space–time continuum. As a consequence we are prompted to understand it and respond to it in ways vastly different from those of our pre-modern ancestors. The dualistic universe, consisting of the tangible, visible, material and finite this-world and the intangible, invisible, spiritual and eternal other-world, is in the process of being replaced in human consciousness by a complex triple-ordered universe. In this the world of our daily life (which we might call the macro-world) is sandwiched between the micro-world of atoms and sub-atomic structures on the one hand and the mega-world of almost infinite celestial space. Our eyes cannot adequately see these other two worlds nor can our minds fully comprehend them.

The cultural traditions, value-systems and religious beliefs which constituted the identity of each of the pre-modern societies and which motivated people to live purposeful lives were all shaped to meet the needs of pre-modern conceptions of the world. Consequently they are all suffering erosion today in spite of desperate attempts to preserve them and even revive them. In countries shaped by Christian culture, for example, an ever-widening gap has been opening up between traditional Christian thinking and that which prevails in public life. The new human consciousness or view of reality which has been emerging with the advent of modernity increasingly permeates the public life of commerce, government, communication media etc. but it has been treated with suspicion, held at bay and even flatly rejected by institutional Christianity. In what now appears to be a post-Christian society, ·

the churches and their teaching have come to be regarded by many as irrelevant.

The transition to modernity has of course brought many benefits. These include not only the more obvious material benefits made possible by modern technology but also the social and spiritual benefits flowing from the succession of emancipations. Emancipation from dogma (supposedly divinely revealed) has brought people the freedom to think for themselves. Emancipation from hampering restrictions based on class, race, colour, religion and sex, are enabling people to make the best of the human potential they all share.

But the advent of modernity has not been all gain. Modern technology has also produced a whole lot of new problems, particularly in the biological sciences and in the field of nuclear energy. It is now possible for humans to control life on this planet and determine its fate in ways never previously even contemplated.

To solve the new problems we cannot simply turn to the value-systems of the past, partly because they were not shaped for present needs and partly because, as we have just noted, they are already suffering erosion. It is for this reason that many of those who welcomed the freedom from the religious dogmas and moral restraints of the past now recognise that if we cut ourselves off from our cultural roots we may throw out the baby with the bath-water.

Back in the eighteenth century when the dawn of the modern world was already being heralded in Western Europe, there were people who felt that if only they could strip away the cultural accumulations of the past they would arrive at a solid core of religious beliefs (natural religion) and moral precepts, which all humans would find self-evident. It has not proved that easy. Each living culture is more like an onion than a nut; if one keeps peeling away the outer skins to reach the core one finds oneself left with nothing. There is no kernel of self-evident beliefs and values which is culturally neutral. If we are to respond to the challenges of today's world and live purposefully for the good of all, we must go back to the culture which has shaped us and draw from it where we can without allowing ourselves to become enslaved by it.

It is this approach to human existence in the modern world which is to be regarded as the basis for the essays collected together in this book. They try to address a variety of current topics, problems and issues raised by science, technology and life in the modern secular world. Since references are made to the work of depth-psychologist Carl Jung, the book concludes with a sketch of the way his analytical psychology throws light on human self-understanding and growth to spiritual maturity. Jung, also, was concerned with breakdown of traditional religion and with the growing rift between it and the modern world. He made very fruitful suggestions as to how to resolve the crisis for faith being experienced in the modern world.

All of this material was originally delivered as public lectures and consequently retains the simple and (hopefully) lucid style most appropriate to the oral medium.

In 1984, on the initiative of the Revd John Murray, minister of St Andrews-on-the-Terrace, Wellington, there was established as an autonomous body the St Andrew's Trust for the Study of Religion and Society. The first five sections of this book were delivered as lunch-hour lectures under the auspices of this Trust. In a slightly different form they were subsequently broadcast by Radio New Zealand and they were published in independent booklets by the Trust.

The section on Jung originated as lectures delivered under the auspices of University Centres of Continuing Education, where they were accompanied by the screening of the BBC films 'The Story of Carl Gustav Jung' in which Laurens van der Post is the narrator. It is now nearly twenty years since I first began conducting one-day seminars on religious topics in University Centres of Continuing Education. Of the many I have now done that on Carl Jung has easily been the most popular. These lectures in one form or another have been delivered in Auckland, Hamilton, Wellington, Christchurch, Dunedin as well as some smaller centres, and in some places the programme has been repeated several times. The lectures appear for the first time in print.

Thus all the material was prepared with a broad cross-section of the New Zealand community in mind. While it draws upon the Christian roots of our cultural past, it is not concerned with expounding, let alone defending Christian orthodoxy. Hopefully it will be of interest to all who have a concern for our cultural and spiritual future, irrespective of whether readers see themselves currently as Christian, non-Christian, humanist, atheistic or agnostic.

Science, Religion and Technology

1. Science and Religion in Conflict

Our age is characterised, and even dominated, by science and technology. This is hardly open to dispute. The word 'scientific' has come to be associated with the highest authority universally recognised. A certain mystique has even come to be associated with the word. Advertisers on our television screens are making capital out of it almost every night. 'It has been scientifically proven,' they say, as they commend their product.

By contrast, the word 'religion' has been declining in the popularity stakes. Until a century or so ago, religion, and everything associated with it, was almost universally looked up to with honour and respect. Most people regarded themselves as religious believers. The rest felt some inward guilt that they were not. Today increasing numbers confess openly and casually, 'I am not a religious person'; 'I am not a Christian'; 'I don't believe in God'. According to a recent opinion poll in Britain, the number of people there professing belief in God has dropped from about 60 per cent to 40 per cent in only 20 years. Two hundred and fifty years ago there was hardly an atheist to be found in the whole of Europe.

Today no educational curriculum which excludes science would be regarded as adequate. Religion on the other hand, which formed the basis of Western education until 150 years ago, has been largely eliminated from the educational curriculum.

There is a significant correlation between the rise of science and the decline of religion. By the end of the nineteenth century some observers were openly interpreting this correlation as the transition from the age of religion to the age of science. For example, James Frazer, who amassed the myths and folklore of so many peoples in his famous *The Golden Bough*, concluded that human culture had progressed through three successive stages. First there was the age of magic, then the age of religion and finally the age of science.

The conflict between religion and science reached its most heated stage of debate in the latter part of the nineteenth century. We live in its aftermath. There is, of course, more than a grain of truth in the widespread belief that science has superseded religion. But if that were totally true, then religion of all kinds should be progressively disappearing, in much the same way as Karl Marx prophesied it would. This in fact is not the case. Both in the Christian and the Islamic worlds (to name but two) there is today a resurgence even of the more traditional forms. But more importantly than that, there is springing up today a bewildering myriad of new forms of religion. Many of these no longer conform to the popular stereotype of what religion ought to be. This is partly because they actually came to birth in the new age of science. Even many people who say they are not religious are often trying quite desperately to find some practical philosophy or faith to fill the vacuum left behind by the erosion of traditional religion.

Before we begin exploring the changing relationship between religious faith on the one hand and science and technology on the other, it is necessary to clarify the two basic terms — 'religion' and 'science'. When I refer to 'religion' here I shall be using it in its more popular sense to mean all that has been associated with Christianity in belief and practice in the past. But it must be remembered that traditional Christianity is only *one particular* form of religion. Religion has taken many diverse forms in the past and is today taking new forms which have never been known before. This diversity calls for a broader definition. In this broader sense, religion has to do with finding a life style and a belief system which is personally and ultimately fulfilling.

Science, by its derivation, simply means 'knowledge'. In the days when theology proudly called itself the queen of the sciences, it did so because the knowledge of God studied in theology was, by definition, the highest form of knowledge possible. But when we use the word 'science' in the modern world we are referring to a special kind of knowledge. It is knowledge arrived at by a particular method — the scientific method. In this the phenomena being studied are carefully observed and their connections noted. Traditional explanations are temporarily suspended. New theories to account for the phenomena are then tested. Modern science is thus more properly called empirical science.

There are more ways than one, however, of understanding the word 'knowledge'. By no means all that we speak of as human knowledge is open to the testing methods of empirical science. Before the rise of empirical science the need to distinguish between different kinds of knowledge had not become apparent. It seemed self-evident that knowledge was knowledge was knowledge! The Bible, for example, does not attempt to draw any distinction between knowledge of God and of spiritual truth, on the one hand, and knowledge of human history, of human origins, of the world, on the other.

Moreover all this knowledge had been part of the inherited tradition for so long in the Western world that there was little reason for anyone to question it. It actually says a great deal for the quality of the Hebrew account of world origins that people found it utterly convincing for more than 2500 years. During that time the Bible had come to be accorded an authority given to no other known book in the Christian world. It was not thought to have been written by human beings in the way other books were. Its writers had been inspired by God in such a way that what they wrote was divinely revealed. Because the Bible was thought to rest on the foundation of divine revelation, the knowledge it contained was eternal and absolute. Nothing would ever be able to overturn it.

With the gift of hindsight we can now say that the church's dependence on a supposed source of divine revelation made it very vulnerable to the rise of empirical science. But in the days when modern science first began to surface it did not seem that way at all. Possession of the Bible made the church so confident of its position that it could welcome the developing sciences in the seventeenth and eighteenth centuries. It expected them simply to provide further evidence of biblical truth. When the Royal Society was founded it included many clergy. Theologians and scientists saw each other as allies.

The rift between science and religion did not really occur until the nineteenth century. It came about not so much because of a conflict between the divinely revealed knowledge and the new empirical knowledge (though that was a factor) but because of another change taking place, both more subtle and more radical. We may call it a change in human consciousness. It may be alternatively described as a fundamental shift in world-view between the medieval mind and the modern mind. This change has been taking place over 400 years.

This change of consciousness involved three revolutions in thought, each of which is scientifically based. They have been called Copernican revolutions, after the name of the man who sparked off the first one.

We may call the first one the revolution in cosmology. It concerns the way in which we conceive and understand the cosmos or total universe. We often associate the change with Galileo more than Copernicus and in his case two things become clear:

(i) Galileo provides the very first good example of what it means to be a scientist. His theories were being tested by the new instrument of his day, the telescope. The sight of the mountains on the moon impressed him greatly and added strength to his convictions about the nature of the heavenly bodies and the centrality of the sun, rather than of the earth, for the planetary movements.

(ii) It led to a confrontation with religious authority — the irony of the situation was that the conflict was not so much that his views were in contradiction of the Bible as they were a rejection of the ancient science of Aristotle, which had become part of the world-view of the Christian medievalist.

This revolution in the mental picture of the cosmos has proved much more radical than at first appeared. Most people, even today, do not realise how far-reaching that shift in consciousness has been. It is not just that we now all know that the earth revolves round the sun and that the earth is not even the centre of the solar system, let alone of the universe. It is this. The work of Galileo, followed quickly by that of Newton and Kepler, had the effect of adding a new dimension to the tangible, visible world in which we humans see ourselves living.

Up until this time people saw their known tangible world as basically two-dimensional. The human world was a relatively small area of flat earth. When they looked up to the sky, it was not recognised as part of *their* material physical world. It was *God's* world in contrast with the earth. The sky and heaven were synonyms. 'In the beginning God created the heavens and the earth'. The heavens were God's dwelling place. The hosts of stars they saw at night served as clear proof of the reality of the divine domain. It is just as if they observed, from afar, the lights of the eternal city. Up there was to be found their own ultimate dwelling-place. The cosmological revolution brought the heavens into *man's* world. The world of mankind ceased to be two-dimensional and became three-dimensional. It introduced what we now call the space-age. In doing so, it had the long-term effect of dispossessing God of that spacial heavenly realm once thought to be uniquely his. Newton and Kepler, followed later by the much more advanced astrophysics, showed that the so-called heavenly bodies operate according to the same kind of natural laws as the physical earth.

Previously when special imagery was applied to God it could be understood at face value. God did actually seem to live above the earth. But if such spacial imagery is used today, it has to be recognised as metaphorical. The cosmological revolution had rendered the medieval view of the created universe obsolete.

We moderns of the Western world have all become adjusted to the first Copernican revolution. We may not have recognised all its implications, but, in so far as we have absorbed it into our consciousness, we are already one giant step removed from our ancient and medieval forbears, including the people who wrote the Bible.

The second Copernican revolution is only about 150 years old. It is associated with the name of Darwin. The theory of evolution, greatly refined and modified since his day, is still debated among Christians. It conflicted, much more blatantly than the first Copernican revolution, with the supposedly revealed knowledge contained in the Bible. Of course science itself is on somewhat less certain ground here, because evolution is not something which is readily open to demonstration by experiment. For that reason those who want to adhere to biblical teaching often feel free to dismiss evolution by saying, 'It is only a theory!'

In this second revolution we are again dealing not so much with a conflict between scientific knowledge and divine revelation as with a radical shift of consciousness. To appreciate this we must turn not so much to zoology as to the new science of geology, which provided the necessary data to make the theory of biological evolution a viable possibility. So long as we think in terms of an earth age of the order of 6000 years, biological evolution is impossible to contemplate as a theory of origins.

Geology, however, has assembled convincing evidence that the age of Planet Earth is much more in the order of four to five billion years. Geological time has had the effect of multiplying our previous concept of time by the factor of a million. Of course it is easy to speak of a billion years (and since the rise of geology we have learned to speak in terms of millions of light years) but it is much more difficult for us humans, who have personal experience only of a human life time, to absorb the significance of geological time. It is partly due to this difficulty that the second Copernican revolution has not yet been universally accepted. As we do gradually absorb it, however, it has the effect of adding to our consciousness of reality a still further dimension to our three-dimensional world. It is the dimension of cosmic time.

The originating cosmological revolution, continuing in the science of astrophysics, has added further convincing proof of the second Copernican revolution. We look up at the stars at night, and we actually look back into time, not just by years but by millions of years. What we see in the night sky is not how this great space universe is at *this* moment but how it was at the time when the light left each distant body on its long journey to us. If there is anything which completely prevents us from taking the opening chapter of Genesis at face value, it is astrophysics even more than the theory of evolution. The more one puts together the reasonably assured data of the relevant sciences, the more we are led into a radically different view of the universe—a new cosmic consciousness.

The implications of this second Copernican revolution are just as far-reaching as those of the first. Let me mention only one. As the first Copernican revolution displaced the earth from being the centre of the universe, the second displaced the human species from being the central key to life on this planet. Human beings have existed on this planet for not much more than about 100,000 years, and in a civilised state, for a great deal less. But *life* has existed on this planet for about 3500 million years. The dinosaurs and other giant reptiles roamed this earth for 200 million of them. This raises alarming questions about the traditional view of God. If God created the planet for mankind (as the Bible everywhere implies) why have we arrived so late on the scene? Why were we preceded by so many species now extinct?

This second revolution caused many to feel they were on the horns of a dilemma. Either the religious tradition was true or else science, but not both. Many have rejected science, at least in part, to remain faithfully committed to the Christian tradition. Many others have felt the compelling evidence of science and abandoned commitment to religion. This second revolution, much more than the first, has left an unresolved rift between the way of science and the way of religion.

The third Copernican revolution concerns the inner workings of the human mind. Here we come to one of the frontiers of science where even the scientific world is very much in the process of exploration and is yet by no means unanimous in all its conclusions. Sufficient progress has been made, however, in the new human sciences, and in psychology in particular, for them already to have become a permanent part of the new consciousness of the human condition. Yet the significance of this revolution for the traditional interpretation of religious experience has hardly yet begun to be realised.

In a book little known in New Zealand called *The End of Conventional Christianity*, a Dutch Roman Catholic scholar said, 'The consequences and implications of modern psychology have not yet reached the general public and have yet to cause a shock in the circles of conventional Christianity.' It will be a greater challenge to traditional Christianity than even the first two revolutions. Modern psychology, which literally means the 'study of the soul', has largely outdated what traditional religion affirmed about the human soul and, as a consequence, the way in which the soul was believed to be influenced by divine power or spirit.

There are two main ways in which this has come about. The first is that the sciences of psychology and neurology have largely rendered untenable the dualistic view of the human condition — a spiritual soul dwelling for the time being in a physical body. The sciences which study the human condition all point to the fact that each human being is a unified psychosomatic organism. We may call a person either a body or a soul depending on which aspect of the human organism we happen to be thinking of. Thought and spirituality are not entities but dimensions of human existence.

Secondly, depth psychology, though it still has a long way to go, has already shown conclusively that there is a great deal more content and activity within the human psyche than ever comes to the surface consciously. This has very far-reaching implications for what used to be called 'religious experience'. When people heard voices which no-one else heard, saw visions which no-one else saw, found themselves speaking with a voice and in a language not normally their own, the obvious explanation used to be that they were under the influence of spiritual power from an external unseen world. Now a quite different and natural interpretation is possible. At such times it is the forces of our own psychic unconscious which are invading our consciousness and motivating our behaviour.

I have sketched briefly the three Copernican revolutions which have brought into being what we may call the *'modern mind'*, *'modern consciousness'*. Because they have been challenging, with increasing success, the traditional mind, associated with traditional religion, it is not at all surprising that religion, and science had come into open conflict on several fronts by the end of the nineteenth century. They had been clearly set on a collision course for some time.

There is a time lag, however, before the reality of the conflict slowly penetrates all levels of a society and before the consequences of such revolutions in thought are completely recognised. In popular thought this conflict is more widely recognised today than it was a century ago and may well be one of the factors in the recent accelerated decline in church allegiance. And let us be under no illusions about the reality of the conflict between traditional religion and the modern consciousness, itself the fruit of the scientific age.

A great deal which is still being affirmed and proclaimed by preachers and religious teachers is quite inconsistent with the new consciousness. It has been rendered outmoded and anachronistic. It will not bear close examination under the bright lights provided for us by the sciences. There is no future for teaching what can be so readily countered, dismissed and proved to be false.

If the matter were as simple as this, however, we could agree with Sir James Frazer and shout, 'The Age of Religion is dead. Long live the Age of Science'. But though traditional religion, at many vital points, has been shown by science to be vulnerable, it does not mean that science is equipped to ascend the vacant throne. At the end of last century there were a few scientists who claimed that science held the key to the world's future, that science could be hailed, in effect, as the world's new saviour. But no good scientist claims that today. Indeed in the academic world today there is no longer any obvious and open conflict between religion and science. This is partly because scientists and theologians have both become considerably more humble and are openly acknowledging the limits within which they work. But the fact that there is less awareness of conflict today, does not mean that there can be any return to the pre-scientific age. Certain traditional forms of religion have become outmoded for all time. The only viable forms are those which take fully into account the fact that we have entered the age of science.

2. The Constraints of Science

The conflict between religion and science is not felt so sharply in academic circles today as it was at the turn of the century. One reason for this is actually misleading and could have serious consequences. Many in the scientific world have simply ceased to give any serious attention to the traditional world of religion. The debate has ceased because they view religion only as outmoded superstition. On the other hand, many in the religious world simply shut their eyes to the implications of scientific knowledge. They confine their life and thoughts to a somewhat narrow horizon of interest, within which they feel secure. This ostrich-like obscurantism is unfortunately all too common. It may temporarily give spiritual and mental relief but there is no future in it.

The division of conscious interest and activity into two mutually exclusive compartments of science and religion is not confined to society at large. It may occur *within* a person. Then such persons are forced to live a kind of schizophrenic existence, finding spiritual comfort in the religious world at certain times and for certain purposes, and earning their living in the technological world at other times, but never allowing the two to meet.

It is much healthier, both for the individual and for society, when the conflict between science and religion is brought out in the open. This, among other things, is what I am attempting to do briefly here.

There is another reason, however, why the tension between religion and science is not so frequently discussed in the public arena today as it was at the turn of the century. Scientists and religious thinkers are no longer so inclined to make the dogmatic assertions their respective forebears were making in the late nineteenth century. It is not too much to say that in the worlds of both science and religion quite revolutionary changes in thought have been taking place.

Let me, for a moment, discuss a little further the very character of science. As I have already indicated, it is a special kind of knowledge. There are two reasons why we find it cogent. The first is that science is never content to rest on past tradition or any other external authority. The scientific enterprise starts by casting doubt on all traditional knowledge and claims which are not self-evidently true. This includes scientific hypotheses themselves. The good scientist is not trying to prove his theories to be true. He is trying to falsify them. This capacity for doubt has proved one of the greatest assets of science. It prevents one from putting trust where it should not be put. In this respect science has arrived at its body of knowledge by a method diametrically opposed to all dogmatic forms of religion. These latter have made constant appeal to external authority. Scientific knowledge, on the other hand, should not be accepted unless (at least theoretically) one can be convinced of its truth for oneself. Although in practice we tend to accept a great deal, simply on the authority of the scientist, yet the latter should be always saying to us, 'Don't accept these conclusions on *my* authority. Test them for yourself!'

The second important aspect of science follows from this. Scientific theories which have withstood continued testing constitute a body of reliable knowledge. And this is *public* knowledge, accessible to all. Scientific experiments and demonstrations, if true, will yield the same results no matter who performs them. It does not matter whether the scientist is a Christian or an atheist, a Russian or an American; the results should always be the same. If not, it is not a scientific conclusion. It is because of the public and universal character of the body of scientific knowledge that we humans have become dependent on the ongoing pursuit of science, whether we like it or not. We are not in a position to lightly dismiss or ignore publicly attested scientific findings, unless we can falsify them to our complete satisfaction.

It is largely these two aspects of the scientific enterprise which have quite rightly caused people to have such confidence in it. Because of this confidence there has been a tendency for some people simply to transfer an allegiance of blind trust, from the Bible or the Church, to the scientist. This is dangerous. The scientist is no more infallible than the Pope or the Bible. Every scientist is fallible and may err. All scientific theories and findings remain open to review and revision. None are final. It is not any particular scientist or scientific conclusion upon which we have become dependent, but rather the method and character of the scientific pursuit. Science is an ongoing pursuit. Its results can never be taken to be *absolute*. But they *can* be taken to represent, at any one time, the most reliable knowledge available to us at that moment.

This body of reasonably assured knowledge transcends all our human divisions of race, nationality, religion and ideology. Modern science, though it emerged in Western Europe, has transcended the particularities of its own cultural origin and become universal. That is its great strength. That is the reason why, for our knowledge of the natural physical world (including all planetary forms of life), we have become dependent upon it. Science is today pursued by an international fellowship of scientists in each particular field of expertise. No good scientist is willing to modify his conclusions simply to conform to any political ideology any more than to a dogmatic religion said to be divinely revealed. The conviction that divine revelation is an adequate channel for knowledge of the natural world has been rendered untenable by science.

As the sciences have taken root in the programmes of universal education all around the world they have become the common core, the most universal component in the curriculum. The languages, literature, and cultural interests studied vary from place to place. The sciences are universal.

A few years ago, on a visit to Iran, I came across some students studying for their examinations. They had found a quiet corner in one of the large mosques. They showed me their textbooks. They were written Farsi, but I could recognise, because of the symbols and diagrams, it was the same mathematics and physics that are being taught everywhere else.

Moreover, in many non-Christian cultures, the modern sciences have been accepted more readily and with less conflict than they were in Christian Europe, the home of their origin. Muslim thinkers, for example, have asserted that Islam has always encouraged the scientific understanding of the natural world and they point back with pride to the Early Middle Ages when Muslim scholars led the world in their knowledge of the natural world. In today's resurgence of Islam there is no rejection of the sciences and technology. These they have been glad to borrow from the West. They reject only the cultural dress which has sometimes accompanied the introduction of the Western sciences.

In a parallel but different way some Buddhist teachers have been proclaiming that empirical science does not raise for Buddhism the same kind of problems it raises for Christian orthodoxy. A Buddhist scholar, Professor K. N. Jayatilleke writes, 'One of the great attractions of the early Buddhist theory of the nature of man and his destiny in the universe is that, long before the advent of modern science, it presented a picture of man and the universe which is consistent with basic findings of science and it encouraged an outlook, even with regard to matters moral and religious, which closely approximates what we today call the "scientific outlook".'

In particular Buddhists point out that the last words of the Buddha were: 'Work out your own salvation with diligence.' In other words, although he had, as he believed, found the way to enlightenment, he did not ask his followers to accept it on his authority. They were invited to test it for themselves and come to their own first-hand conclusions. And that, as we have seen, is the key to the universal appeal of modern empirical science.

As pointed out earlier, the entry of the human race into the age of science has been marked, not so much by the discovery of new knowledge about the natural world, as by the new dimension to human consciousness which it has brought about. One aspect of this is the spread of autonomy. The scientific method encourages us to think for ourselves, to carry out our own investigations, and not to rest content until we reach what we find inherently self-convincing.

As an example of the universal character of this change of consciousness we should note that even conservative Christians who are trying to defend traditional views which have been undermined by science, very often appeal to scientific criteria to support their case. Anti-evolutionists, for example, have established an institute which exists for the express purpose of trying to demonstrate by scientific means that the earth was created in basically its present form and that all the known species of life were created as such and did not evolve. It is very evident from the outside that these people are already convinced by the infallible authority of the Bible and are therefore not genuine scientists at all. Nevertheless they are unconsciously acknowledging that in today's world supposed divine authority on such matters must take second place to the way of science.

A similar example is found in the modern appeal to historical evidence as a defence of the truth of traditional Christianity. (Strictly speaking history is not a pure science like physics and geology, but its methods for establishing reliable knowledge of the past are scientific in the general sense of that term.)

It is very noticeable that, when Christian orthodoxy came increasingly to be threatened in the nineteenth century, its new line of defence was to use the Bible, no longer simply as the divine word of God, but as a source of supposedly reliable historical evidence. Take the resurrection of Jesus from the dead, for example. This received relatively little attention during the Middle Ages. Indeed the crucifix, the figure of Jesus hanging on the cross, was the dominant symbol. Even at the Reformation this did not change. In John Calvin's 1800-page *Institutes of the Christian Religion* we find less than one page devoted to the resurrection of Jesus. But since the middle of the last century, whole books have been devoted to it, for defenders of Christianity saw it now as one of the firm foundations of the faith, for which they believed they possessed convincing historical evidence.

In such ways, whether we are conservative Christians, radical Christians, Muslims, Buddhists, humanists or agnostics, we are all being shaped by the age of science we have entered. To a greater or lesser extent, whether we are aware of it or not, science has become an important component of our universal human consciousness.

Those who find its conclusions unpalatable may choose to shut their eyes to it and temporarily withdraw into a small ghetto world of their own. But, for the human race as a whole, there can be no return to the pre-scientific world. If we choose to live in the real world of all humanity, we are forced to acknowledge the value of the scientific method and the cogency of its more important conclusions. Let us now look at some of them.

First of all, science has provided for us a new mental image of the universe. We see the universe in a radically different way from our ancestors. Our mental apprehension of it is different. We may still see and even speak of the sun rising and setting. But when we think about it we hold in our minds a mental picture of what the solar system would look like if we could view it from the nearest star.

But perhaps the way in which science has changed our mental view of the universe most drastically is that it has stretched out the known horizons of the universe to almost infinite dimensions both in space and in time. As pointed out earlier, the effect of this was to swallow up the dimensions of time and space which previously were felt to belong exclusively to the divine or spiritual world.

The great difference between the scientific picture of the vast space–time universe and the relatively tiny human world conceived by the pre-modern human mind strikes home as soon as we read a few well-known biblical passages. They reflect a very different world-view, one in which the tangible, visible world is very small by comparison with today's view of a universe of mind-boggling dimensions, and one which the divine creator views from the outside.

If we are still going to speak of God in association with today's view of the cosmos, then the reality of God must be conceived *within* the universe. The universe no longer possesses any kind of outside, either spacially or temporally. This is why, as the new view of the cosmos began to emerge, new ways of conceiving God began to evolve with it. It started with the Jewish philosopher Spinoza, usually regarded as the father of pantheism. This is the view that God is in everything and everything is in God.

There is another reason why the advance of science threatened and eventually undermined the traditional concept of God. Empirical science has thrown new light on how the changing phenomena of the physical universe constitute an exceedingly involved complex of 'cause and effect' inter-relatedness. Whereas in the pre-modern world the only satisfactory explanation was to postulate that all cosmic movement and life did what it did because it was controlled behind the scenes by a personal mind of divine proportions, it slowly became unnecessary to make such a postulation. When Napoleon asked Laplace where, in his model of the planetary system, he found a place for God, he replied, 'Sir, I have no need of that hypothesis.' For a time there were still other places where people felt such a need, and the view of God as the solution of unsolved problems became known as the 'God of the gaps'.

But this was no answer. It is not as if the gaps have at last all closed. If anything, it has been the other way. Scientists often discover a satisfactory explanation as to why things are as they are, only to find in our ever-expanding view of the universe, that new problems have appeared which were earlier quite unknown. But, although there is just as much as ever in this vast universe awaiting a satisfactory explanation, the credibility of attempting to explain it all in terms of an infinite divine mind has diminished more and more. In two centuries, modern science has caused a still accelerating decline in the cogency of postulating an objective spiritual reality called God. It has undermined what was taken to be the self-evident nature of an independent spiritual world and of the ontological character of the human soul or spirit.

As the decline of belief in a spiritual world (including spiritual beings whether divine or human) came about, it was first assumed that what was left as solid reality was the physical universe. Thus, the dualistic world-view of pre-modern mankind, consisting of a spiritual and a material world, was replaced simply by the remaining physical world. This was the dominant view in the late nineteenth and early twentieth centuries. Philosophically we call it materialism. The physical world served to provide the solid basis of reality. Then the splitting of the atom changed all that. The word 'atom' means the smallest bit of material substance which cannot be divided further. It *has* been divided further, revealing a strange new microcosmic world. Although we speak of the elements of the sub-atomic reality as particles, they are no longer 'bits' at all. So what we have learned is that even the most solid-looking material substance is composed mostly of empty space.

Whether we call the simplest and most basic stuff of the universe energy or something else is of no great moment. What's in a name? The fact is that, though we can in part track down and measure the basic stuff of the universe, it also eludes us. The investigation of sub-atomic nuclear energy has meant that the materialistic, mechanical world-view of Sir Isaac Newton has become almost as outmoded as the medieval world-view which it replaced. Instead of a dualistic world we have in its place not just a material world but a cosmos which at heart is neither wholly physical nor wholly spiritual but somewhere in between.

Conservative Christians have been inclined to rejoice at the overthrow by scientists of the mechanical, materialist world-view of Newton. But it does not mean at all that we can return to the world in which the traditional Christian once felt at home. Like the lone traveller in *2001: A Space Odyssey*, we are speeding through a cosmos whose basic reality is as strange and mysterious to us as ever. There are no certainties, no solid ground, no known facts which will be true for all time.

So far I have sometimes coupled the terms science and technology together, but it is useful to make a clear distinction between them. Science tries to learn the how and the what about everything which can be empirically observed. Science is the pursuit of true knowledge of the tangible world. It has changed our views out of recognition and we have come to depend on it. Technology is the practical application of that knowledge to whatever use we may find for it. We can go a long way in technology even when our knowledge is partial and incomplete. When our ancient human ancestors found how they could make and harness the mysterious phenomenon of fire they were taking early steps in technology. Human technology has been very slowly evolving over thousands of years. Now and again there has been a significant leap forward, as with the invention of the wheel.

The advent of modern science, however, has greatly accelerated technological development, so much so, that today a new invention has sometimes become outmoded a year later. First, there was the harnessing of steam, then electricity, then radio and electronics. Now, the silicon chip and the computer. Before the end of the century something as equally epoch-making will most probably appear. In medical science, rapid technological advance has led to such things as heart transplants and *in vitro* fertilisation. Examples of modern technological advance surround us at every turn.

In modern life we have come to depend on technology. The power loom and improved methods of agriculture enabled Europe to clothe and feed more people. The population rapidly expanded. Coupled with that technology, medical science greatly extended the average length of life. Life styles changed, economics changed. Less and less of the community's time was taken up with simply keeping ourselves fed, clothed and housed. Technology made it possible. Now we have become dependent on that technology, if we and our descendants are to be kept in the manner of life to which we have become accustomed.

But modern technology has been a mixed blessing. With the spread of industrialisation came also the 'dark satanic mills', the ravished forests, the polluted streams, the greedy and thoughtless exploitation of the earth's non-renewable resources. More recently we have become aware that we are not only polluting our planetary home, we are upsetting the delicate balance of planetary ecology, upon which each form of life depends for its survival. We have not only already caused the extinction of many living species, and endangered others. We are even endangering our own species by the very technology devised to improve life and defend it. The most alarming example of this is the amassing of stockpiles of nuclear missiles. These have, as their sole purpose, destruction on a grand scale. Already destruction has been caused by technology designed for good and useful purposes, simply because we did not fully understand all the consequences of what we were doing. How much greater is the disaster from such nuclear warheads because of our blind and inadequate thinking? We have reached the point where our technological cleverness may rebound upon us with unthinkable results. We have become dependent on technology and yet it may destroy us. That is our dilemma.

What has gone wrong? It is true that it was science which made modern technology possible. Science has opened doors to knowledge previously hidden from mankind. That knowledge in itself is neither good nor bad, but what we do with that knowledge is another matter. Sometimes we may fervently wish that we had never split the atom and found out what was inside. But Pandora's box, once opened, can never be closed. Yet there is nothing wrong in possessing the knowledge. The problem is that it greatly increases the responsibility we must shoulder, responsibility which we may not yet be spiritually mature enough to bear. The questions of good and evil arise not from the scientific knowledge itself, but from the use to which we put it by our technological devices.

This is the point of the biblical story of Adam and Eve and of the tree of the knowledge of good and evil. The myth of the Garden of Eden has peculiar relevance to the technological age for it describes the dire consequences which follow for those who do not show trustworthy responsibility. Our technological cleverness has evidently outstripped our wisdom. Firstly, we have mostly failed to discern the good from the evil use of knowledge, and secondly, where we have discerned the difference, we lack the courage, purity of intention and moral responsibility to choose the good.

Is it possible, in spite of all the benefits which science and technology have provided for us that in the end they may fail us? Yes, it is possible! Yet in no way must we undervalue their importance. For our knowledge of the world we live within the constraints imposed by empirical science, and for our material standard of living we are dependent upon technology.

A wise man once wrote, 'Mankind does not live by bread alone; mankind lives by everything that proceeds out of the mouth of the Lord.' In this post-traditional and scientific age, we may paraphrase that to read, 'Today we are dependent for life on science and technology, just as much as man has always been dependent on bread. But mankind cannot live by science and technology alone, for these do not of themselves supply insight, wisdom and spirituality. These latter are even more essential for the life and preservation of the human spirit, both in our day and for the generations, as yet unborn, who have the cosmic right to succeed us.'

3. *Where Science Fails Us*

We have come to depend on science and technology. There can be no return to the pre-scientific age. An irreversible threshold has been passed over. But this does not mean that science can simply usurp the place once occupied by religion, just because it (i) has been so successful and (ii) has undermined a great deal of what formerly served as religion. As some people see it, this is exactly what has happened. In their case traditional religion has simply been replaced by a new form of religion, which is often called 'scientism'. This is the belief that science can provide answers to all of our hopes and problems and be the new saviour of human-kind. But scientism is a false religion, at best only pseudo-religious.

Let us look, for a moment, at the nature and purpose of religion. The traditional form of Christianity (which science has done so much to undermine) is only one *form* of religion, and is not to be identified with religion as a whole.

No understanding or definition of religion is adequate which applies to only one of its forms. We must look for a definition which is equally applicable to all the known forms in the past and to whatever new forms may be emerging in the present. This is no easy task. It has become one of the notorious problems in the modern study of religion to find such a definition. Let me give two or three. Paul Tillich described religion quite simply as: 'the state of being grasped by an ultimate concern'. An Italian historian of religion defined it as: 'a total mode of the living and inter-preting of life'. In order to spell out such simple statements with a little more content let me offer this. Religion consists of the system of meaning, the code of values, and the styles of life by which a person responds in faith to the ultimate issues encounter-ed in human existence.

Notice that in these definitions there is no reference to God, miracles, prayer, the supernatural and so on. It is for the simple reason that already in human history there have been recognisable religions in which these concepts have played little or no role. We should also notice that in these definitions there is no reference to knowledge (revealed or otherwise) of the universe, of the natural world. But knowledge of the natural world is exactly what forms the content of empirical science. It is too extreme to say that religion is not at all concerned with knowledge of the natural world, but it is true to say that this is not the primary concern of religion. What has just been outlined as constituting the substance of religion can only become a reality when it takes root, and becomes the motivating force, within what is taken to be knowledge in a particular culture or human society.

In the case of traditional Christianity, for example, what we may call the Christian system of meaning, code of values and style of living took root among people around the Mediterranean. It became integrated with what was at the time the current state of their knowledge of the natural world. In the light of what we know today that knowledge was extremely limited and often quite false and it did affect the way they appropriated and interpreted the meanings and values which lie at the heart of Christianity. But it did not supply those values and meanings. What science has done is to undermine the pre-scientific understanding of the natural world which constituted one component in traditional Christianity.

Now it is one thing for science to have shown to be false or inadequate the knowledge of the world which our Christian forebears believed to be true, and which is deeply embedded in the Bible. It is quite another to expect that same science, having convinced us in one area, to provide what traditional religion gave us in another area — its most essential area — a system of meaning, a code of values, and a style of living which brings a sense of fulfilment.

The contrast between science and religion, properly understood, can be set forth in this quite simple way. The role of science is to help us answer the 'how' and the 'what' in connection with the world and its phenomena. What is lighting? What is magnetism? What is gravity? How does water turn into ice or into water vapour? How does the human body work? Science helps us to understand the inter-relatedness of the empirical universe, how one thing is related to another.

By contrast, it is the role of religion to help us answer the 'why' of everything which is found to exist. For what purpose does it exist? Why do we exist? What is the meaning of life? Why is there good and evil? All of these questions focus in some way or other on human existence. Religion has to do with human goals for living, with the values and styles of behaviour by which those goals will best be reached.

Science is particularly well equipped, because of its empirical method, to deal with the questions of 'what' and 'how'. But in order to continue to be successful, science must remain as objective as is humanly possible. It must try to keep the scientist's own presuppositions out of the picture. Science, theoretically, must try to remain value-free. Consequently the scientific method cannot answer questions of value, of ultimate purpose and meaning.

Science *does not* and *cannot* provide us with a value system.

We may sharpen the contrast between science and religion even more. The scientist, in his objectivity, is studying something other than himself. In religion the personal subject is central. Religion must always be subjective. One simple way of showing this is to say that religion is concerned with certain basic questions: Who am I? Where have I come from? What am I here for? Where am I going? What does it mean for me to exist as a human being? How can I best achieve my human potential?

These questions cannot be answered by science. They are not even the kind of questions that science asks. Of course, a particular scientist might ask them and even offer answers. But when he does so, we should carefully note that he has taken off his scientist's hat and speaks as a human being. The fact that the scientist is also always a human person, encountering the universal human issues, is a fact all too readily forgotten. Only some people become professional scientists but all people, by virtue of the humanity they share, ask, however superficially, the basic religious questions. That is why religion, when defined more broadly as I have done, is universal to mankind.

Indeed, as philosopher Ludwig Feuerbach pointed out last century, religion is the essential difference between human beings and all other animals. Only human beings have the capacity to reflect on the nature of their own existence and to ask the basic religious questions. It is common to speak of these questions today as existential questions for they arise out of our awareness of our existence and the recognition that in this existence we have choices to make. These choices largely determine our destiny in life, the kind of persons we become and the degree to which we find life fulfilling.

It is this personal or subjective component, so central to religion, which takes it outside of the scope of scientific enquiry. It may be illustrated by the fact that science has been most successful in those areas of study where it can be most objective — the so-called pure sciences such as physics, chemistry, astronomy, geology and so on. When we come to the so-called human sciences, it has been a different matter. In sociology, psychology, anthropology, political science, economics, it has been a different story. Conclusions have always been more vague and predictions less certain. The reason is that the human being is never wholly predictable. In spite of this handicap the human sciences have been very helpful, but they will always lack the exactness and certainty of the pure sciences. The subjective component in the human condition defies objective enquiry in any final way.

We should note in passing that religious questions are not the only human interests which lie outside scientific enquiry. All the human arts and the many products of human culture also defy scientific prediction, just because they all arise out of that subjective reality we call the human spirit. In each of us there is an element of free choice. It may be smaller than we think. But it is there. And associated with it are hopes, yearnings, inner urges, personal loves and hates, all of them often known only to ourselves, and some of them not even known to us. All of this is basic to our humanity and it lies outside the scope of scientific investigation.

Religion has to do with the phenomenon of human freedom and the way we exercise it, with the choices we make, with the personal identity we become and the destiny which we shape for ourselves. Important as science has become, it cannot provide for us the answers to our basic religious issues. Science can serve us but it cannot save us. Science can enlighten us on many things — and I say *things* advisedly, whether objects or objective processes. Science can enlighten us but it cannot bring us that enlightenment which the Orient speaks of as the religious goal.

But if science cannot help us: cannot provide the answers to our religious questions, who can? That in itself is a religious question. The only answer that can be given to a religious question, is a religious answer. In our cultural tradition the answer which has been most commonly given to this religious question is this — 'Only God can give us the answers to the most basic questions we ask!'

But this response is expressed in religious language. It is essential that we do not forget this. It is very easy to assume that 'God rules' and 'Queen Elizabeth rules' are two sentences of the same order of language just because the construction is almost identical. But in fact in these sentences we are speaking two quite different languages. The statement 'Queen Elizabeth rules' is an observation which can be made by anyone who has an elementary knowledge of current affairs. It does not matter whether one is British, American, or Russian. The only person who can say 'God rules' is the person for whom that statement adequately expresses an answer to one of his religious questions. In other words the statement 'God rules' tells you something about the person who makes it, whereas the statement 'Queen Elizabeth rules' tells you nothing about the person who makes it.

Another way of showing how these two sentences belong to two different languages is to say that anyone who wants to question the statement can do so very easily in one case by going to London and seeing who Queen Elizabeth is and what she does. But that is not possible with the statement 'God rules'. God is not an object of the empirical world in the way Queen Elizabeth is.

Religious language often looks like ordinary language because it uses the same grammatical constructions and many of the same terms. But it is using these in a metaphorical or symbolic way. Religious language is a meta-language. It is a language which has evolved as a way of verbalising our existential answers to the basic religious questions. It is the language of faith and it has evolved out of ancient mythology.

Another way to clarify the distinction between religious language and ordinary language (a way which some modern philosophers use) is to say that whereas ordinary language is descriptive, religious language is expressive. A good example of expressive language is the communication which takes place between two lovers. Hours may be spent in the whispering of honeyed things. No objective information may be communicated but the language is powerfully expressive of the love the two feel for each other.

In religious language one is expressing how one feels about, and wishes to respond to, the basic issues which human existence raises. This is why religious language is most clearly recognised for what it is in hymns, liturgies of worship, in prayers, meditations and other spiritual exercises. Let us take the verse of a hymn, chosen at random:

> Immortal, invisible, God only wise,
> In light inaccessible hid from our eyes,
> Most blessed, most glorious, the Ancient of Days,
> Almighty, victorious, thy great name we praise.

As soon as we look at the words of any such hymn we recognise that religious language has much more in common with poetry than it has with exact description. Indeed religious language often goes to great pains to assert that what ultimately concerns us human beings is invisible, intangible and beyond all description. What the words do is not to describe, but to express our attitude towards the indescribable, towards the mystery of life—an attitude expressing wonder, hope, trust.

Religious language does not convey information, as scientific language does and as all descriptive language does. This distinction, however, is something we have been learning to make only within the last hundred years and it is the advent of science which has helped us to make it. Indeed we may say that it is the advent of science, because of the particular kind of knowledge that it is, that has helped us to distinguish clearly between faith and knowledge.

Up until recent times faith and knowledge were so intermingled that they were often thought to be one and the same, just as the Christian system of meaning and code of values were thought to be all of a piece with the pre-scientific picture of the natural world with which they had long become integrated. Under these conditions Christianity came to be conceived as a body of knowledge. This knowledge was taken to be infallible and eternally true because it was believed to have been divinely revealed. Thus the process of becoming a Christian seemed to consist of giving assent to this knowledge. For Protestants this knowledge was contained exclusively in the Bible. For Roman Catholics it was contained in the living tradition of the Church, which included the Bible. Until the advent of science there was little reason for doubting the validity of that body of 'revealed' knowledge.

We can be thankful to science that we have been forced to distinguish between knowledge and faith, and to see that religious affirmations do not constitute empirical knowledge but are expressions of faith. For this reason we must clearly distinguish between faith and belief. Christianity has frequently been conceived, and even taught, as if it were a collection of such beliefs. Christians have even been tempted to defend the truth of some of these beliefs by appeal to reason, to historical evidence, or to universal human experience. When these have failed, as they often do, they have appealed to divine revelation. This brings us back again to an affirmation of faith, for which there can be no rational or empirical demonstration.

The great affirmations made by Christians in the past did not originate as empirical statements but as spontaneous expressions of faith. 'God is love', 'Jesus is the Christ', 'Jesus Christ is the Son of God', 'Jesus died for the sins of men', 'Jesus was raised from the dead' 'Jesus will come to judge the living and the dead'. These are not statements which are open to public demonstration. Neither are they ever open to disproof. They are not descriptive statements about the natural world. They are statements expressive of faith. And in one way or another they are all symbolic.

Now it is quite true that faith does not come to verbal expression in a cultural vacuum. The faith of every human comes to expression within the context of that person's beliefs and state of current knowledge. Beliefs and knowledge vary from age to age and culture to culture. One draws one's beliefs from the culture in which one is shaped. But genuine faith has been present in all cultures and in all ages.

Faith is universal to the human species. Faith is not knowledge but an attitude of trust. Some may have great faith, some may have little. But all humans have some modicum of faith. Faith concerns one's orientation towards life. Faith is an attitude of confidence and trust to life, to people, to the future. Faith is a quality of human living. At its best it leads to serenity, to courage, to service. It is by faith that a person is enabled to find meaning and purpose in life, to live by a satisfying set of values and to discern ultimate goals most likely to bring a sense of fulfilment.

Faith expresses itself verbally in religious language, which is both symbolic and poetic. In our cultural tradition the most important word used to express faith, to talk about it and to communicate faith to others, is the word 'God'. This is not the name of some unseen object. It is misleading to speak of God as a person. It is misleading to debate the existence of God. To say that God exists and to say that he does not exist are both equally false. Both statements carry the hidden assumption that God is an object in the world like any other object which may or may not exist.

The word 'God' is symbolic and every statement we make about God is symbolic. There can be no definition of God — except the paradoxical one, that God is the symbol for the ultimately indefinable. By this symbolic term we are referring to the ultimate mystery of life, to the mystery which ever transcends us. It is because this mystery lies always beyond our human knowing that our human spirit is enlivened, our hopes kindled, our creativity stirred and we are motivated to live our lives to the full.

Because the word 'God' is a faith symbol, it will be conceived a little differently by everybody. There is always something of ourself in the way we use the word, for it is expressive of our response of faith to the demands of human existence. Some may choose not to use the word at all. But simply to abandon the word as outworn or meaningless does not remove the mystery nor does it do away with the need for faith. Today the human race stands in need of faith as much as it ever has in the past.

4. *Science and Faith in Partnership*

There was another reason why, a hundred years ago, the 'religion versus science' debate seemed to be irreconcilable and why extremists on both sides were over-confident and dogmatic. They had two different views of reality. Religious people remained utterly convinced of a spiritual world greatly superior to, and independent of, the physical tangible world. God was the name of the ultimate spiritual reality. Human beings, by virtue of their immortal souls, also participated in the life of the spiritual world. The spiritual world explained human consciousness. It contained ideas, values, abstract truth. The more liberal religious thinkers no longer saw this spiritual world as the source of infallible knowledge about the physical world as their forbears had earlier done. But they still believed that knowledge of the ultimate truth and of the way to human fulfilment came from this world by way of divine revelation.

At the other extreme to this was the materialistic world-view which asserted that the only reality is physical reality, which behaves according to a few basic laws of nature that empirical science will eventually be able to uncover. In this view of reality there is absolutely no place for the operation of a divine will. The whole spiritual world of traditional religion is simply an illusion. Indeed Sigmund Freud who, like many other scientists of his time, embraced this materialistic philosophy wrote a book in which he dismissed all religion as an illusion — a social neurosis, from which humankind needs to be delivered.

Now it will always be impossible to reconcile a purely materialistic view of reality with that which asserts a spiritual reality quite independent of the physical world. What has been happening during the course of this century at the growing edges of both science and religion, is the recognition that in their dogmatic forms of a century ago, they were both wrong. In both science and religion, less rigid and more fluid positions are being arrived at.

Science and religion are today in dialogue. They are both more ready to listen to what each other is saying. Both are now less confident that they have access to the respective absolutes which made them so dogmatic, whether absolute natural laws or an absolute deity. There has been a growing recognition of the human dimensions of both science and religion. Let me illustrate.

It is of course self-evident that scientists on the one hand, and all people of religious convictions on the other, are all human beings. What is less self-evident, is that their very humanness has shaped a great deal, if not all, of what they have said or done, whether in a scientific or a religious way. The reason this was not more fully realised earlier is that religious persons were so convinced that the truths they proclaimed were of divine or non-human origin that they did not recognise even the particular human content which was clearly visible, let alone its more subtle forms.

In a similar way, the scientist was so impressed by the apparent confirmation of his theories that, when the stage was reached that those theories were called the 'laws of nature', he forgot the particular formulation of them had originated in his own mind. There are no absolute laws written into the fabric of the universe. What we call natural law is a useful human construction to help us understand and make use of the natural phenomena we observe. There is no finality about any of these so-called laws. Any of them may have to be revised or replaced by others in light of further evidence. Science is a human pursuit. Science never knows with certainty. Scientific knowledge is the human way of constructing order in the observable phenomena. It is a human product which we regard as reliable for present use because of the way we keep testing it. But at any point some long-standing conclusion may become superseded by something else.

Moreover it used to be thought that scientific explanation consisted of reducing complex phenomena to the operation of a few simple principles. As anthropologist Levi-Strauss has pointed out, scientific explanation rather consists in opting for one complexity which is more intelligible than one that is less so. Scientific advancement has often come about by a progressively complicated analytical picture, by comparison with which the earlier quite simple explanation has come to be seen as far too simplistic. Human intelligibility is now recognised as an essential ingredient in the scientific pursuit. More than anything else this brings out the essentially human character of science. Intelligible to whom? Intelligible to us, of course. We humans supply the criterion of intelligibility, which is an essential ingredient for science.

But just as the human character of the scientific enterprise has forced the scientist to surrender any claim to infallibility or to the absoluteness of scientific conclusions and constructions, so the human character of religion has forced a similar surrender. In the last 200 years, partly due to the historical and scientific study of religion, it has come to be recognised with increasing clarity that religious concepts, beliefs, tradition and rituals all originated in the human imagination. This fact does not in itself destroy the practical efficacy of those religious phenomena. What it does challenge and undermine are those particular religious convictions which asserted that certain truths and practices were revealed and commanded, respectively, by an absolute authority external to the tangible world.

This kind of appeal has been much stronger in the monotheistic traditions originating in the Middle East than it ever became in the religions of the East. The trouble begins as soon as different religions make parallel claims which conflict. For the orthodox Jew, the Torah was delivered by God to Moses on Mt. Sinai. For the orthodox Christian the Bible was inspired and personally guaranteed by divine authority. For the Muslim the original Qur'an, which is in heaven, was orally delivered to Muhammed, through the angel Gabriel. In the modern world it has become self-evident that the holy scriptures of traditions other than one's own bear the unmistakable marks of their human origin. What are the grounds, if any, therefore, for claiming that one's own tradition is uniquely different in this respect? Only personal conviction can defend any uniqueness which is not self-evident to all, and such conviction is not recognisably different from prejudice.

The human origin of religious traditions is not confined to Scriptures. When one remembers that human language itself is a human product (the result of the slow evolution of attempts by humans to communicate with increasing clarity), and that names and concepts are an essential part of language, then all belief systems and mental construction, religious or otherwise, are seen to be human products. This applies even to such basic terms as God, love, justice, good and evil.

An important step in the contemporary process of reconciliation between religion and science has been the recognition therefore, that both these activities in their respective ways are human products. They are both human responses arising out of the experience of human existence. While science and religion arise, respectively, out of human response to different kinds of questions, there are also certain things that they have in common. The reason why they do share common components is to be found in the fact that they are both human enterprises.

The first thing they share is a faith component. By faith, of course, I do not mean blind acceptance but an attitude of trust. That faith is a component of religion is of course self-evident, so much so that religion is even better referred to as a path of faith. The religious quest for meaning and fulfilment is pursued without any guarantee that it will reach a successful conclusion. There is no certainty that questions of meaning and purpose are worth asking and are capable of being answered with satisfaction. It requires an act of faith.

The scientist also has faith in the intelligibility of the empirical data he is studying. This also implies that if he is successful in discovering the empirical truth he is seeking it will remain constant. In other words, what is true one day will be true the next day. The scientist approaches the data in the faith that this is not a crazy chaotic universe which changes its character at random. Indeed German physicist and philosopher Carl Friedrich von Weizsäcker has maintained that the reason why empirical science arose in Western Christendom is because the belief in the unity and constancy of God supplied that essential faith in the constancy of the world, which is the necessary pre-supposition of the scientific enterprise.

Science and religion both require faith, though not in the same proportion, simply because the scientist is usually dealing only with a segment of the physical world, whereas in religion one is dealing with the human response to the whole world as personally experienced.

Secondly, science and religion both rely heavily upon the creative power of the human imagination. In religion once again, this fact is fairly obvious. The religious figures which religious traditions of the past conceived as the inhabitants of an unseen world — angels, demons, spirits, gods and goddesses — were all creations of the human imagination. It is for this reason that the visual arts, music, and the performing arts have always played an important role in religious activities. Religious language is more like the language of poetry than anything else. Ritual is a religious drama.

Of course it is true that religious language relies heavily on the poetic tools of symbol, metaphor, and visual imagery, whereas scientific language strives to excel in logic, precision and measurable, quantifiable terms. Nevertheless workable scientific theories do not emerge of their own accord out of the quantified data. They arise in the imagination of the scientist, who then puts them to the test. To be a great scientist one also needs a fertile imagination. Let me quote Philippe Frank: 'The main activity of science... consists in the invention of symbols and in the building of a symbolic system from which our experience can logically be derived... the work of the scientist is probably not fundamentally different from the work of the poet.'

That brings me to the third component common to science and religion. Each creates its own symbols and its own terminology. These terms, concepts and symbols are intelligible only in the context of the language and human activity where they belong. One can no more jump readily from one to the other, and expect to make sense, than one can start a sentence in English, finish it in Chinese, and expect to be understood. With their specialised symbols and concepts, scientists construct models. Those which prove unsatisfactory they discard; others they continue to use as long as they appear to work.

Similarly the religious imagination creates symbols and myths.

These myths remain alive while they have the power to communicate, to express meaning and purpose, and help people cope with the enigmas of human existence. The myth of the resurrection of Jesus, for example, dealt in a creative and positive way with the stumbling block of the unexpected death of Jesus as a common criminal.

Science and religion, though having clearly distinguishable aims, thus have common ground. They are both human products. They both call for faith. They both require the exercise of creative imagination. They both create and use their respective symbols and languages.

Can we go further in the rapprochement of science and religion? I believe we can. I have tried to show that we stand in dependence upon them both. We depend upon science for the way we understand the nature of the physical world and the way it works. We depend on religion for the way it helps us deal positively and creatively with the demands of human existence. Can we conceive the possibility of a complementary synthesis of science and religion? We can! Some syntheses have already been attempted and further exploration in this field is exercising an increasing number of minds today. The man who has produced the most exciting synthesis to date — breathtakingly vast in its scope — is almost certainly the French scientist and Jesuit priest Teilhard de Chardin. I do not mean he has wholly succeeded but his efforts will repay close study and are certainly not to be dismissed too lightly.

In 1934, six years before Teilhard completed his magnum opus, *The Phenomenon of Man*, he wrote this, 'It is a curious thing: man, the centre and creator of all science, is the only object which our science has not yet succeeded in including in a homogeneous representation of the universe. We know the history of his bones, but no ordered place has yet been found in nature for his reflective intelligence.'

At the time he wrote those words, the scientific world was largely conditioned by the materialistic philosophy that the only ultimate reality consists of what is physically solid, stable and measurable. Taken to its logical conclusions, this not only left no room for the operation of a divine will; it led to a philosophy of physical determinism, which also eliminated human free will. It turned human consciousness into a delusory epiphenomenon of no significance. This kind of science left no room for the scientist himself.

Teilhard asked himself, 'Why in this scientifically constructed view of a totally physical universe is there no place left for that most important aspect of the human condition — consciousness and the capacity for human reflection?' So Teilhard turned the whole process round and made man the key to the nature and purpose of the universe. This clearly has its dangers, not all of which Teilhard managed to avoid. But for the scientist who rejected Teilhard's vision, Teilhard held a trump card. 'Well can you propose a better way of explaining the phenomenon of human reflection in an all-physical universe? For any materialistic science which does not do this is clearly inadequate. It has the effect of nullifying both the scientific enterprise and the scientist.'

Teilhard sketched a vision of a spiritually evolving universe. The potential for consciousness is present everywhere in cosmic matter, the basic stuff of the universe. In mankind this potential has reached its highest level of manifestation to date, so far as this planet is concerned. Since Teilhard wrote, some forty years ago, the physical sciences have been moving in a direction which lends even more support to his basic thrust than they did earlier. Ever since the splitting of the atom, and the investigation of sub-atomic structures, the physical sciences have been seeing the physical world much less as a static, solid edifice constructed out of hard building blocks, and much more as a delicate fabric of dynamic relationships. The universe is no longer seen as static and unchangeable but as a dynamic process. And the very basic matter of the universe is conceived not so much as bits as events. We have known for some time now that 'matter' can be transmuted into energy and vice versa. It seems now that neither matter nor energy is the 'basic stuff' of physical reality. Matter and energy are simply two different states of the basic stuff of reality, just as water and ice are two different states of H_2O.

But much more importantly than that, this basic stuff shows the capacity to evolve out of itself new and more complex structures which are quite different in character from the original parts, just as water is uniquely different from the hydrogen and oxygen of which it is composed. Again and again in the physical world we find cosmic reality organising itself into more complex structures in such a way that the new whole is something more than the sum of its parts. We may say that the basic stuff of physical reality manifests two distinct but related drives: (i) to move from simple relationships and structures to more complex ones, and (ii) to move qualitatively from poverty to richness. A living cell is more complex than the megamolecules of which it is composed. It manifests life in a way which they do not. An organism is a complex structure of cells and it manifests a quality of life higher than that of the single cell. The human being is the most complex organism we know and has the capacity for reflection and spirituality. Because these successively complex structures are all composed of the same basic physical reality we need a new name for this basic stuff which does justice to its mysterious complexity.

Let me quote Harold Schilling, past Professor of Physics at Pennsylvania State University, 'Nature means for men, as I believe it does for most scientists, the whole economy or system of observable phenomena and things, including man and his social institutions, having space-time relations and held together in a field of cause and effect relationships. All the individual realities of nature are manifestations of one grand comprehensive physical reality which may be called 'the matter-energy-life-mind-spirit continuum.'

A great deal more could be said along these lines. I hope I have said enough to show that the physical sciences have been moving towards a view of reality which is dynamic, open-ended, inclusive of human free will, human consciousness, human reflection and human spirituality and not exclusive of these factors as it once tended to be. Reality is one, and yet it incorporates what was previously conceived as two mutually exclusive realities, matter and spirit.

This changing view of reality from the angle of science is one which religious thought can respond to positively, though not of course without undergoing quite radical changes itself. There is time to mention only one such change — the new religious thinking about the chief religious symbol, God. Catholic theologian Schillebeeckx has said, 'The situation requires us to speak of God in a way quite different from the way we have spoken of him in the past.'

Just over twenty years ago Bishop John Robinson shocked the world of conventional Christianity by declaring, 'Our image of God must go.' His little book *Honest to God* introduced many Christians for the first time to theologians like Rudolf Bultmann, Paul Tillich and Dietrich Bonhoeffer. These had already explored radically new ways of conceiving God in the light of a scientifically shaped modernity. They all abandoned the traditional picture of God as a supernatural creator who exists independently of the physical world he had created. God is no longer conceived as a substantive reality. Just as physical reality itself consists more of structured forms than of substance and the more complex the structure, the higher the quality of consciousness and spirituality, so God is to be conceived in terms of structure and relationships. One could even say that God is the name for the dynamic and basic thrust towards complexity and quality which we observe in the matter-energy-life-mind-spirit continuum. To believe in God means the same thing as to respond in trust to the universe as it truly is.

More recently a young Anglican theologian of Cambridge, Don Cupitt, has written a book entitled *Taking Leave of God*. In it he persuasively argues that we must abandon the traditional image of God as an authoritative commanding external figure, not only because scientifically based modernity is leading us to the view that no such figure exists. We must abandon it in the interests of our own spirituality and personal salvation. Perhaps we would feel a great deal safer if there were such a strong divine parental authority who would always ensure that we come to no ultimate harm. But by the same token, we would be kept forever in a state of child-like subjection which stunts spiritual growth and breeds a race of slaves. For our own spiritual growth as human beings it is necessary to take leave of the former image of God and learn to shoulder adult responsibility.

This is not so much to push God out of the world as to let God emerge in and through human consciousness. For we human creatures are not only a part of the one ultimate reality, but in our complex structures, in our capacity for thought and spirituality, we represent on this planet the highest level yet reached of those basic thrusts. In other words we have reached the stage in this planet's evolving life where there has been placed on our shoulders the kind of responsibility we have traditionally projected on to an external deity.

The delicate and critical stage through which this whole planet is today moving cannot be over-emphasised. On the one hand, accelerating advances in science and technology are putting into our hands the knowledge and the tools with which we shall be able increasingly to direct the destiny, not just of ourselves but of the whole planet. On the other hand, the many choices to be made demand from us a grasp of ultimate values, an insight into eternal purposes and a level of spiritual maturity which at present we clearly lack. Yet, for better or for worse, these responsibilities have been thrust upon us and we cannot avoid them. To quite a large extent the religious forms we have inherited were shaped for the pre-modern world and are sadly out of date. Yet they are the only things we have to guide us and we must draw upon them for the task ahead.

Because of the critical stage we have reached in our assuming control of planetary development, it is essential that science and religion grow rapidly together in a complementary relationship to build a synthesis of knowledge and values which will enable life on this planet not only to continue but to reach an even higher quality than hitherto.

Machines, Computers and People

1. The Use of Machines

The time in which we live is often described as the age of advanced technology. Human technology itself is by no means new. More than 5,000 years have passed since the discovery of the wheel and the harnessing of fire for the making of pottery and for extracting metals from ore. What is new about technology today is the speed with which it is now advancing and the bewildering complexity of its products.

For these reasons it should not surprise us if people of my age find modern technology in general, and the electronic computer in particular, to be rather unsettling and even threatening; whereas pupils at our schools gain mastery in the use of a home computer with remarkable ease. In a similar way I observed fifty years ago that my parents, born in the 1870s, never really became adjusted to the use of the telephone, and avoided the use of it if they possibly could.

The suspicion and fear of things mechanical is as old as technology itself and is reflected in the oldest traditions of the Bible. Metalworking was held in contempt by the ancient Semitic nomads and regarded as a magical black art. It was traced back to Tubal-Cain as its originator. He is described as the first ever to hammer and chisel with bronze and iron. In other words, according to the Bible, he was the father of technology. His mode of life was sharply distinguished from that of the tent-dwelling pastoralist and that of the musician, with the unmistakeable hint that technology endangers our humanity and the promotion of the cultural arts.

From that day to this, all new technology has been welcomed with both wonder and suspicion. That is why in this essay I will attempt to examine the relationship between humans and the technology they have developed to see in what ways, if any, technology is changing the character of the human condition for better or worse. Does technology interfere with human relations and choke the human spirit? Is it possible that the technology we have devised may become a macro-Frankenstein which will assume control and crush us? In attempting to answer such questions we shall be led back to the basic question — what does it mean to be human anyway?

Although the recent advent of the computer must inevitably be a dominant theme, it is not with it that I intend to start. I believe we shall arrive at a more balanced appraisal of the computer if we look at it in a much vaster chronological setting, sketching briefly the long development of human technology through three successive ages — the tool-age, the machine-age and the computer-age. It may still be true that only God can make a tree, but it is quite undeniable that tools, machines and computers were conceived and made by humans. Why? And what has been their effect?

To differentiate us from other earthly creatures, the human species has sometimes been defined by anthropologists as the tool-users. There was a dramatic moment portrayed in the opening of the film *2001: A Space Odyssey*, when our pre-human ancestors first made the discovery that a bone could be used both as a hammer and as a deadly weapon. It was the first step into the tool-age.

Up until that point our human ancestors, along with so many other kinds of creatures, had been solely dependent upon their limbs with which to respond to and cope with their environment. Our legs and arms are not, of course, as essential to biological existence as are some of our inner organs. We can live without our limbs — and a very few do so, as a result of accident or arrested embryonic development. But loss of limbs makes us more dependent on others. It deprives us of the self-reliance which our legs and arms give us. Our legs provide us with mobility; our arms enable us to manipulate external objects for our advantage. From mammals down to tiny insects the possession of limbs has great survival value.

Now look at what happened to those limbs as different species, in the course of their evolution, adapted themselves to their particular environment. Some animals, such as moles, developed limbs which were amazingly efficient for digging into the ground. Some, such as members of the cat family, developed limbs which enabled them to leap speedily on to their prey. The giraffe developed long legs and a neck to enable it to reach the highest foliage. Monkeys developed versatile tails. The elephant lengthened its nose to a most useful trunk. Birds retained their back legs for walking but their front limbs became wings.

Thus limbs developed to become more highly specialised and efficient — but for fewer purposes. Increase in a particular skill was matched by a decrease in the variety of uses to which those limbs could be put. Now the front limbs of the mole cannot be used to fly, nor can the wings of a bird be used to dig holes. The biological development of limbs has had the effect of locking the creature into a particular style of life in a particular environment. That's a lesson worth remembering.

The human species was evolving biologically as part and parcel of this total life process when, at some point, a most important transition took place. Our ancient ancestors stumbled on to the use of tools. Simple though those first tools were, their advent was to mean that, in the long run, there would be no further stimulus by way of natural selection for the limbs of the human organism to evolve further in a biological way. Tools made that unnecessary — for tools are, in fact, artificial extensions to limbs. They have increasingly given humans a tremendous advantage over other animals. Whereas the forelegs of one animal could evolve to dig like a spade and those of another could become excellent for climbing, human tools extended the use of our limbs in a way which combined both efficiency and versatility.

Gardening shops these days provide a range of gardening devices, each of which can be fitted on to the same handle. It was like that with the discovery of the tool. The human arm can now be extended by an endless variety of interchangeable parts, each designed for a particular skill. Tools may thus be regarded as artificial extensions of our limbs. A skilled artisan, such as a carpenter, is not just a human — but a human plus his or her particular set of tools. Take away the tools and the human can no longer operate as a carpenter.

From the discovery of the first tool, right down to the present, may be called the tool age. The artefacts which constitute the visible, tangible products of any human culture are almost completely dependent on the fact that humans became tool-users.

Much more recently, mainly in only the last 200 years, the tool itself was transformed by humans into what we call a machine... and humankind entered the machine age. The machine may be regarded as a special kind of tool. Not only is it usually more complex in that it has more moving parts; more importantly, it has access to a source of energy other than manpower, which gives it the capacity to go on working by itself with the minimum of human oversight, and perhaps even none at all. The earliest machines were water mills, windmills and clocks, where energy was supplied by gravity, the wind and the winding of springs. But the machine age really came into its own with the invention of the steam-engine, followed rapidly by the combustion engine and the electric motor. The machine age has revolutionised the way in which we live, so much so that we speak of the period of its most rapid advance as the Industrial Revolution. It had the effect of raising quite dramatically the material standard of living. It is not too much to claim that the advent of the machine has brought about more change in 200 years than occurred in the 10,000 years or more of the tool age.

While tools enabled us to do things we could not do with our bare hands or our unaided legs, machines have enabled us to do things we could not do with tools alone. For example, the wheeled vehicle may be regarded as a tool, the invention of which enabled us to travel further and faster than our legs would carry us. But for a long time the motive power had to be supplied by other living creatures — humans in the case of rickshaws, horses in the case of chariots and carts. Only with the use of petroleum in a combustion engine was the wheeled vehicle turned into an *auto*mobile. In other words, the tool became extended into a machine, with a consequent dramatic increase in speed and range.

People long tried to invent a tool which would enable humans to fly, as the ancient Greek legend of Icarus illustrates. Human flight only became a reality with the advent of the flying machine. Thus the arrival of the machine age led to the construction of an automated set of wings greatly more powerful than those of the strongest eagle. This mechanical bird can carry more than 500 people at one time.

In many similar ways the advent of the machine age led to a massive increase of production in a whole variety of areas, such as woven fabrics for clothing, food production, and communication through the written word. Now just as an artisan is not just a human but a human plus his or her tools, so the advent of the machine age has done something to humanity which is very important and too little recognised. Human society, as we have come to know it, is no longer simply a group of human beings relating together with a common purpose. Human society consists of human beings, plus our machines — which have become an essential part of our collective life. As a person without tools ceases to be an artisan, so the human way of life we have come to take for granted in this machine age has become dependent on the machines we have constructed. They are artificial extensions of our natural physical abilities. If all our machines were to be suddenly rendered inactive, life as we know it in the Western world would quickly collapse. All communication systems would cease to operate and all transport systems would come to a halt. The only part of the world about which we would have any continuing knowledge would be our immediate vicinity. In urban areas our food supplies would soon be exhausted. We would not be able to reclothe ourselves. We rarely stop to think how dependent we have made ourselves upon the machines we have constructed. We are no longer the self-reliant individuals our ancient ancestors were. We have become part of a complex system consisting of humans-plus-machines.

But this is not the end of the story. Some 10,000 or more years ago humans entered the tool age. Some 200 years ago humans entered the machine age. During the last twenty years we have been entering the computer age. We all have a clear idea what a tool is and what a machine is. Many of us have only a vague or ill-defined idea what a computer is. Because of the sense of magic and superhuman power that has come to be associated with the computer, it has tended to take on an identifiable personality, just as the steam locomotive did in the nineteenth century — and still does for railway enthusiasts. The computer is treated as if it were an intelligent being. It is sometimes held accountable for the errors it has supposedly made. It is said to suffer from fatigue. It is even feared as one which will usurp control, as it did in *2001: A Space Odyssey*.

The reason for these impressions and fears (some of them false) is quite simple. Whereas the tool extends the range and efficiency of the functions of the human limb, and whereas the machine supplies that extension with a form of self-automation; the computer is an extension, into an external machine, of two of the functions of the human brain.

The simpler of these functions is the capacity of the computer to store raw data or facts. We even name this faculty by its counterpart in the human brain — memory. Our own personal memory is an essential part of our humanity. We could have no awareness of self-identity, nor could we function as self-conscious beings if we did not retain in our memory a certain minimum body of facts drawn from past experience. These include such obvious but extremely important things as the use of language, the meaning of words, recognition of familiar faces and places, and so on.

In some respects the average human memory is a much vaster storehouse than any computer yet constructed, simply because of the wide range of things it contains. Even so, our memories are finite in capacity and are fallible. That is just where the computer can prove to be an invaluable artificial extension of our memory bank, so that at the press of a button we have instant recall. Our memories are storehouses of instant information. The computer is a greatly increased databank for instant information. Every day we observe the use of this memory facility in our banks, airline offices, libraries and so on. The human memory is occasionally capable of great feats. One of New Zealand's great mathematicians, known affectionately to his fellow students as 'Swotty' Aitken, had such a memory. During World War I (so it was reported) the records of his regiment were destroyed by enemy action. Aitken could recall, without error, the full name and rifle number of every man in the regiment. A large computer can completely outstrip that feat and have ready for instant recall a great deal more raw data in chosen areas than any human could ever retain.

The second, and probably the more important, function of the computer is its facility for processing the raw data it is fed, in such a way as to produce a great deal of new information, logically deduced from that data. And it can do this at lightning speed when compared with the equivalent operation in the human brain. 'Swotty' Aitken could add up long-tot sums of six-figure numbers faster than we ordinary mortals can add up single figures. But in a few minutes computers can process data which would take humans many years to perform by mental and manual calculation.

In the Western world we have been used to the practice of numbering our years from the supposed date of birth of Jesus Christ and to speak of all time before him as B.C. It may well be that people of the future will tend to think of the division of human time into *before* and *after* the arrival of the computer, in which case the abbreviation B.C. could take on a strangely unexpected new meaning. We are only at the beginning of the computer age and no-one can predict what it will lead to. But we know enough of its potential to know it will revolutionise the character of human civilisation. No other technology known to humans has advanced at such a rapid pace as has computer technology in the last thirty years. This technology is almost beyond the understanding of the average individual and even the experts have trouble keeping their skills up to date. As one of them once wryly remarked, 'If we really understand it, it must be obsolete.'

Why will our entry into the computer age have such revolutionary consequences? Let me put it this way. The most important function of the human brain is to store and process the raw data it is receiving all through life, from impressions received through the five senses, and from the ideas and thoughts taken in from our cultural heritage. Our brain processes these in such a way as to put them into some sort of order, rarely ever perfect, so that we can respond to the demands of human existence in some kind of purposeful way. The human brain is a most marvellous data processor. Yet it has limited capacity in any one field. What the advent of the computer means is that we can now transfer certain specified areas of data processing to a machine. This machine can process vastly more data of a particular kind than the human brain can; it can process it with unbelievable rapidity, and it can do it with infallible accuracy.

The computer has been described as a 'steam engine' for the mind. Just as the steam engine greatly increased the physical energy at human disposal, so the computer has greatly magnified the brain power at human disposal. Just as people could not have foreseen the Industrial Revolution which was to result from the invention of the machine, so we cannot really see where the computer revolution is taking us. But already it is being applied to business, industry, communication, education, medicine, engineering, the detection of crime and the social sciences.

Where does all this leave us as people? Some may be inclined to think that it really makes no difference. We are still human bodies with two arms and two legs, who have to think for ourselves. I want to suggest that this is only half true. Each of the three ages I have described has had the effect of changing us as human beings in very real, though subtle, ways. This is because 'no man is an island', as John Donne said. None of us is an individual isolated from the culture and civilisation in which we live. When that civilisation undergoes a radical transformation we also change with it. Incidentally, what I have called the tool age, the machine age and the computer age closely parallel what Alvin Toffler in *The Third Wave* describes as the three successive waves of human civilisation. And we are the children, he says, of the next transformation—the 'third wave'.

In what ways are we humans changing as a result of these three successive ages? The first is this. Each of these ages has further increased the distance between us and our nearest animal relatives. It has placed us in such a position of authority and power on this planet that we should tremble. Even in the tool age the ancient psalmist could marvel at the human condition and speak of humanity as being only a little less than God. The machine age and computer age have enthroned the human species in a very godlike relationship towards the life and resources of this planet.

It is not only between us humans and the higher animals that the machine age and computer age have widened the gulf. These two most recent ages have created a gulf between what are euphemistically called the 'developed nations' and the 'developing nations'. These terms really mean the industrialised nations and the non-industrialised nations. Moreover, that gap is said to be widening. Because of the speed of industrialisation, followed now by computerisation, the underdeveloped countries are losing ground in relation to the developed nations. Of course there are many economic factors which may be advanced to explain this widening gulf, but these factors are themselves a direct consequence of the fact that the advanced nations happened to be the first to enter the machine age and then the computer age. The growing rift is all the more serious in that, even with the best will in the world from liberally-minded people in the developed countries, we seem to be almost powerless to reverse the present trend. It is just as if the developed nations on the one hand, and the developing nations on the other, are on two enormous ice floes which are being carried further apart by invisible currents, and any attempt to throw lifelines is of little avail.

The third and last point I wish to make is this. Earlier I pointed out that as (in the course of biological evolution) each of the living species developed special expertise with their limbs to deal with a particular type of environment, so its life and future became locked into that environment. That is why environmentalists keep warning us that when we interfere with the ecology of an environment certain species die out. There is a kind of law which operates like this: efficiency and versatility are related in inverse proportion. The more efficient for a particular purpose become the limbs of an animal, the less versatile it is when it comes to coping with change.

The advent of the tool age enabled humans to break this law and combine efficiency and versatility. Or so it seemed. Really, it was only a partial victory. So successful was the development of the tool, that human life became dependent on the use of the tool. Even more so have the machine and computer made us also dependent upon them. We people of the sophisticated urban civilisation have become locked into the kind of age we have created. We have become highly efficient because of these extensions of our natural abilities but we have lost some of the simple versatility of the ancient cave-dwellers. Perhaps a few of us could recover it if forced to, but certainly not all of us, for modern society as a whole has become dependent on the machine and is becoming dependent on the computer. It is rather ironical that at the very time when we at last feel free of the unseen 'principalities and powers' which people feared in the days of St Paul, we have actually rendered ourselves dependent on a new set of powers, which this time turn out to be things of our own creation.

2. *Machines in Control?*

Most of you will be familiar with the story of *The Sorcerer's Apprentice*. It began as a fable more than 1800 years ago. The German poet Goethe used the theme for a ballad, perhaps in the light of the Industrial Revolution. Paul Dukas composed a piece of symphonic music around it and finally Walt Disney combined both music and story for a screen version.

The favourite trick of the travelling sorcerer was to turn a broomstick into a human figure, which then did all the duties of a servant, such as making meals and carrying water. His young apprentice found a hiding place so that he could overhear the words of the charm. When the sorcerer was safely out of the way he tried out the magic words, changed a stick into a human figure and ordered it to fetch the water from the well—a chore his master had asked him to do. At first all went well. But when enough water had been brought and the apprentice ordered the slave to become a stick again, the automaton did not understand —for the apprentice had not bothered to learn the words which put the magic in reverse. The senseless servant continued to fetch water until the room overflowed. In desperation the apprentice split the stick in two with an axe, only to find he now had two obedient creatures fetching water. Only the arrival of the sorcerer saved the day, once again bringing that magical power under control.

This fable vividly illustrates the danger of unleashing forces one does not fully understand. It is all the more relevant to our study of advancing technology in that the practice of magic was a primitive form of technology. In a cultural context where supernatural forces were assumed without question, magic was the supposed method by which one could release them and use them to achieve one's own ends. Even to this day, each amazing, new technological advance strikes the uninitiated as a new burst of magic. We have become very blasé about handling a tiny electronic calculator or watching a television screen, but if these had been suddenly presented to people hundred years ago, they would have stared in disbelief and declared it to be magic made real. And advancing technology, like ancient magic, has been treated with both awe and suspicion on the grounds that it can be as dangerous to dabble with new forces as it is to play with fire.

Let me illustrate this by reference to the three successive stages of advancing human technology, described earlier as the tool age, the machine age and the computer age. Even the simple tool can occasionally cause us physical harm if not properly used, as everyone who has hit their thumb with a hammer has only too painfully learned.

When we move into the machine age, however, the potential dangers increase tremendously. Because the machine has its own source of energy it is not under the direct control of humans in the way hand-tools are. It can often do untold damage before it can be brought to a stop. Fifty years ago Upton Sinclair was alerting the unsuspecting American public to some of these dangers by recording some hair-raising stories of human disasters which had occurred in the industrial world. It has become necessary to ensure by legislation an ever-increasing number of safety devices along with careful supervision.

The dangers we may suffer as a direct result of computer malfunctioning are of a different kind — but are no less serious. Some time ago a business firm with which I occasionally deal billed me for $5000 for a load of bricks I had supposedly purchased. When I complained that I had no knowledge of such a purchase I received a quick apology, with the explanation that it was due to computer error. No harm resulted on that occasion, but it will be a very different matter if computer error sparks off a nuclear war. In any case we shall never really know how much an incorrect computer setting contributed to the Mt Erebus disaster.

Strictly speaking, computers do not make errors, any more than machines make the accidents they cause. It is no more just, to blame the machine and the computer, than it is to blame the hammer which has hit your thumb. Tools, machines and computers have all been conceived by humans, been constructed by humans, and remain subject ultimately to human control. What these technological devices do is to reflect the imperfections and errors of their makers. Moreover they have the capacity to magnify those errors. The more complex the device, the more it may lead to unintended calamity on an ascending scale. A machine which is out of control can do more damage than a tool. A computer could do more widespread damage than a machine if, for example, a government were to base its economic policy on computer conclusions which were seriously in error.

Because tools, machines and computers are (logically) simply extensions of our own limbs, we are just as responsible for what they do as we are for the actions of our arms and legs and for our own mental reasoning. It is very tempting to disown them when it suits us, shift the blame to them and protest our own innocence. We humans have been doing that ever since we developed sufficient ethical sensitivity to experience guilt, as the myth of Adam and Eve so clearly portrays. The man tried to shift the blame for having eaten the forbidden fruit on to the woman. The woman in turn claimed it was the serpent who beguiled her. Since the serpent was as low as one could get, there was no other creature to which it could pass the buck.

Even in the tool age it was not uncommon for a man to blame a poor job on to his tools or for a housewife to blame her burnt cakes on to the range she had to work with. Yet it was said to be the mark of a good craftsman never to blame his tools. He alone controlled them and was responsible for their use.

There are two reasons, however, why it is easier to persuade ourselves that the machine or the computer is at fault rather than ourselves. The first is that, unlike the hand-tool, the machine and the computer are constructed and operated by a group of people. The responsibility for the operation is shared. It is much easier to hide oneself in a group and avoid the full force of the accusation than to have to face the complete responsibility by oneself.

The second most important reason is that advancing technology has had the effect of bringing a veil of ambiguity over the question of responsibility. Machines and computers give the appearance — however false that may ultimately be — of doing things by themselves. It is just as if the machine or the computer is an embryonic self. Sherry Turtle, in her recent study of the effect of computers from the point of view of one who is both a psychologist and a sociologist, called her book *The Second Self.* The computer becomes a kind of other self, from whom one can also distance oneself. Whether a computer can be legitimately regarded as possessing intelligence we will leave until later. But complex machines — and now computers — are often treated by humans as if they *were* living beings, which must consequently bear responsibility for what they produce. This new grey area in our relation to machines means that instead of our ultimate responsibility being *direct* and hence, quite clear, it has become blurred by a veil of ambiguity.

This may be illustrated by referring to a well-known theological problem. Many may regard the theology as a bit outmoded, but if so, this is partly because the logic of the problem remains as poignant as ever. It is this. If God created human beings who are not only free to sin but have in fact sinned, then God himself cannot be wholly free of blame for what has befallen the world. God must be held indirectly responsible, not only for the so-called natural evils like earthquakes, storms and plagues, but even for the evil which humans themselves have committed. Adam simply passed the buck downwards, like the stereotype of a public servant. He did not think to counter God face to face with this divine responsibility. But that is exactly what Job did do! Ever since the time of Job theologians have wrestled with this problem, trying (rather ironically) to get God off the hook. No satisfactory solution has ever been found. There is no way in which an almighty, all-wise and all-loving Creator God can be reconciled with the present state of the world. If God wholly created the world out of nothing, then that God must, indirectly at least, bear some responsibility for the way it is.

But this very same problem has now landed on our human plate. As the creators of advancing technology we cannot avoid bearing full responsibility, indirect though it may be, for all that tools, machines and computers are doing to the world... for better or for worse. Yet the two factors I have referred to — first, the shared character of our responsibility and second, the indirect nature of our responsibility — combine together to give us a sense of helplessness. We must collectively bear responsibility for our technology and yet we feel we are no longer in control.

Let me put it this way. In normal health we feel that our legs and arms are completely under out control. They do what we wish without our even thinking about them. In certain failures of health, however, our limbs do not so respond to our intentions. We say we feel as if they do not belong to us. And because of this we feel helpless, even disoriented.

It can be like that with the technological extensions to our limbs. It may occur in various ways. When the engine of our motorcar suddenly splutters and stops on a lonely road and we face a motionless silence, how helpless we suddenly feel. At one moment we are in control, moving to our destination at a rapid speed; the next moment our ability to control our circumstances has been suddenly reduced. It is just as if our legs have suddenly crumpled beneath us — and the car is in fact our artificial legs.

It is even worse if the steering suddenly malfunctions and we find ourselves at the mercy of a mindless machine hurtling forward with absolutely no sense of direction. I shall never forget a moment I had some forty years ago, when I was driving eight or nine children home from a picnic. It was a gravel road, deeply corrugated by heavy traffic, with not even a fence between it and the fast-flowing Waitaki river. Suddenly there was a blow out and the car careered madly from one side of the road to the other until I finally brought it safely to a stop.

But there are other ways in which our technology makes us feel helpless. As the annual toll of deaths on our roads so tragically reminds us, the entry into the machine age has meant that, along with all the benefits our machinery has brought us, there has also been a magnification of human tragedy. There is instructive aspect of this, which I first heard expounded some years ago by zoologist and Nobel Prize winner, George Wald, of Harvard University. What he said went something like this. For some 200 million years this Earth belonged to the reptiles. The dinosaurs were the lords of the Earth. They were the biggest land animals that have ever existed. They were well-protected with armour-plate. They were well-armed with horns, teeth and claws. Those dinosaurs looked impregnable.

But back among the trees were a small group of tender, defenceless animals — the first mammals. They did not have much to offer except that they had rather large brains for their size. The dinosaur had a very small brain for *its* size. After some time there were no more dinosaurs, the age of the reptiles having given way to the age of the mammals. The mammals grew and flourished and kept improving that wonderful brain. About two million years ago humankind emerged and the human became a fine animal, versatile, gentle, altogether in control.

Quite recently, that human has built himself a car. You can hardly *see* the man any more as the car drives past, making a roar and spewing out poisonous gas in the streets. Once again the pro-portion of brains to brawn has suddenly decreased. The human and the car together have become like a medium-sized dinosaur — and just as dangerous. Cars kill more than 50,000 on American roads every year, more than were lost in the whole Vietnam war.

'That is the problem of technology,' said George Wald. 'While we were not looking we humans have become dinosaurs again. For it is not only cars, but juggernauts, and trains and jumbo jets and nuclear bombs and computers to run them all. The propor-tion of brains to brawn has sunk very low and is still sinking.'

All this strongly suggests that we humans are not quite so much in control of our technological inventions as we thought we were. There are indeed some grounds for the fear some people have: that we are caught up in a technocratic process which is develop-ing a momentum of its own, and over which there is no indivi-dual or group exercising an all-embracing control according to some predetermined purpose. Rather, it may be the case that at this moment technocracy is moving steadily onwards in a pattern-less path, according to its own internal functioning, and in an impersonal and purposeless way. It is only in each of its many local parts and areas that we humans are in some partial control.

An analogous situation, which may help to illustrate the point, is to observe the ways in which many cities grew in the days before town-planning. Each builder had some kind of plan of the house or other building he wanted to construct. But there was no plan for the development of the city itself. Impersonal forces such as the lay of the land, old animals tracks, and haphazard chance determined the growing shape of the city. Then came to be recognised the need for an overall plan for the benefit of all who lived in the city. Thus the art and practice of town-planning was born. At last some kind of control, however imperfect, was being brought to bear upon city growth.

We have already begun to develop some counterpart to this in the area of technology on the national scale. What we need is something on the global scale. The higher up the scale we go the more reluctant we are to surrender our traditional local liberties. Even town-planners struck fierce resistance from indignant and obstinate individualists. A plan for the control of advancing technology is needed most of all at the global level, yet that is the level where it will become effective last of all.

A good example of this is to be found in the very urgent problem of the arms race, where we are dealing with highly efficient and highly destructive technology. Each nation, including the superpowers, is able to exercise some control over its own production and further technical advance. But because the nuclear powers are in competition and fear each other, this national control is ineffective as long as there is no global body exercising overall control. There is a global body of course — the United Nations. But its individual members will not permit it to operate in this area. They will not surrender their autonomous control in the interests of the greater good.

At the moment, therefore, with the problem of advancing technology in general — and of the arms race in particular — we do seem to be in the position of the ancient dinosaurs. We have built the largest and most complex machines ever known. We have built impressive lines of defence. We have developed the most deadly weapons of offence. But our brains have remained the same. Relative to what we have created our mind-power has become much smaller. Or, like the sorcerer's apprentice (partially at least), we have lost control.

What is the solution? Where do we go from here? There are two blind roads we can immediately rule out. The first is this: it is quite useless to attempt to turn the clock back. There can be no going back to a pre-technological age or even to a simplified technology. Neither is the answer to be found in attempting to peg down the advance of technology at its present level. There would be some psychological benefits from such a course, in that it would give us some time to catch our breath and think out where we want to go. But this approach is also impossible because it begs the question. In order to halt the advance of technology we would need to be in control. But gaining control is actually the very problem we are trying to solve.

A simple analogy would be this. What do we do when we find ourselves in a moving vehicle in which there is suddenly no driver because, say, he has had a heart attack? We look for those ways in which we can influence the direction and speed of the vehicle, so that its present momentum will cause least damage and we can move forward to a state in which we have finally gained control.

This is an immense and multi-faceted problem so far as the advance of technology is concerned. I do not have the knowledge even to name the many aspects of the problem, let alone provide the solution, but I shall make two or three points by way of illustration. There is a direct correlation between advancing technology, the standard of living and patterns of employment. The arrival of the tool age led to a leisured non-artisan aristocracy. The machine age led to an ever-wealthier merchant middle class. Just who will be the élite in the developing computer age, is as yet hard to say. But what we can say is that each advance of technology means that as soon as the initial benefits have been absorbed as far as they can be in an increased standard of living for at least a majority, unemployment for a minority will be an inevitable result of the changing pattern of employment. Unemployment is not just a passing phase but will become a permanent feature of the age of advancing technology unless it is dealt with in a more radical way. The trade unions are right in sensing this to be the case, though in most cases they do not really have the long-term solution.

Another long-term problem of an uncontrolled technocracy arises from the impersonal character of our technology. Tools, machines and computers are impersonal objects which come between people and have the effect of making more difficult — and on occasions even eliminating — the fostering of natural human relations. Telephones are enormously useful but they are never quite the same as talking to a person face to face, and talking to an answering service is decidedly off-putting. But even more than that, our increasing association with machines is also having the effect of making us more machine-like. We may be more efficient but we become less human, less spontaneous, less able to develop the exclusive traits of our humanity. If we do not take more care to control our technology we shall find ourselves shaped by, and eventually sucked into, its very mechanical style of existence.

At the same time as we critically examine advancing technology we must not ignore its many benefits. Control of it does not mean imprisoning it or holding it at bay like an enemy, but learning how to use it for maximum benefit. It is just here where the computer, properly used, may turn out to be of immense help. It is an extension and magnification of some aspects of the human brain. If it is true that the rise of modern technology has meant that we have returned to some extent to the disadvantages of the age of the dinosaurs, in that the ratio of brain to brawn has greatly declined, then the advent of the computer may be the way to remedy this and to restore the ratio to what it ought to be. This partly depends on what we can and cannot expect from the computer and whether even the computer itself is part of the problem to be feared.

3. Are Computers Intelligent?

Twenty years ago a professor of computer science at the Massachusetts Institute of Technology, Joseph Weizenbaum, composed a computer programme which enabled one to converse with the computer in English. The human partner would type out his or her conversation, and the computer was programmed to analyse the message, compose a response and type out the reply. Weizenbaum chose the name ELIZA for his programme after Eliza Doolittle (who was taught to speak increasingly well).

The programme was constructed in two tiers, the first consisting of the language analyser and the second of a script, or set of rules, of what one might expect in a particular language context. In his first experiment he gave ELIZA a script which enabled the computer to play the role of a non-directive psychotherapist. The conversation went something like this (computer's responses in capitals):

Men are all alike.

IN WHAT WAY?

They're always bugging us about something or other.

CAN YOU THINK OF A SPECIFIC EXAMPLE?

Well, my boyfriend made me come here.

YOUR BOYFRIEND MADE YOU COME HERE?

He says I'm depressed much of the time.

I AM SORRY TO HEAR YOU ARE DEPRESSED.

It's true. I am unhappy.

DO YOU THINK COMING HERE WILL HELP YOU NOT TO BE UN-HAPPY?

I need some help, that much seems certain.

WHAT WOULD IT MEAN TO YOU IF YOU GOT SOME HELP?

Perhaps I could learn to get along with my mother.

TELL ME MORE ABOUT YOUR FAMILY.
My mother takes care of me.
WHO ELSE IN YOUR FAMILY TAKES CARE OF YOU?
My father.
YOUR FATHER!
You are like my father in some ways.
WHAT RESEMBLANCE DO YOU SEE?
You are not very aggressive but I think you don't want me to notice that.
WHAT MAKES YOU THINK I AM NOT AGGRESSIVE?
You don't argue with me.
WHY DON'T YOU THINK I DON'T ARGUE WITH YOU?
You are afraid of me.
DOES IT PLEASE YOU TO BELIEVE I AM AFRAID OF YOU?
My father is afraid of everybody.
WHAT ELSE COMES TO MIND WHEN YOU THINK OF YOUR FATHER?
Bullies!
DOES THAT HAVE ANYTHING TO DO WITH THE FACT THAT YOUR BOYFRIEND MADE YOU COME HERE?
... and so on.

This experiment soon became very famous round the MIT and was rapidly circulated round the nation. Weizenbaum was so shocked by this enthusiastic reception and by the conclusions people jumped to as to what a computer could do that he was led to write a book, *Computer Power and Human Reason* to press home what he believes to be the essential difference between humans and this new machine, the computer.

There are three reasons why Weizenbaum was shocked by the interest so quickly generated by ELIZA. First, a number of practising psychiatrists seriously believed that his computer programme could be quickly improved and refined to become a completely automatic form of psychotherapy, and he asked himself, 'What must a psychiatrist really think he is doing if he believes this simple mechanical parody can capture the essence of a human encounter?'

Secondly, he found that people very quickly became emotionally involved with the ELIZA-programmed computer. Even his own secretary, who had observed him creating the programme over many months, after her first few interchanges asked him to leave the room, so that she could freely converse with the computer. Weizenbaum realised that only short exposures could induce powerful delusional thinking into quite normal people.

Thirdly, the belief quickly spread that he had solved the problem of whether a computer would ever be able to understand natural language. Weizenbaum insisted that no absolute solution to this problem will ever be possible because human language can only be understood in particular contexts. Even humans themselves sometimes have difficulty in verbal communication because of this. How much more so will mechanical computers! It is in fact quite false to assume that behind the computer's verbal response there is anything comparable to what we call the human mind, the human thinking process.

This, in any case, is what Weizenbaum firmly believes and he insists that an absolute line will always divide human intelligence from machine intelligence. In other words computers will never be able to think in the way humans think.

But not all computer experts agree wth Weizenbaum. Whether human beings are able to create artificial intelligence, equal to and perhaps even superior to their own, was first raised 100 years ago. Augusta Ada Byron, daughter of Lord Byron, maintained that machines will never be able to achieve any task which they have not been programmed to do. But that question is hotly disputed today. Pamela McCorduck in her book, *Machines Who Think*, records some of the criticism which followed Weizenbaum's negative conclusions.

It is true, however, that computers have not lined up to the more optimistic forecasts of the early 1950s, when it was confidently being asserted that humanity would ultimately face the danger of being taken over by machines. In spite of the remarkable things which computers can do — feats of memory recall and calculation far beyond the ordinary human mind — it is nevertheless true that no computer is in a position to make important decisions. Computers can only do what they are programmed to do and cannot go beyond what their programmers intended. In other words, they must remain a valuable tool, and will never be able to replace the creative capacity and the decision-making role of the human mind.

I shall consider presently whether computers may be said to possess intelligence and the capacity for human thought. First I wish to take up the question of whether our increasing fascination with computers may not be having the subtle effect of changing our understanding of our human condition without our realising it. There is in fact an important correlation between how we understand ourselves as human beings and how we understand computers. This can best be illustrated by looking back briefly to the understanding of the human condition which we have received from our cultural heritage.

Ever since humans began to engage in critical reflection on the nature of reality, they have asked the question: 'What is human-kind?... What does it mean to be human?' The Bible discusses this question at the very beginning. In well-known words it asserts that 'God created humankind in his own image.' Humans reflect the very character of God. And what is that character? This is answered in part in Genesis 2 where God is literally described in terms of a potter, taking the clay or dust of the ground and shaping it into a human form before giving it life by breathing his own breath into it.

The activity of God the Creator was seen then in the terms of a potter, and that was reflected very clearly in some words of Jeremiah. But it was really not until the nineteenth century that we humans began to realise that whatever truth there may be in the assertion that God created mankind in his own image, it is even more correct to say that we humans conceived God in *our* image. And in the tool age, the dominant image our ancestors had of themselves was that of artisans, workers with tools creating and shaping new objects which previously did not exist. One can imagine how impressed the ancient human mind was by watching the potter bring out of a shapeless lump of clay a creation beautiful to behold and handy to use.

Throughout the long tool age humans saw themselves, not exclusively but quite dominantly, as artisans proud of their skills. And God was conceived as the cosmic artisan. Indeed this symbolism was adopted even more specifically in the liturgical rites of the Masonic Order which have lasted to this day.

But some 200 years ago we entered the machine age. We became the makers and operators of machines, not simply tools. A subtle but very deep change came over the way we began to think both of ourselves and of God. From Isaac Newton onwards, the world itself came to be seen as a great machine, operating according to its own internal laws. God ceased to be conceived as the potter and was seen as the machine maker. Having put together his machine and set it going, God simply had to watch his machine at work from a distance, having no more need to interfere with the way it worked. This is the kind of God-belief which became dominant among intellectuals in the eighteenth century and is still found in a lot of folk-religion today. It is known as 'deism'.

Similarly, the entry into the machine age began to affect the way humans thought of themselves. The human organism began to be seen as a complex machine, operating according to its inner design. This design was seen as being determined by forces over which we have no control. These forces are partly hereditary, partly our cultural conditioning, and partly our past actions and thoughts. When this view is taken to extreme it eliminates all personal free will. In philosophy it is known as 'determinism'. Everything down to our very thinking is determined for us. We are nothing more than machines and our awareness of freedom is simply an illusion of consciousness. Leibniz, one of the great philosophers of the early machine age, claimed that if we knew the position and velocity of every particle in the universe we could predict every single thing which would happen in the whole universe.

More recently we have entered the computer age and the computer has already begun to affect the way we think of ourselves. It is frequently being asserted that our minds are internal computers, each with its memory bank and its capacity to process the large amount of data being continually received through the senses. The more we become familiar with computer concepts and jargon, the more we unconsciously apply them to ourselves. Two women were overheard in a coffee shop discussing the bereavement one of them had recently experienced. She said, 'The hard part is reprogramming yourself to live alone.'

As the influence of the computer penetrates ever more deeply into our lives and our thinking, it is causing us to recast the world in its own image, transforming all of nature into bits of information to be processed and programmed. The computer has created a new context within which we try to organise our human existence. As we start to compare ourselves with computers we run the very serious risk of reducing ourselves to mechanical computers, just as earlier our forefathers began to see themselves as complex machines. Either way we are in danger of losing our unique character as humans. That is certainly the fear of Joseph Weizenbaum.

Just what the computer age may do to our understanding of God is as yet hard to foretell. Perhaps it is just as well that, to date, computer experts are not so much interested in the question of God as were Newton and Leibniz. Yet the spread of computer jargon and thought is certainly going to reach folk-religion, and be reflected there before long. One shudders to think what it may do to the electronic churches of the United States, churches which in my view already practise religion in quite a debased form. One can even imagine hearing one of those radio preachers pray: 'O thou great programmer of the cosmos, flash on to the inner screens of our minds your instant commands and so programme our minds, hearts and wills that we may obey those commands in every respect.'

Of course this is rather a caricature, but I mention it in order to point out that not only in the computer age but also in the machine age and the tool age before it, there was always a strain of traditional religion which was afraid to acknowledge the most unique thing about our humanity, and that is the capacity for autonomous and spontaneous creativity. This is our most precious human possession and we must jealously guard it and foster it, lest we lose it in subservience to the tool, the machine and the computer.

It is in the light of this warning that we now turn to consider whether or not computers may be regarded as possessing intelligence. There is considerable ongoing discussion on this subject under the term AI or 'artificial intelligence'. But first we must ask what we mean by the term 'intelligence'. Unfortunately, a far too simplistic and misleading notion of human intelligence has long been dominant at not only popular but even scientific levels. This is exemplified in the well-known term IQ or 'intelligence quotient', which is measured by various tests devised by educational psychologists. This gives the impression that a person's intelligence is measurable on a simple scale, remains constant through life, and is quite independent of the cultural context in which the person lives. All of these things are false if taken to be absolute.

It was Einstein who first taught us there is no such thing as absolute motion. It is a meaningless term. We can speak of the velocity of an object only in relation to some other object, some external frame of reference. In the same way human intelligence is a meaningless concept in itself. It needs a frame of reference. This necessity often does not strike us because our frame of reference, i.e. our cultural and social setting, is all around us. When we speak of intelligence we are referring to our ability to respond in a purposeful way to our cultural environment. There is nothing absolute about our environment. If we were suddenly transposed to northwestern Australia and left to survive on our own resources we could well appear decidedly unintelligent by comparison with the Australian Aborigine. What our current IQ tests chiefly measure is our ability to respond to the kind of world *we* live in and, more particularly, to cope with the kind of problems which arise in Western education. Indeed it is preferable not to speak of intelligence but to refer rather to intelligent behaviour.

Once we recognise that what we are measuring in IQ tests is not the whole range of human consciousness and capacity to respond to one's environment, but rather a much narrower range of mental activities — namely our ability to solve a selection of practical and abstract problems — we are in a better position to see why, at first sight, the computer may appear to show some intelligence. We can programme it to deal with a selection of such problems. But here we strike a problem. The more expert it becomes, the more it is able to exceed our human ability, the narrower must be the range of the problem.

Now one of the things we normally associate with intelligent behaviour is the ability to handle quite diverse situations, to move from the known to the unknown and still cope, to deal adequately with the unexpected. Now it is just in these aspects that computers have an unbelievably long way to go even to come within range of intelligent human behaviour. Weizenbaum asserts, 'It is simply absurd to believe that any currently existing computer system can come to know in any way whatever what, say, a two-year-old knows about children's blocks.' There is, after all, a lot of information which humans know simply by virtue of having a human body, so that not even another organism, let alone a machine, could know these things in the same way we humans know them.

Another way in which the gap has been made clear, is this. Mosquitoes are not generally thought of as being intelligent creatures. Yet even today's largest and fastest computers cannot match the data processing power of a mosquito by virtue of its ability to fly, navigate and land; identify targets, mates and breeding areas; and survive as a species over millions of generations in a changing and unpredictable world. Yet the mosquito possesses only a few tens of thousands of neuron brain cells; a human being possesses something like a trillion. (See Tom Alexander, 'Artificial Intelligence', *Popular Computing*, May 1985).

There are some computer experts who are not daunted by this. Hans Moravec is a research scientist still in his mid-thirties, who has spent four-fifths of his life constructing robots, having built his first at the age of seven. He believes that by the year 2000 we shall have computers which will be able to perform a trillion operations a second, and that this is the level required for human performance. He insists that by then anything a human can do, a machine will be able to do, and of course it will have to possess mobility comparable to ours.

But most academic researchers in artificial intelligence deny that computers, however expert in certain data processing skills, will ever really qualify as intelligent in any legitimate sense of the word. For one thing, a computer would have to grasp meaning in order to display intelligence. The computers we know are essentially symbol manipulators in which the manipulations are logically valid irrespective of the meaning of the symbol or whether the

symbol has any meaning at all. The computer has no more idea of
the meaning of its operations than the cash register understands
the meaning of the total it has just rung up for you to pay at the
checkout counter.

In order to be able to grasp the meaning of something, one not
only requires something like human consciousness (which computers do not have) but one needs to be aware of the context in
which a statement is to be understood. The meaning of any
statement is not only dependent upon the words used and the
grammatical structure in which they are placed, but also on the
context in which they are heard. A telegram saying, 'Am arriving
on the last plane tonight love, Bill', delivers important information to Bill's wife, who knows he is coming home but not
precisely when. It would convey quite different information to a
girl-friend who was not expecting Bill at all, and who is agreeably
surprised by his declaration of love. The computer has no awareness of contextual meaning and that is why it may keep sending
out monthly accounts demanding that the recipient immediately
pay the sum of $0.00 which has been owing for some time. Of
course one could programme the computer not to do that any
more. But it would be the programmer who would be showing
the intelligence, not the computer.

Computer researchers seeking artificial intelligence have come
increasingly to conclude that computers can never really be called
intelligent until they learn to learn. At Stanford University a
programme called Eurisko has been constructed with the intention
of enabling the computer to copy the kind of introspection
(thinking about one's own thoughts) which goes on in the human
mind a great deal of the time. We are constantly churning over
our own observations and stock of data, linking them together,
reshaping them in an endless variety of ways, discarding some
thoughts and pursuing others.

Programmes like Eurisko may come to be of increasing assist-
ance to people in suggesting new ideas and identifying the most
plausible ones within a complex, but strictly narrow, domain. But
anything like a general purpose intelligent machine is out of reach.
Computers do not think on their own. That means they are not
autonomous thinkers as we humans are. Computers are manipulators of the data they are fed, and their behaviour is strictly determined by the code of directions they are given in each programme.

Why is it then that we humans have been so quick to treat the
computer as if it had personal traits and intelligence superior to
our own? This may be illustrated by returning to ELIZA. The
reason why people who conversed with ELIZA soon came to be

convinced that they were being understood is that, unconsciously, they themselves were supplying the meaning to what ELIZA said. This also happens very often when a person consults a fortune-teller. All the fortune-teller, or horoscope writer, needs to do is to make general statements which are sufficiently plausible—and the eager listener does the rest. Those who had personal encounters with ELIZA had very little knowledge about computers and they attributed to ELIZA a great deal more capacity than it actually has. They projected into it their *own* consciousness, because it appeared to be conversing on the same level as they were. In this way they experienced a self-induced illusion. It is important that we go into the computer age under as few illusions as possible as to what computers may or may not be able to do.

On the one hand the computer is going to become more complex in its operation and more versatile in the kind of tasks it can be set. By means of it we can arrive at information we could never have reached otherwise. It may be regarded as a mechanical extension of the data processing skills of the human brain, an extension which is greatly magnified, but operating only within strictly defined limits. As a servant, the computer will probably prove to be the most important thing which humankind has ever constructed. But it can never be anything more than a servant, comparable perhaps to the genie of Aladdin's lamp.

On the other hand, by comparison with the computer, we humans should come to realise that, in spite of the particular skills in which the computer is vastly superior to us, we possess unique traits and capacities which we must come to value all the more. Just as no person should ever be content to be the slave or tool of another—not even of a divine being—so also human beings are much more than machines and more than computers. There is much more to human existence than logical calculation. It is not surprising that we so often speak of logic as cold. For we humans are also *feeling* creatures with emotional responses and intuition, which can never be captured and repeated by a mechanical apparatus. As creatures with great capacity for intelligent behaviour we are looking for something beyond the information which comes from computer-processed data. We are looking for wisdom. Joseph Weizenbaum said, 'What emerges as the most elementary insight is that since we do not have any ways of making computers wise, we ought not now to give computers tasks that demand wisdom.'

4. Are People Wise?

On a cold January morning in 1800, a boy aged about thirteen came out of the woods which bordered a small village in southern France. It subsequently appeared that from very early childhood he had lived on his own and had somehow managed to survive even the rigours of winter. He could not speak, uttering only strange and meaningless cries. He came to be known as the Wild Child. He was undoubtedly human in form, the offspring of human parents, but having lived in isolation from human language and culture he had not advanced beyond the existence of a sub-human animal.

This happened shortly after the French Revolution. As he must have been a child of two in 1789 it is just possible he was a tragic casualty of the Revolution. This was also a time when, through-out Europe, there was a growing interest in all things natural. This strange phenomenon offered a grand opportunity, so it was thought, to find out about human existence in its wild, natural state, uncontaminated by civilisation.

A young French doctor took responsibility for the Wild Child, renamed him Victor, and commenced the task of educating him in order to find out what he knew of his past and present experience. The doctor worked with Victor for seven years with painstaking patience. The boy never learned to speak. He was never able to tell what he knew. It never became clear whether or not he did know, in the usual sense of that term.

Of course one must avoid jumping too readily to conclusions on the basis of one example. Nevertheless, when we couple this with the odd one or two instances in which infants have been reared by animals, we are led to the tentative conclusion that the process of becoming an intelligent, self-conscious and reflecting human being is not simply a matter of genetic instinct and of ongoing biochemistry and physiology. Growth to *physical* maturity may be assured by these things alone — but growth to *personal* maturity is not.

Most of the things we associate with human maturity are not physical at all, but intellectual and spiritual. They include the capacity to communicate at the highly sophisticated level of human language, and the capacity to think and reflect in the abstract ways made possible by that language. Just as the prenatal embryo is not yet a child but has the potential to become one, so the newborn infant is not yet a fully-developed human being but has the potential to become one. Each of us is born with the potential to become a mature human person but, for develop-ment, that potential must have the stimulation provided by an environment of human society and culture. To become human, it is as necessary for us to breathe in the atmosphere of human culture as it is for our lungs to breathe in oxygen from the physical atmosphere. Moreover, as the phenomenon of the Wild Child suggests, if our potential for human maturity does not receive the appropriate stimulation at the right time, it may atrophy so that it may never again be re-activated.

Earlier we examined the issue of intelligence, and looked at the similarities and differences between the computer and the human mind. I suggested that the more we understand what a computer may or may not be able to do, the more we are led to a deeper appreciation of the unique character of the human condition. Whether or not one should describe a computer as intelligent is partly a semantic problem. If one thinks of intelligence solely in terms of logical reasoning, then one could refer to a computer as intelligent. But if one thinks of intelligence in terms of under-standing and awareness of meaning, then it is quite a different matter. In any case, I question whether the power of logical reasoning is the most important — or even necessary — component of what it means to be human. Some of the finest human beings I know are often quite illogical in their reasoning but this does not make them less human. There is a great deal more to human understanding than logical reasoning.

I have introduced the phenomenon of the Wild Child because it helps to illustrate that the essential differences between humans and computers is even greater than at first might be thought. In learning how to survive under the most adverse conditions the Wild Child may be said to have manifested intelligent behaviour. Yet the Wild Child never reached the intellectual and spiritual stature of humanity, though his body was well on the way to reaching physical human stature. What was missing was the human social environment. The human being is essentially a social creature, part of a larger living whole — human society. The computer is not dependent on other computers; that is its strength but also, *vis-a-vis* humans, its essential weakness. There is no society of computers. It is human society from which the computer receives its input and to which it delivers its output. A cynic once described university education in these terms. It's a process in which students carefully write down what the lecturer reads to them from his notes in order that they may later communicate it back to him in their examination papers, without the content going through the minds of either lecturer or students. This is exactly what the situation would be if computers were ever to converse.

Or so it would seem... for this may not be quite true. We have yet to look at one other way in which computers and living organisms have something in common. Some forty years ago a new science was born, called Cybernetics. The man who founded and did much to spread cybernetic theory was a mathematician from MIT, Norbert Wiener. He subtitled his classic book on the subject, 'Control and communication in the animal and the machine'. He pointed out that living organisms are continually receiving innumerable little messages from their environment, causing them to respond to it in particular ways and thus, in turn to have an effect upon it. Cybernetics is the theory of the way those little messages, or pieces of information, interact with one another.

The term 'cybernetics' is derived from the Greek word which means 'steersman'. A very simple example of cybernetic control in a machine is a thermostat. It continually measures, say, the air temperature of a room and turns the heat supply on and off to keep the temperature relatively even. The thermostat is that part of the whole heating system which enables us to call it self-regulating. Small children are inclined to think there must be a little man in there operating the controls. There is no little man or ghost in the machine. The heating system is cybernetic.

In a similar but much more complex way, living organisms — from the simple cell to the human being — are cybernetic systems which enable the organism to maintain the steady-state of equilibrium, so essential for life, known as homoeostasis. The cybernetic system steers the organism between the Scylla of overgrowth on the one hand and the Charybdis of destruction on the other.

Cybernetics is not only applicable to self-regulating machines and to organisms. It opens up quite a new way of understanding the nature of life itself. Whereas the ancient and primitive mind was always looking for the hidden spirit, the soul, the god, the 'ghost in the machine', in every manifestation of life, we are coming to see that every such manifestation of life is a cybernetic system. The secret of life lies in the network of relationships.

A French biologist, Pierre Grassé, has spoken of life as a circular process in which the genes, the organism and the environment are continually feeding information back and forth, allowing the organism to regulate itself in response to changing external cues. A living organism is no longer seen as a permanent unchanging form but as a network of activity. Thus the philosophy of *being* has been superseded by the philosophy of *becoming*. The very concepts of life and of mind are now seen to be intricately bound up with the changes taking place in the course of time. Indeed cybernetics is changing the way we conceive the nature of reality. Nothing exists except in relation to other things and every event in some way affects everything else. Not only is the whole greater than the sum of its parts, but nothing exists which is not the part of some whole.

Of course seminal thinkers were expounding some of these things long before they came to be assembled in the science of cybernetics. Jewish philosopher Martin Buber, for example, taught that relation is the key to the nature of reality. 'In the beginning is relation,' he said, and, 'Relation is reciprocity.' Reciprocal human relationships are the key to personal growth. That is why the Wild Child never became a human person.

Teilhard de Chardin, another creative thinker of our century, was taking some of the basic steps toward cybernetics when, out of his perceptive observations, he noted that the basic stuff of the universe — whatever it is — shows the strong tendency to organise itself into more and more complex forms. He expressed this tendency in his Law of Complexity-Consciousness, which may be expressed in this way: the more complex the organisation of the basic stuff of the universe, the higher the level of consciousness reached. Human consciousness is not the only form of consciousness to be observed in life on this planet, but it is the highest known to us. And, in human beings, physical matter is organised in the most complex way known to us, chiefly because of the human brain.

Donald MacKay, Professor of Neuroscience at the University of Keele, has tried in the following way to give us lay people an idea of the complexity of our brain. Imagine one cubic millimetre of your cerebral cortex magnified to the size of a lecture hall. Here we would expect to find 100,000 nerve cells. Each of these have anything from 1000 to 10,000 connections. Thus in this building we would see a tangled mass of a thousand million functioning parts. But that would visually portray only a tiny part of the brain. To do justice to the whole brain we need 600,000 of these lecture halls, all equally complex. That's the kind of complexity which has made human consciousness possible.

Now it is true, as we have already seen, that there are some clear analogies between the human brain and the computer in the way they operate or process information. Indeed, the rapid advance of computer technology has been of some help in enabling us the better to understand the way the brain works. But it does not follow thereby that, if we were able to construct a computer as complex as the human brain, it would acquire a self-consciousness of its own. In any case we are so far away from such a feat, even if it were feasible, that it is rather idle to speculate.

It is more important to examine the ways in which humans and computers are alike in some respects, and unalike in others. We are alike in the way we process data. Computers can handle much vaster quantities of information, and work much faster, provided the range is extremely limited. Humans deal with an exceedingly vast range of information by comparison and show a versatility quite unmatched by any computer.

In so far as a computer can be equipped with negative feedback mechanisms, it can become a cybernetic system, as a human is, but at a relatively simple level of operation. The human organism unites into one overall system many different levels of systems stretching from the innumerable cells, through the organs, to the human self-conscious self which we refer to as 'I'. Because of this, human behaviour is operating simultaneously at many different levels. Even the human psyche, as depth psychologists have been teaching us this century, operates at different levels, including at least both the conscious and unconscious levels.

Computer operations are much closer to the way in which lower forms of life operate, and to the lower levels of the human cybernetic system. We human beings have come to recognise, for example, that some aspects of our behaviour are not motivated by conscious choice but by instinct. The lower we move in the hierarchy of living forms the more is behaviour dictated by instinct and less by conscious choice. We can see a very clear parallel between the genetic code, which partly determines what we become, and the programme which determines how the computer will process the data.

All this is true. But now we come to the crux of the matter. The higher up we go in the hierarchy of complexity-consciousness, the more aware we become of having to make choices. It is interesting to observe that those who want to interpret human behaviour entirely in terms of a complex machine or a computer usually end up in philosophy of determinism. Behavioural psychologists, for example, usually see human freedom as an illusion which has no reality.

If it is true that human beings have no real freedom of choice, then we would indeed be no more than highly complex automata. And it would have very serious consequences. We could no longer speak of intelligent behaviour, certainly not with the connotation 'intelligence' usually has. Nor could we hold people morally responsible for their actions. Morality and genuine intelligence are both ruled out where there is no conscious choice being made.

Why are we so sure for the most part that we do enjoy some

freedom (however limited) — certainly living our personal and social lives on this assumption? However much we may be personally conscious of free will, it is rather more difficult to demonstrate than one may imagine. Let me try to do so in a rather unusual way.

We can programme a computer to make a choice. It is what we humans would call an informed choice. It is directed to look at all the possible alternatives and select that which best meets certain criteria. Now in one sense it is making a choice but the choice has really been predetermined by the criteria we have set. In that sense the computer did not of itself make a choice and it displayed no freedom. Many of the choices we make as humans may be of that kind.

But there is something over and above that with us. We too can work out by a set of criteria what would be the best choice, the logical choice. And then we can quite illogically choose the opposite. The computer cannot be illogical and cannot make bad choices. That is its strength. Humans are free to be illogical and to make the bad choice. That's the glory of human freedom, though it may sound a very Irish way of trying to demonstrate it.

The point I am making was first expounded by the nineteenth century philosopher Hegel in the quite novel interpretation he brought to the ancient myth of the Fall of Adam. The Garden of Eden portrayed, in a picturesque, symbolic way, the life of animal-like innocence in which there is no awareness of good and evil, no awareness of choice, no awareness that things might have been otherwise. To become human it was necessary for the eyes of humankind to be opened. It was necessary to become a decision-making creature. It was necessary to become aware of good and evil. The experience of guilt and spiritual suffering which are everywhere present in human existence represent the dark but necessary side of the greatness and the destiny of humankind. The myth of the Fall is an attempt to describe the transition from animal to human status. In making the first bad choice and becoming aware of it, our human ancestors took an irrevocable step into becoming human. This does not mean, of course, that making bad choices now becomes commendable behaviour. Rather it means that *because* we can make bad choices — and frequently do — we can also make *good* choices. It is because we can make bad choices that we can become morally sensitive and responsible creatures.

Computers, like sub-human animals, make no conscious choices and experience no guilt. They exist in that paradisiacal state of innocence which theologians used to call ante-lapsarian, i.e. 'before the Fall'. If computers make mistakes, it is not they who bear the responsibility but we, their makers and their operators. The faults of the computer are *our* faults. That is *our* problem, but it is the dark side of our human greatness.

That is why, however much information the computer can deliver to us (and we are going to become increasingly dependent upon it for information), wisdom — even more so than intelligence — is something which remains applicable to humans alone.

But what is wisdom? The *Shorter Oxford Dictionary* defines it as 'soundness of judgment in the choice of means and ends'. Notice the emphasis on choice. Ever since humans became aware that we are decision-making creatures and that not only our own welfare but that of others (indeed the destiny of the world) is affected by those decisions, our ancestors have been searching for wisdom.

The search for wisdom figures very prominently in the Bible. Yet for some curious reason it has often been largely neglected both in the Jewish tradition and even more so in the Christian tradition. In ancient Israel, alongside the priests and the prophets and the kings, there were the wise men. They have left their deposit in the Bible in what is today called the Wisdom literature: the Books of Proverbs, Job, Ecclesiastes and Ecclesiasticus, the Wisdom of Solomon, and some Psalms. These books stand apart from the rest of the Bible in quite surprising ways. There is no mention of altars and sacrifices, no mention of the Exodus and the great historical events which shaped the religious thought of Israel, no mention of coming Messiahs — and indeed, for the most part, there are only incidental references to God. Not surprisingly these books have been called the documents of Hebrew humanism.

It is here we find the human search for wisdom so brilliantly expressed, and yet in such a way as to the supply no easy answers.

Where shall wisdom be found?
  Where is the place of understanding?
Humankind does not know the way to it.
  It is not found in the land of the living.
The watery chaos has said, 'It is not in me.'
  The sea has said, 'Neither is it with me.'
It cannot be delivered for any amount of gold,
  and silver cannot be weighed out as its price.
It is hidden from the eye of every living creature,
  and concealed from the birds of the heavens.
The underworld of the dead has said,
  'We have heard of it only by rumour.'
God understands the way to it,
  and he knows its place.

That, of course, is an answer at one level—and at another level no answer at all. For do we not sometimes say when we cannot find something we have lost, 'God knows where I put it!'

And it is like that with wisdom. It is continually to be searched for, to be striven for. It cannot be bought. It cannot be prescribed. It cannot be read in a book, not even in the Bible. It cannot be obtained from a computer.

Yet, we need wisdom. And the more we are faced with choices the more we need it. Throughout human history, from the mythical Fall onwards, the opportunity for making choices has been steadily accelerating. In the Third World the number of choices available is still very small, relatively speaking. In the affluent West they are multiplying rapidly, so that on occasions we become weighed down with decisions, decisions decisions!

And more and more is the destiny of this whole planet coming to rest upon our decisions. During the long tool age we exercised choice as to what tools to make and how to use them. We chose to make swords and spears as well as hammers and chisels. In the machine age we chose to make warships and tanks as well as weaving looms and washing machines. We are only at the beginning of the computer age, unable as yet to see clearly where it will lead us—or rather, where we shall choose to go by means of it.

At each stage we have put ourselves, as the human species, in a position of ever-greater control over the planet and its future—often with disastrous results. It has been estimated that, during the long age of the dinosaurs, animal species became extinct at the rate of about one per thousand years. At the beginning of the machine age animal species were dying out on the average of one per decade. Today they are being rendered extinct at the rate of one every 60 minutes. According to one wildlife expert, 17 per cent of all remaining plant and animal species will become extinct by the year 2000.

But there are hopeful signs. We are becoming increasingly aware of the ecological character of the biosphere and of the far-reaching character of every decision we make. The computer will greatly multiply the information at our disposal and help us to calculate the long-term effects of the choices before us.

Moreover, through the advent of biogenetic engineering, again aided by the computer, we have begun the process of creating new living species, first in plant life and more recently in animal life. It is just as if we were taking control of the evolutionary process on this planet—all, of course, for better or for worse.

We have already changed the face of this Earth quite considerably, first with our tools, then by our machines and now by our computers. We humans, the most complex organisms which 3000 million years of biological evolution have produced, have ourselves in some 5000 years made this planet an even more complex network of relationships.

We should be trembling with tension over what we have done and what we now have the power yet to do. We should be approaching at least each major choice before us with a sense of awe and wonder as to what it means to be human. For this is what the ancient wise man meant when he said, 'Reverence for the Lord is wisdom, and turning aside from the evil choice is understanding.'

Images of the City

1. The Wicked City

As each year goes by, more and more people live in cities and find themselves more or less cut off from surroundings in which the forces of nature predominate. Nearly two-thirds of all Australians live in only five cities, leaving a vast continent largely uninhabited. Even in New Zealand there are rural areas which are less populated today than at the beginning of this century.

If this trend continues worldwide, the time may come when all human beings will be city dwellers. If so, our descendants will dwell not just in one of many cities but in one vast global city. So we need to ask ourselves — where are we really heading with rapid urban growth? Is city dwelling so wonderful that we can have no doubts about this trend?

For a generation or so — but for not much longer than that — various professional people, such as town planners, economists, sociologists, anthropologists and even theologians, have been turning their attention to the rapid expansion of city dwelling, as some of the titles of their books make clear — *Cities in Transition, The New World of Urban Man, The Secular City*. They have been looking critically at this modern process of urbanisation and asking some fundamental questions.

The scientific study of the city is a modern phenomenon. But long before this the Bible has been helping to shape the way we think about the city. Quite unconsciously, no doubt, and for better or for worse, we have inherited various images of the city.

The Bible speaks very frequently about the city. Even more interesting is the fact that the Bible is ambivalent. It provides quite contrasting images. The reason for all of this is that the Bible was being written within the long period in which the process of urbanisation has been taking place.

The oldest part of the Bible is between 3000 and 4000 years of age. But the first cities began to appear 5000 to 6000 years ago — in Mesopotamia, Egypt and Indus Valley. Cities had been in existence for some 2000 years before the Judeo-Christian path of faith began and, in part, as I shall show, this faith originated as a kind of response to the evolution of the city.

We should note in passing that though 5000–6000 years seems a very long time, it is relatively short compared with the length of time our human ancestors have been on this planet, which is at least 100,000 years and probably more. The advent of the city, then, has been relatively recent. It had the effect of introducing a new dimension to human existence. To understand this we must ask what it is which constitutes the essence of a city.

In part, of course, it is numbers. Yet the first cities were quite small in population compared with some of our great metropolitan centres today. The first cities in ancient Sumeria had a population of between 7000 and 20,000. But the city is not just a matter of numbers. We have to ask what factors occurred which allowed such numbers of people to live together in close proximity. Then we must ask — what resulted from this concentration of humanity? How could it give a new dimension to existence?

The simple answer to the first question is that the fertile river valleys of the Tigris, the Nile and the Indus yielded food in such abundance, through agriculture and stock-breeding, that no longer was it necessary for all persons to spend most of their available time in gathering sufficient food to keep themselves alive. The growing food supply freed a section of the population for other pursuits. While the majority remained food producers, forming a kind of peasant class, there developed, in addition, an aristocratic ruling class and a professional class of craftsmen.

Of course there had been some form of art and craft in the pre-urban era but these had to be pursued on what we would today call a voluntary or part-time basis. Because they could now be developed as full-time professions, the skill of the craftsmen also increased at a much more rapid rate. Another important factor in this was that the city enabled a community of craftsmen to work together and to learn from each other's improvements. The solitary craftsman was replaced by the community craftsmen. Indeed, one of the chief reasons why urban life was bringing a new dimension to human existence was this — the greatly increased opportunities for personal contact, dialogue and stimulation brought a new heightened awareness and sophistication.

There was now provided, at least for a few, both the freedom, and stimulation to think, which were necessary for the first attempts to philosophise. This in turn led to the invention of writing. Writing provided a new means of communication. In oral speech one communicates only with those who are within hearing distance, and, even then, there is no permanent record of what has been said. By means of writing one can communicate with people much further away both in space and in time.

Here was a new way in which cultural traditions could be inherited from the past and handed down for the future. It gave rise to the phenomenon of Holy Scripture. All these things make up what we call culture. The seeds of culture had long been there in pre-urban mankind. It was the advent of the city which nurtured those seeds to mature growth and flowering. What we call civilisation is the direct product of the advent of the city as the very word 'civilisation' reminds us, being derived from the Latin word for 'citizen', a city-dweller.

But the advent of the city led quite naturally to a sharp division being made between city dwellers and country dwellers. The city dwellers saw themselves as the sophisticated people, the civilised. The rude simple folk of the hills and mountains were the barbarians, the uncivilised. When Christianity spread through Europe it was the country dwellers who were last to be influenced by it: that is why they were called 'heathen', i.e. people of the heath. As late as the early part of this century people of tribal cultures were still being referred to as savages.

Moreover, even in countries of western culture like New Zealand the division of people into urban and rural classes still lingers on. Country folk are sometimes referred to by their sophisticated city cousins as hayseeds and country bumpkins. We find the differences caricatured in comic sketches like those of the 'Two Ronnies'. Dressed in the smocks of country peasants they make us laugh with their childish simplicity and lack of logic.

It is quite true that from the very first city until now, urban life has led to a particular kind of sophistication, by the variety of personal contacts it makes possible, by the mental stimulation it provides, by the variety of professional pursuits it offers, by the cultural and entertainment opportunities it makes available. Only in the cities are to be found the libraries, the theatres, the opera houses, the art galleries, the universities and other places of higher learning. There is a great deal which we owe to the emergence of urban life.

But there is another side to the city, a side which the country dweller is often more acutely aware of than the city dweller. First, there is noise and there are cramped living conditions. There is the complexity of traffic. How many country people say they would not dream of driving their car in the city? The city can be very impersonal in comparison with the country. It is full of strangers. One can become very lonely. The loneliest place in the world, it is sometimes said, is in the middle of a large city where one knows not a soul. Shopkeepers often appear to want your money rather than your custom, for they may never see you again.

Cities quickly become drab and dirty. Some areas deteriorate into slums. What is more, the city becomes the place in which the anti-social tendencies, always present in the human heart, begin to breed and multiply in the same way as that in which diseases strike our plants under hothouse conditions. The city becomes the place for the spread of burglary, drug trafficking, gang warfare. The city produces a criminal underground.

For all these reasons, country people often feel thankful they are not city dwellers but belong to the country. There they enjoy the freshness of nature—clear air, clean water, quietness, honest toil, mutual trust and a network of sincere personal relationships. To the rural mind the image of the city which is often uppermost is that it is a breeding ground of wickedness.

The wicked city is the very first image of the city which occurs in the Bible. The reason is simple. When the city had been in existence for 2000 to 3000 years, it was already beginning to manifest some of its worst by-products. The semi-nomadic wanderers who lived no settled existence visited the cities for trading purposes but were often not at all impressed by what they saw. It was to such pastoral nomads that the ancient Israelites belonged. Indeed, the very word Hebrew is said to be not an ethnic term but one which simply describes a migratory class of peoples. Their modern survival is to be found in the Bedouin, who still value their freedom above all else, and who contemplate with horror the sedentary, tightly packed life of the city. They and their ancient counterparts saw the city as a wicked place.

It is this image of the city which is reflected in that very quaint but fascinating myth which the Israelites told about the origin of mankind. Our mythical parents, Adam and Eve, had two sons whom they called Cain and Abel. Cain became a tiller of the ground, an agriculturist. For this purpose he had to settle in one place. Abel became a keeper of sheep, a pastoralist. He was free to move with his flocks and herds. The ancient Israelite mind saw human beings divided from the beginning into these two types, the permanently settled and the free. Curiously enough something of that class distinction between the pastoralist and agriculturist occurs even to this day. I know parts of New Zealand where the high-country run holder treats the agriculturist (whom he calls the dirt-farmer) with a slightly superior air. It is reflected in the well-known musical, *Oklahoma*, in the song which urges the cowman and the farmer to be friends.

Animosity between the two is evidently very old indeed. In the biblical myth Cain killed Abel. At this point in the story we are told that Cain went off with his wife into exile. Many people get side tracked here and say, 'Hang on. If Adam and Eve and their surviving son Cain were the only human beings on earth, where did he get his wife from?' That is the kind of problem which would only occur to the prosaic logical mind of the sophisticated city dweller. The ancient poetic mind of the pastoral storyteller was just not interested in that kind of logic. What we should take notice of is not what he omitted to explain but what he *did* say. 'Cain went off with his wife, fathered a son and built a city'.

Here there are three quite fascinating insights into the nature of the city. First, the ancient nomad saw the settled life of the agriculturist as the transition from the pure and free life of the nomad to the beginning of city life. Secondly, he saw the city as something man-made unlike the natural world. Thirdly, the founder of the very first city was Cain the murderer. That being the case, could one expect the city to be anything else but a cesspool of iniquity?

The image of the wicked city is further reflected in the myth of the Tower of Babel, where the very building of a city, with its accompanying tower, was seen by the nomad as a human monstrosity which reflected the wicked pride in the human heart and which was an affront to God, who made the earth in its natural state. In similar vein, the cities of Sodom and Gomorrah became so wicked that according to ancient folklore God destroyed them by raining down fire and brimstone from heaven.

In later Israelite tradition it was the Assyrian city of Nineveh which became the symbolic embodiment of all the evil a really great city was thought to engender. When it fell, the prophet Nahum cried out victoriously:

Woe to the bloody city
all full of lies and plunder.

In those days the great powerful empires were often known by the name of the city which was the seat of the Emperor. Assyria, ruled from Asshur, was succeeded by the Empire ruled from Babylon. From that time onwards Babylon became the chief symbol for the wicked city, partly because Jewish exiles were held in captivity there. These symbolic associations long survived the destruction of the city itself and were later used by both Jew and Christian whenever they wished to refer to the wickedness they both deplored and feared in the later city of Rome. It is really Rome which is being referred to in the New Testament Apocalypse where the writer in the following words looks expectantly for its imminent destruction:

Fallen, fallen is Babylon the great
It has become a dwelling-place of demons,

a haunt of every foul spirit...
for all nations have drunk the wine of her impure passion,
and the kings of the earth have committed fornication with her.
She shall be burned with fire.

The writer of the Apocalypse hears the voice of God calling:

Come out of her, oh my people,
lest you take part in her sins,
lest you share in her plagues.

In view of the frequency of the image of the wicked city in the
biblical tradition, it is not surprising to find it accompanied by a
divine call to move out of the city, to start somewhere else a new,
purer, freer life. Because the city was associated with wickedness,
immorality, filth, murder, crime, sexual aberrations and slavery.
It was beyond redemption and had to be destroyed. The only
hope for mankind was to make a clean break with urban existence.

Something of that is embryonically there in the opening of the
saga about Abraham, 'Go away from your country and your
kindred and your father's house to the land I will show you.' And
later tradition did embroider this story of Abraham by saying that
he was called to abandon the ancient city of Ur because of its
idolatry and other forms of wickedness.

The story of Abraham has come down to us almost wholly in
legend. But there is another and more important biblical tradition
which is much more firmly based on historical events. It is the
Exodus from Egypt of a group of Hebrew slaves under the
leadership of Moses. The city of Pharaoh had become for them a
prison, where they had lost all freedom, and where they lived as
forced labour under a foreign ruler. Moses came with the promise
of a new land of freedom even though it meant years in which
they suffered the rigours and hunger of an unwelcoming wilderness.

The rejection of the city for one reason or another and the
return to the simplicity of rural and even desert environment has
been no isolated occurrence in past human experience in general
and in religious traditions in particular. Several of the great
religious traditions originated in just such a move. As the Judeo-
Christian tradition is founded on the Mosaic Exodus from the city
of Pharaoh, so Buddhism is founded on the experience of
Gautama, who abandoned the princely comforts in which he was
born to take up the life of a wandering mendicant, seeking the
answers to the questions of life. Finally he found them, as he
thought, not sitting at the feet of the wise men of the city, but

sitting in solitude under a bo-tree. Jesus of Nazareth, so the Gospels tell us, really began his ministry to mankind by going out into the loneliness of the Jordanian desert for a long period. There, like the John who baptised him, he lived on locusts and wild honey. Muhammad, unlike Jesus, was actually born in the city — the rich, commercial centre of Mecca. But it was only after he had made a practice of frequently retiring in solitude to a cave on Mt Hira, that he received the divine revelations which became the heart and soul of the Islamic faith.

The flight from the busy, frustrating and wicked city has continued from time to time. It led the Christian St Anthony in the third century to leave completely the wickedness of Egyptian city life and retire in solitude to the desert. His move became the beginning of the monastic orders which became such a feature of medieval Christendom. Behind monastery walls monks and nuns found a haven of peace.

Most of us can identify with this rejection of the city even though with us it takes a different form. It is city people, not country people, who complain of the pressures and stress of modern life and who want to get out of the 'rat race'. It prompts people, if they possibly can, to acquire a bach, a weekend cottage, where by the seaside, the lake, the countryside, they can catch their breath, regain their equilibrium, amid the quietness of natural surroundings.

For most, it is but a temporary respite, but a few go further. They turn their back permanently on the city, sell their homes and find a quiet uninhabited spot, where on their own, or as members of a small commune, they live a simple existence close to the soil and the forces of nature. Some would say they are going back to God. Others would say they are going back to nature. They are certainly turning their backs on the man-made city.

But for most people that is not possible and never will be. The human species is becoming more and more urbanised whether we like it or not. Even the decreasing minority who still live in rural areas are becoming more and more dependent on what goes on in the city. In some respects we can say that just as city dwellers receive their bread from the country, so the cultural fruits of the city are being increasingly distributed in the country. This inter-dependence between city and country began from the very origins of city life.

However frustrating, uninviting and wicked we may come to view it, wholesale abandonment of the city is not a practical solution. What, then, can be done? Are we humans doomed to become imprisoned within the urban social structures which we have built? What kind of positive hope is there for us city dwellers? Is the future to be all downhill? There are certainly some who think so. Go to Hong Kong, New York, Philadelphia and Sydney, to name but a few, and you will find much evidence to support such a gloomy picture.

2. The Secular City

In 1965 a Baptist theologian in the United States called Harvey Cox wrote a book which was intended for a fairly confined audience. It was to provide the basis for discussion in a series of conferences organised by the National Student Christian Federation. He called it *The Secular City*. To his great surprise it suddenly took off. It began to be read by many people for whom it was not specifically intended. Both American and foreign theologians began arguing about it. Sociologists and city planners began discussing it. It reached an unexpectedly large Roman Catholic audience. Within a short time it had sold half a million copies in America alone—and had been translated into seven other languages. By the following year a book appeared called *The Secular City Debate*. It presented a sample of the wide diversity of responses which Cox's book had brought forth—some of them appreciative, some of them harshly critical.

Why was the book so widely read? And why did people come to such different opinions about it? Cox had put his finger on an issue which, though sensitive, pinpointed the most dominant trends in today's city. The issue is two-fold: the *spread of urbanisation* and with it, the *process of secularisation*.

Cox defined this process as one in which people turn their gaze away from a supposed other-world and fasten their attention on *this* world and *this* time. For *saeculum* is the Latin word which means 'this present age'.

These two dominant processes he put together in the term *The Secular City*, with the implication that this is the dominant image of the city which operates today. Many refuse to acknowledge that there is any good in this secular city. They see it as an enlarged and grotesque form of the wicked city. This is particularly so with many church people who, though they live in the secular city, keep contrasting it with their ideal city, which they call the holy city. Cox set out to allay what fears Christians may have about the increasing manifestation of the secular city. He tried to show it is not the wicked city many take it to be, and that there are many advantages it has given to us for reaching more fruitful levels of human existence. Instead of being seen as an enemy to be fought and held in check, it should be seen as the logical development of certain trends deeply embedded in the Judeo–Christian tradition itself.

Cox's book is a little dated now and should certainly not go unchallenged. But it raises issues which are still with us.

What is the character of the modern secular city? There are three we may usefully observe. The first we may call *mobility*. Cox notes that there are two visual images which we frequently associate with the city: the switchboard and the cloverleaf. Since his book was written it has become necessary to add the computer. The telephone switchboard means that in spite of the very large population of the city, we have the opportunity for instant communication with the person of our choice. And the arrival of STD in most cities of the western world illustrates better than anything how fast the globe is becoming one city.

In our main cities there are now many examples of the cloverleaf intersection of two motorways. In the big European and American cities, these intersections are much more complex. They manifest the variety of directions in which people choose to travel. Not only are there many geographical directions, but these in turn symbolise the variety of career directions one can take and the variety of opportunities for life fulfilment.

Compare the city with the village. There was one main street— the High Street. It led in and it led out. And life in the village was often just as confined. One tended simply to follow in one's father's trade, if a man, or become a housewife and mother, if a woman.

The cloverleaf of city life keeps presenting us with choice after choice. Further, it symbolises the fact that, as a result of increased choices, we are people more frequently on the move. City people less commonly put down their roots for long periods, but move from suburb to suburb, from city to city.

In the age of the village, life was sedentary. One spent one's whole life very often within an area perhaps only 15 kilometres in diameter. So it was in the first cities. But in the modern secular city there is great mobility. Instant communication, constant change and instant information. First it was access to knowledge stored in libraries. Now it is the computer. Knowledge which once took a lifetime to amass is now instantly available.

From mobility we turn secondly to *anonymity* as a characteristic of the secular city. This aspect of city life is what often first strikes a person from a rural area, where everybody knows everybody. By contrast, in the city it first appears that nobody really knows anybody. Other people become nameless faces we pass in streets, sit with in a bus or theatre. In our contacts we do not speak of people by name but by the role in which we meet them — the 'person on duty', the 'girl at the counter', the 'rubbish man', the 'paper boy', 'the milkman'... Even at work it can be the case we do not even know by name people working close to us, let alone have any kind of personal relationship with them.

Of course in one sense the great numbers of people in a city make this essential. A city mayor who set out to know all the citizens on a personal basis would never get anything else done. Nor is this phenomenon completely without its advantages. Because it is not possible to know all our contacts personally, it frees us to be highly selective in those whose friendship we do want to cultivate. Although the city can be the loneliest place in the world, its anonymity means also that there we have greater opportunities for living our private lives than we have in the country. There your presence cannot fail to be noted and you are talked about, whether you like it or not.

Let us now turn from the mode of life in the modern city to its secular character. I have so far defined secular as 'this worldly' in orientation, compared with the alternative of being 'other worldly'. Another term we could use as the polar opposite of the secular city is to speak of the holy city.

There are three cities which in the course of history have come to be regarded as the chief claimants of this title. First, there is Benares in Northeast India, on the River Ganges, the holy city of Hinduism. Secondly, there is Mecca, the holy Muslim city towards which every faithful Muslim turns several times a day in order to say his prayers. Thirdly, there is the city of Jerusalem, revered as holy by all three faiths of Middle Eastern origin, Judaism, Christianity and Islam.

Any religious tradition which acknowledges one city to be a holy city keeps focusing attention on that city — going there if it is at all possible on holy pilgrimage. That city provides for the devotee a centre to his world. This is very clear in Islam where every mosque has its Kibla, or apse, which marks the direction of Mecca. The central point provided by the holy city symbolises the fact that the religious faith stemming from that city gives direction and meaning to life.

One of the reasons why Jews built synagogues, Christians built churches and Muslims built mosques is that the further one lives from the holy city the more difficult it is to go there. So the church, synagogue or mosque becomes a holy place which serves as a centre for the village, town or city where one lives. As Christianity spread through Europe and Western Asia, the church became the village centre and the cathedral the city centre. The market square, where business and trade were carried on, where celebrations occurred, was very often directly in front of the church or cathedral.

This meant that every pre-modern city of the Christian West had a holy centre. Such was the magnificence of the buildings of the European cathedrals during the High Middle Ages that one was left in no doubt as to where the centre of the city was. The one city of New Zealand where this state of affairs is still clearly visible is Christchurch, where the Cathedral still dominates the city, remains the centrepoint of the city and is faced by a large open square, now a pedestrian precinct. But in most cities today it is very different! Even in London the great dome of St. Paul's, which long was visible from almost everywhere in London, has now become hidden among large blocks of post-war commercial buildings.

The secular city, unlike earlier cities of Christendom, has no holy centre. Indeed it tends to have no real centre at all. When the modern city first began to emerge the city hall tended to become the centre. In the late nineteenth century it was the railway station. Each city may develop its own idea of a centre. In Dunedin, for a long time, in spite of the presence of First Church with its imposing Gothic spire, it was actually the Stock Exchange which was the centre. By and large the modern secular city has no centre — certainly no permanent and universally acknowledged centre. Each person sees and finds their own centre — depending upon interests. That means that the city no longer supplies us with a kind of architectural model of our world, of an ordered cosmos, which conveys to us a strong sense of direction and purpose. The city of Christendom once used to do that. The spire to be seen from everywhere, was a constant reminder that eyes should be continually turned to God above. The bells which were rung from the church or cathedral were a call to prayer. Indeed the tinkling of bells still heard at the Roman Catholic Mass is only the relic of the practice of ringing the great bells so that all within hearing distance would know the moment in which that miracle had taken place once again by which the bread and wine had become the body and blood of Jesus.

Many Christians look back nostalgically to cities of European Christendom with their holy centres: for these give, both visually and in sound, a clear sense of direction and order to life. Such people deplore the fact that those characteristics have been choked to death by the rise of the secular city.

But there is another side to it. The homogeneity and uniformity of life in a city with a holy centre was fine for all those who whole-heartedly embraced the Christian faith. But what of others, the Jews for example? They could not be citizens of that city. They could be allowed no part of that city. They had to be herded into a ghetto and sealed off, as it were, from the Christian community.

What also of those solitary individuals, who from time to time, followed their own independent thoughts, exerted their individuality and questioned one aspect or another of the foundations of the Christian city? They too could not be tolerated. Stern measures were often taken to ensure that all conformed. That is the other side of the Christian city of the Middle Ages. It was selective, not wholly human. It limited personal freedom. It curbed initiative. At times it even imprisoned the human spirit. Since the Renaissance and Reformation, which mark the first clear beginnings of the modern world, personal freedom has been growing in successive stages, resulting in increasing diversity of thought and conviction.

As the modern world emerged it became necessary to break out of the boundaries and rigid forms into which the Christian tradition had become fixed. While on the one hand these had given security, on the other hand, they were becoming a prison. This is why in the late nineteenth century the prophetic insight of Nietzsche charged Christianity with teaching a slave morality.

The result of this outburst of human freedom and of the emancipation of western society from ecclesiastical control necessarily meant that the modern city had to become secular. There could no longer be a holy centre. To allow freedom for the individual, the institution both of city and of the nation, had to become religiously neutral. The only kind of a human society consistent with the freedom of the individual human spirit is one of religious pluralism.

This brings us to a new important meaning of the word secular. It should not be equated with 'non-religious' far less with 'anti-religious' but with 'religiously neutral'. The modern secular city, like the modern secular state, must be religiously neutral in order that its citizens may be religiously free. Good examples of the modern secular state are India, United States and New Zealand. England and Sweden are secular in practice, but, in theory, they are still religious states. Russia, in theory, is a secular state but, because of its official commitment of an anti-religious ideology, it is actually a 'religious' state of a negative kind.

The secular city, like the secular state, has therefore become religiously necessary in the modern world. Many traditional

Christians find that hard to accept and feel great nostalgia for the former holy city or the city with a holy centre.

One of the reasons Cox wrote his book was to expound two main theses. The first is that the modern secular world was a product of Western Europe. The second is that the secular world, far from being an enemy of the religious tradition out of which it has emerged, is in fact the logical development of certain trends which have been present in the Judeo-Christian stream from the beginning. His arguments may be briefly described as follows.

First, Cox contended, the Hebrew teaching about creation had the effect of separating God from the forces of nature. Whereas primal man treated the very forces of nature themselves as sacred, the Hebrews saw them as having no ultimate power over mankind. Rather, mankind was given legitimate control over them.

Secondly, the Exodus from Egypt under Moses was a dramatic rejection of the conviction that hitherto had been unquestioned, namely that royal houses and aristocratic classes rule by divine right. Moses led the first of what was destined to be a long series of social revolutions before the truth was to be universally recognised. The Exodus was the first step, said Cox, in the process of taking the 'sacred' out of politics.

Thirdly, the ancient covenant at Mt Sinai between the Israelites and their God, Cox saw as the relativism of all absolutes. This is expressed particularly in the first two commandments which call for the iconoclastic destruction of anything from this world which begins to assume the absoluteness, the holiness, the finality, which belong to God alone. Cox called this the deconsecration of values. He meant that all our value systems are relative to a time and place. They are open to criticism. They must not be treated as eternal and unchangeable.

In short, it was Cox's contention that the process of secularisation which is the dominant trend in modernity really found its origin in the very foundations of the Judeo-Christian faith and that is why the modern world emerged out of the Christian West and from nowhere else. This means that though the term 'secular city' cannot be termed an image of the city which is *explicit* in the Bible, it is nevertheless one which is *implicit*.

There is one strange confirmation of this in the Bible. It is in the Book of Revelation, that last book of the New Testament which has both puzzled and yet fascinated Christians ever since it was written. Right at the end of the book (and consequently of the Christian Bible itself), the writer describes a vision he saw of a new kind of world which was to replace the present world. He described it as a holy city, a new Jerusalem. One of the features of this city was that there would be no temple in it—there was to be no holy centre!

Why was this to be the case? He explained! It was because the only temple would be the Lord God Almighty. But where was this God to be found, if not in a temple or church? He would be found among his people. He would be found *among* and *in* human beings. The very same Greek language is used here as we find in the prologue to St. John's Gospel in the passage that gave rise to the term 'incarnation'. There it says that the logos or word of God became enfleshed in Jesus. But here it says that in this city of the future, God will cease to be the transcendent divine ruler in heaven above and will be *in* and *among*, not just one particular person, but in all people.

All this is expressed in ancient mythical language. Yet it is in many ways the most daring thought in the whole Bible. The implication is that in the city of the future the dichotomy between holy and secular will have disappeared. There will be no difference between the secular city and the holy city. There will be no difference between God and the human community.

It is abundantly clear that we are still a long way from the realisation of that ancient vision. Yet it may help us to see that, although the modern secular city must not be regarded as any final product, it may well be an important stage on the way towards a yet more satisfying and fruitful form of human existence. Already in the modern secular city there is increased freedom and choice of opportunity. But at the same time we must assume increased responsibility for our human future. We participate more and more in the prerogatives which formerly were attributed to God.

3. The Doomed City

A few years ago two Italian students of archaeology and I hired a taxi from Baghdad and travelled south about 100 kilometres until we reached the Euphrates River. The countryside was only sparsely populated. What I had gone to see was quite uninhabited. It was the ruins of the ancient city of Babylon. First I climbed and walked over a shapeless mound of dry earth. Although only about twenty metres above the completely flat landscape, one could nevertheless see quite a distance—to the palm trees growing on the bank of the Euphrates. This mound is all that is left of what legend calls the Tower of Babel.

Archaeologists call it a ziggurat. Several were built in ancient Mesopotamia and some remain in much more of their original shape than this one, for after this one was destroyed for the last time it served as a quarry of sun-dried brick for builders for centuries to come. This ziggurat once stood about ninety metres —a most imposing structure. It started as an ancient Sumerian village some 5000 years ago.

Then the invading Semitic Akkadians built a tower-like ziggurat as a temple to their goddess Ishtar and they gave it the name *Babel*, which means Gateway of God. The name of the city which grew up round about took its name from that tower and became Babylon. The story of Babylon is the story of construction and destruction—more than once. The earliest destruction of the tower gave rise to the biblical legend of the Tower of Babel.

There were two great periods of Babylonian prosperity. The first was about 1800 years before Christ when it became the religious and administrative capital of an empire ruled by Hammurabi. His law-code carved in rock can be seen in the British Museum to this day. But that city of Babylon was destroyed and rebuilt by successive waves of foreigners. More than 1000 years after Hammurabi came the second great flowering. We may call it the New Babylon. It was the capital of the greatest empire the world had then seen. This Babylon was the city of Nebuchadrezzar who, in his victorious marches, captured, among many other cities, the holy city of Jerusalem. It was to this Babylon that he took into exile as captives the Jewish priests and aristocracy. It is probably in this Babylon that the first five books of the Bible were compiled into their present form.

I thought of all these things as I walked through the ruins of what was in its day the greatest city mankind had ever built. The hanging gardens of Babylon were long regarded as one of the seven wonders of the world. All that I could see were toppled, broken-down walls of sun-dried brick. It needed the expertise of an archaeologist even to discern what was left of temples, palaces and theatres in this heap of rubble. It was not hard to conclude that in the course of time all the greatest and noblest of human constructions ultimately end like this. The words of the Bible came to mind:

Fallen, fallen is Babylon: and all the images
of her gods the Lord has already shattered to
the ground.

The Jews, because of their close association with this city of Babylon seized upon it as an image of the wicked city. The early Christians inherited this image. But Babylon also became the chief example of the doomed city. Babylon thereafter became a symbol of every city doomed for destruction.

More than 400 years after the time of Nebuchadrezzar, when the enemies of the Jews were no longer the Babylonians but the Hellenistic kings of Syria, an anonymous Jew tried to encourage his persecuted fellow Jews by writing of the fate of Babylon. He portrayed Nebuchadrezzar strutting proudly over the roof-top of his royal palace saying, 'Is not this great Babylon which I have built by my own mighty power for the glory of my own majesty?' While the words were still in his mouth a voice from heaven called to him, 'Your kingdom had departed from you— you will be driven out from humankind and forced to live like an animal.'

But though Babylon became the chief symbol of the city doomed for destruction, it was not, of course, the first to suffer that fate. Rather it was the largest in a long line of cities which, in Jewish memory and experience, had been reduced to ruins. The pages of the Old Testament are full of stories of doomed cities from Sodom and Gomorrah onwards. The most persistent message in the renowned prophets of Israel is one of impending doom for one city after another. One can open the books of the prophets almost at random and come across such words as:

Behold, Damascus will cease to be a city,
and will become a heap of ruins.

Moreover, this gloomy message of destruction to come was not confined to foreign cities, the strongholds of one's enemies. Finally the prophets told of the coming destruction of their own cities—including the holy city of Jerusalem. This was particularly the case with the prophet Jeremiah who declared 'a destroyer of nations' was already on the way:

to make your land a waste; your cities
will be ruins without any inhabitants.

For this subversive talk he was reviled, imprisoned and tortured. He was regarded as a traitor and was almost put to death, yet he lived to see his words come true. In 586 B.C. the Babylonians destroyed, sacked and burnt both the city and temple of Jerusalem.

A whole book of the Bible is devoted to Jewish lamentation over this ultimate disaster:

How lonely sits the city
that was once full of people...
Women are ravished in Zion
virgins in the towns of Judah.

> Princes are hung up by their hands
>   no respect is shown to the elders.
> The joy of our hearts had ceased
>   for Mount Zion lies desolate;
> and jackals prowl over it.

Now we must ask the question—why has this image of the doomed city been such a persistent one? It is found not only in the biblical heritage, but in human experience everywhere. So many of the cities of the ancient world like Asshur and Babylon, like Byblos and Ugarit, like Memphis and Palmyra exist today only in ruins. Why is this so?

The answer given by the Bible is simple. They long associated the image of the doomed city with that of the wicked city. They firmly believed that human history moves onward according to moral laws because it is ultimately controlled, not by men but by a righteous and all-powerful deity. Therefore all cities, being wicked, must ultimately end in destruction. In the long run this answer has turned out to be over-simplistic and even false.

All of us would hesitate to apply that superficial answer today. Did major earthquakes devastate Lisbon, San Francisco, Tokyo and Napier because these cities were especially wicked? Of course we dare not say so. We need to enquire further to find satisfactory reasons for the phenomenon of the doomed city.

Actually the first reason why the frequency of city destruction led to the prevalent image of the doomed city is very simple. A city brings a lot of people into close and interdependent relationship. Any natural calamity will as a consequence, *appear* much worse and often *be* much worse than it would have been in sparsely settled countryside. Life in the city multiplies the degree of vulnerability already present in human existence.

In the earliest cities fire was the chief cause of destruction. It took a long time to realise that cooking methods which were relatively safe in the country became highly dangerous in the city. As recently as the great fire of London, started in a baker's oven, the lesson had not been learnt. Not only was fire one of the simplest weapons for the ancients to use to destroy the cities of their enemies but some ancient cities such as Persepolis were destroyed by accidental fire (or so it is thought).

Then lack of adequate city planning contributed to urban disaster. The early cities grew up like Topsy as the result of unrelated factors working blindly together. People needed a water supply. So they built beside rivers. This left them unprepared for the 'one in a century' flood which swept the city away. Indeed one of the reasons why the early inhabitants of Mesopotamia built their large artificial towers or ziggurats was to provide a refuge. The surrounding land was so flat that when the Euphrates flooded, as it sometimes did without any warning, cities found themselves in the midst of a shallow sea.

Then thirdly there is the phenomenon of disease and plague. Contagious diseases spread very quickly in the city, not only because people are in closer contact, but because cities which are unplanned and uncared for create the conditions leading to diseases — such as bad drainage, impure water, and no sewerage. More recently it has been air pollution and the hazards of traffic congestion. For all these reasons 'it is little wonder' as one sociologist has said 'all of the early cities were eventually abandoned or overrun by enemies'.

Not just wickedness but ignorance lies behind city destruction. The less planned a city, the more likely it will end in ruin. City planning is a relatively new art, only really in its infancy. Already it has done much to improve the prognosis of the modern city. But this in itself is not sufficient to overcome the challenge of the doomed city.

We must never forget that the city is a human construction. It is artificial. City buildings are themselves lifeless and static and like all human products are finite. They have a limited time span, having a beginning and an end. This is something we could hardly help noticing as we have been walking through the streets of Wellington in recent years, as we have observed one building after another being demolished. The chief features of the countryside result from the living forces of nature. Whereas a deserted city only falls more and more into ruin, a deserted countryside has the natural capacity to re-establish itself. This contrast is strikingly illustrated by the unexpected discovery of Angkor Wat. What had been an impressive structure of Buddhist civilisation, once deserted, became hidden and swallowed up in the encroaching jungle.

This contrast between the natural countryside and the artificially made city leads us to distinguish between two aspects of the city — the buildings and the people. We often refer to each as the city, but in fact a city consists of both. Empty buildings constitute only a dead city. Buildings plus people constitute a living city. A living city, like the natural forces in the countryside, does have the power to grow, to change, to transcend earlier mistakes and disasters, to rise again out of the ruins and partial loss of population, and destruction of buildings. We have seen this happening all over Europe since World War II.

Doom need not be the ultimate end of every city. Because cities are man-made they can not only be rebuilt; they can be remodelled. They can grow into something different. The awareness of the vulnerability of the city and its possible doom can so spur the creative human imagination that the city may grow to be something different from what it has been. It is for this reason that even the Bible itself, in its evolving thought, completely changed its stance on how it saw the city. Its very first image, as we have seen, was that of the wicked city, from which we can expect no good at all. But its very last image was that of the eternal city as we shall later see. The middle step in this metamorphosis of images was the image of the doomed city.

For a long time in history one of the chief ways men attempted to overcome the vulnerability of city life was simply to strengthen its defences by building walls. Cities came to be built in places which were more easily defended from enemies.

This process gave rise to a new image of the city as a fortress. Indeed, in the Teutonic languages, the word for fortress, 'burgh', became the commonly used synonym for city. The relics of this remain to this day in such place names as Edinburgh — and in our own use of the 'borough' for small towns. Both in the ancient world, and in the European world, until two or three hundred years ago, a city always implied a walled city. The gates were closed at nightfall. The walls were manned by night-watchers. People felt much safer in cities than in the countryside. They believed the early vulnerability of cities had been overcome. Cities had become invulnerable. They had become places of safety, fortresses, sanctuaries of peace.

Today cities no longer have walls. They have ceased to be places of safety. The simple reason is that the ingenuity of man can work both ways. The ability to build walls which are impregnable can be matched by the ability to build weapons and machines of war which make walls useless. In the modern world the vulnerability of the city has re-emerged in a starker form than ever before. This was clearly illustrated by the bombing raids in World War II. The city, long thought to be a refuge and place of safety, had become a hot spot of danger. Britain encouraged as many noncombatant and nonessential personnel as possible to leave London for the countryside. Children in particular were sent out of what had become the danger zone.

One of the memories I have of World War II is of the day news reached us of Pearl Harbour. I happened to be living in Wellington then. What I remember was this. At every petrol station there was a long queue of people anxious to fill their cars with petrol so that they could leave the city at a moment's notice. The city had ceased to be a sanctuary and had once again become vulnerable as a place doomed for destruction by enemy action.

This vulnerability of the city has not decreased since World War II but, because of missiles with nuclear warheads, has actually increased many times over. Practically all such missiles if ever used, will be targeted on cities, for their aim is to do the greatest possible damage in the shortest possible time. And that is only part of the story.

The age of nuclear war began, of course, with the dropping of the first atomic bombs on Hiroshima and Nagasaki. That news sent a spine-chilling wave around the world. I know to many it brought a sense of victorious relief in that it would hopefully bring a speedy end of hostilities with Japan — which in fact it did. But that is not how everybody saw it even then. I was living in a small country town in North Otago at the time. The day the news came through I went in to the village store. To my surprise I found the storekeeper almost beside himself with rage and indignation, that the human race could sink so low as to use such a monstrous weapon on relatively innocent citizens. When I think back to that initial reaction of a relatively simple New Zealander whom I would have thought of as possessing only average ability and moral sensitivity, I am amazed how dulled has become the moral sensitivity of the western world today. We seem to have become quite blasé about nuclear war, as if it is something we have become adjusted to, and have learned to take in our stride. Moral aspects of it are rarely discussed any more.

To the extent that this is so I believe we are today living in a fool's paradise. It is true that for a decade after Hiroshima there was a widespread fear of nuclear war. Then in the period of detente, that fear became less acute. Unfortunately, during that lull, the perfection of much more powerful nuclear warheads went on apace until the arms race once again accelerated. Today the threat of nuclear war hangs over us like the sword of Damocles. The image of the doomed city has never been such a threatening reality in all human history as it is today. This time it is not a few selected cities only which are threatened. It is all cities. It is in fact the emerging global city which lives under the shadow of the doomed city.

The reason is that nuclear war, if it breaks out, will escalate so fast that all the fatal decisions may have been made in the first half-hour. From what the experts tell us there seems to be no way of limiting a nuclear war. The only alternatives are: either an all-out nuclear war or no nuclear war at all. An all-out nuclear war would not only produce destruction and death on an unbelievable scale — but its aftermath is likely to spell the end of all higher forms of planetary life. A nuclear war would bring the ultimate end of the city for all time.

Even many of those who support the possession of nuclear arms as a necessary deterrent agree with this Either-Or. They say we must have nuclear arms equal to those of our potential enemies in order to prevent the ultimate disaster of a nuclear war. I respect the sincerity of those who produce this argument but I find the logic puzzling and unconvincing. It is like saying — 'We are living dangerously — we are sitting on a gigantic powder keg which may explode at any moment. Our only hope of survival is to add more explosive so that no-one will dare light the fuse!'

Without realising it, our potential enemies are no longer what they once seemed to be. It is no longer the yellow peril, the Russians, the Communists which constitute the real enemy. Our real enemy today is the gigantic Frankenstein which, because of our mutual distrust and hostility, our own minds and skill have created. It is not our human enemies, but this potentially danger- ous and unstable state of affairs which, if not defused, will destroy both us and our so-called human enemies. The global city of the world stands under threat of ultimate doom.

And the cause? It is not the wrath of a righteous God. It is not the wicked designs of our enemies. It is the fact that human ingenuity has outreached both the moral and rational capacity to control what we have created. The famous Swiss psychiatrist Carl Jung, in his last public interview for the B.B.C., was asked about the human future, and whether there would a Third World War. He made a significant reply. 'Man himself is the origin of all coming evil.' This means that if the ultimate doom falls it will be because the human race through blind ignorance, wilful short- sightedness and narrow-minded self-centredness has brought about its own destruction.

We witness today a growing tide of concern around the world as the image of the doomed city shows up more clearly on our horizon. Yet those who point to what they see are often reviled, sneered at, and dismissed as prophets of doom. Such is frequently the treatment meted out by people in high places. Prophets of doom have never been popular, even in the ancient world. Although the ancient prophets were seen as traitors in their own day their words came to be collected and placed in the Bible because they came true.

It won't be like that this time. If the words of today's prophets of doom come true, because they are not heeded, there will be no one left to ponder and record their words. The global city will lie in ruins, uninhabited, for the last time in the history of this planet.

If you visit Jerusalem you will find halfway up the hill, called the Mount of Olives, a tiny church. There is a window over the altar. Through that window one has a breathtaking panoramic view of the old city of Jerusalem. The church is called Dominus Flevit (The Lord Wept). It marks the approximate point in which, according to Gospel tradition, Jesus paused as he approached Jerusalem with his disciples and he wept as he thought of the destruction which was shortly to befall that city. 'O Jerusalem, Jerusalem, killing the prophets and stoning those who are sent to you! How often would I have gathered your children together as a hen gathers her brood under her wings and you would not. Behold your house is to become forsaken and desolate.' Jesus too was a prophet of the doomed city!

No prophet of the doomed city, either from the ancient world or the modern world, takes pleasure in what they foresee. They weep! Nor are they fatalistic. They know the dangers are real but they see a glimmer of hope.

4. The Eternal City

The secular city has much to be said for it. It has brought to the individual person greatly increased freedom and opportunity for fulfilment. But every increase in freedom carries with it an equal measure of responsibility. The secular city appears to have laid on our shoulders a degree of responsibility for which we are not yet ready. Our cleverness, our technological ingenuity, has outstripped our wisdom. One reason for this is the rapid expansion of science and technology which has characterised the emergence of the secular city.

We have lost our vision. The secular city, as currently experienced, is often flat, uninspiring, cold and inhuman. The secular city lacks vision—that which has the power to stir the human imagination, motivate the human will, and inspire with hope. That is why we must turn now to the image of the eternal city.

There is actually one city in the world which has long regarded itself as the *eternal* city. It is the city of Rome. Why is this so? Most of us think of Rome, either as the capital of modern Italy, or as the even greater capital of the ancient Roman Empire. Why eternal city? Admittedly it is a very old city. It is much older than New York, London and Paris, and even older than Alexandria and Athens. It proudly traces its foundation to the legendary Romulus in 753 B.C. Old and magnificent—yes! But why eternal? After all, it too has known destruction. The reason for this epithet is chiefly to be found in what happened *after* it ceased to be the capital of a great empire and *before* it became the capital of Italy.

For a period of about 1000 years, it was the centre of an empire very different from the kingdoms of this world. After the fall of Rome some of the structures of the empire were inherited by the church and the mantle of the emperor was assumed by the Bishop of Rome. He even took to himself the title once proudly claimed by emperors, Pontifex Maximus, used by the Pope to this day in the form Chief Pontiff.

We may take Christmas Day 800 A.D. as a convenient starting point for the long period in which Rome was to be viewed as no ordinary city but as the eternal city. On that day the Pope crowned Charlemagne as Emperor of a new and Holy Empire. During the next 1000 years the Pope claimed a higher authority than that of all kings and princes of Christendom. From Rome he exercised power both temporal and spiritual. That period came to an end in 1870 when the Italian army entered Rome. The temporal power of the Pope was considerably reduced and is today confined to a few acres known as the Vatican City.

The fact that Rome was the eternal city for 1000 years is due in no small measure to the thoughts of one man — Augustine. When Rome fell to the Goths in 410 A.D. only a century after Constantine had elevated Christianity to be the state religion, many citizens of the old school blamed the decline of Roman power on the spread of the new faith.

Augustine, living in North Africa and the most influential Christian thinker of his day, set out to answer these charges. It resulted in a famous book, written and published in instalments over a period of thirteen years. It became one of the great Christian classics and is known as *The City of God*. These circumstances of its appearance illustrate something mentioned earlier. The doomed city may serve as the middle term between the wicked city and the eternal city. It was the experience of destruction on a grand scale which gave birth to the image of the eternal city. This book was destined to have wide influence on later thought in the West, both political and religious.

Augustine lived at one of the extremely critical periods in the history of the West. He saw the last days of Rome. And he himself was a product of the best which Roman culture had to offer. In some respects he was the last of the great Romans. Yet bleak as the future appeared to many of his fellows, he looked into it with great hope. That hope was expressed symbolically as the City of God — or the heavenly city. His simplest definition of it runs: 'The heavenly city has truth for its King, love for its law and eternity for its measure'.

To appreciate what Augustine was doing we must remember that he was living at a time when people of the ancient world thought in terms of the *Civitas Romana* — the Roman body-politic. That 'city', as it were, was for them the one and only possible society. To this end they had deified the emperor as its living incarnation. They had given a religious sanction to all its claims. As its framework was at that moment cracking into pieces, Augustine said in effect, 'This is not the whole story! There is another and greater society — towards which the whole of creation is moving.' He elaborated a gripping philosophy of human history which inspired new hope! He did this by drawing a sharp contrast between what he called the heavenly city (the city of God), and the earthly city (the terrestrial city).

The city of God was pervaded by relations of righteousness joining together all the righteous on earth, wherever they are, with God and his angels in heaven. This city was universal in extent, but it excluded the fallen angels and the unrighteous. This city was not visible to the naked eye. As he saw it, it did contain most church members but not all. The earthly city was also invisible to the naked eye. It contained the unrighteous — and that included some church members.

These two cities were chiefly characterised by two different kinds of love. In the earthly city was found love of self and contempt of God. Thus wherever people exert power for their own advantage — imperial, civic or economic power — we have the presence of the earthly city. In the heavenly city we have by contrast, the love of God and contempt of self. Wherever people are ready to sacrifice their own personal advantage in the interests of the common good (which is none other than for God himself) there we have the presence of the heavenly city.

It is a mistake to identify the earthly city with, say, the declining Roman Empire (or the civil state) and the heavenly city with the Church. Augustine specifically stated that 'these two cities, based as they are on these two kinds of love, shall live side by side and even intermixed until the final separation shall take place at the end of time at the Last Judgment!'

This aspect of Augustine's teaching is remarkably parallel to Jesus' parable of the need to let the weeds grow up with the good grain until the harvest. However, Augustine's teaching came to be misunderstood. As time went on the church *did* come to be equated with the City of God and all that was not in the church belonged to the terrestrial city. Later Christians looked expectant-

ly to the ultimate dissolution of the earthly city, already symbolised in the historic fall of Ancient Rome. And they looked to
the ultimate victory of the church as the one and only final
society. This is how the new Christian Rome, arising out of the
ashes of the old Rome, came to be seen as the manifestation of the
eternal city.

Yet this was not all. What of those faithful who died before the
consummation? The opening words of Augustine's classic seemed
to put it clearly:

> That most glorious society and heavenly city of God's faithful is
> partly to be found living a pilgrim life amidst the declining
> times of this wicked world. And it is partly to be found in that
> solid state of eternity — which the first part patiently awaits.

Thus Augustine divided the City of God into the Church Militant
on earth and the Church Triumphant in heaven.

In this way Augustine's vision of hope for the city gave rise to
that dualistic view of reality — which dominated the medieval
mind and which has survived for some Christians right up to the
present. In this view final human destiny was transferred from
this world to 'another world'. This world was to remain the
doomed city and the only hope for mankind was to look for
another non-physical world for the realisation of the eternal city.

Although this view of human destiny is less widely held today
than formerly, its residue, where it is to be found, could well have
disastrous consequences. This view is frequently found among
fundamentalists of the 'born again' variety and among those who
form the American Moral Majority. It leads them to say quite
openly that they have no fear of a nuclear holocaust. If it comes,
they have every confidence that they will be transported to the
eternal city of God and only the wicked, who in their view
includes all Communists, will be annihilated. Such people have
little interest in the future of this planet for they, like the
medievalists, have come to equate it with what must ultimately
pass away. Thus should the decision to use nuclear warheads ever
be in the hands of such people (and we are uncomfortably close to
it in the American political scene) we would do well to tremble.

This dualistic view of reality has been rapidly declining in the
last hundred years and for very good reasons. Although Augustine
can be indirectly blamed for it in part, it is a gross distortion of
what he thought. Augustine was a very complex person. Besides
the Christian commitment in his life there were two other great
influences in his thought. First he was a Platonist in philosophy.
Like Plato he believed the eternal realities were not physical things

but ideas. The heavenly city and the earthly city were for him essentially ideas — powerful ideas, controlling ideals. That is why they could both be present at the same time in the everyday world.

Now along with Platonic philosophy there remained in Augustine a considerable deposit from his pre-Christian days when he was a Manichaeist. The religion of Manichaeism stretched right back to the ancient Persian religion of Zoroaster. These two influences, put very simplistically, are the ultimate source of the dualism we find in Augustine. Zoroaster taught that in human existence we are caught up in a cosmic war between the forces of God and the forces of evil. Translated into Augustinian and medieval terms that is the conflict between God and his angels on the one side and Satan with his fallen angels on the other. If people become dominated by Satan then they belong to the earthly city. If they respond in obedience to God, then they belong to the heavenly city.

The elements in Augustine's vision of the eternal city which led to the dualistic world view of the Middle Ages owe much more to Platonism and Zoroastrianism than they do to the Biblical tradition. This was also, of course, an influence in Augustine.

It is in the Bible that the term *City of God* first appears. Of course it appears as a term for Jerusalem, also known as the stronghold of Zion. The Psalmists celebrate the greatness of that city:

> On the holy Mount stands the city founded by God
>> the Lord loves the gates of Zion
>> more than any other of the dwelling-places of Jacob.
>
> Glorious things are spoken of you
>> O city of God.

It was largely because of all the holy associations which Jerusalem came to have for the Jew (from the time David captured that city about 3000 years ago), that the Israelite image of the city underwent a transformation. It came to be accepted into Israelite tradition and the point was reached where they could speak of the city of Jerusalem in particular as the city of God, the holy dwelling-place of the most High.

Now it is true that Jerusalem is a very old city, perhaps 1000 years older than Rome, and it has remained in religious imagination a holy city — first for the Jew, then for the Christian, and finally for the Muslim also. But this does not mean that Jerusalem has by any means remained through history an impregnable fortress of peace and righteousness, impervious to the evil designs of men. In fact, Jerusalem has known destruction many times. It has been fought over by all the great Empires of the ancient world, by Muslim and Christian in the Crusades, by Muslim and Jew in this century.

Jerusalem can, no more than Rome, be identified in any final way with the eternal city. Both, in their respective ways, have been only signposts of a hope yet to be realised. And nowhere is this better expressed than in some words we find in the New Testament. They refer to Abraham. To appreciate them fully we must recall that the very earliest tradition about Abraham reflected the nomadic distrust of cities. It depicted Abraham turning his back on the ancient city or Ur and venturing out to a land as yet wholly unknown. In between that tradition and the New Testament reference lies the long history of how Abraham's descendants dwelt in Israel, made Jerusalem their holy city, saw it destroyed and later returned to rebuild it. Once again it was destroyed, this time by the Romans. Some time after that, an unknown Christian wrote the book we call Hebrews. In recalling the ancient men of faith he singled out Abraham for special attention. He was a model of what it means to have faith for he obeyed when he was called. He went out 'not knowing where he was to go'. But 'he looked for the city which has foundations, whose builder and maker is God'.

What is meant by that city? That city cannot be identified with Rome or with Jerusalem, or with Mecca, or with London, or with any city in God's own country! But neither does it refer to some actual but unseen city in another world. That city exists only as a symbol of hope. The 'eternal city' is an image, a product of human hope and faith, created by the human imagination. We should not think any the less of it for that. The same applies to all the images we have been looking at.

How those images relate to reality depends upon us. The images of the wicked city and of the secular city refer more particularly to ways of seeing and understanding the present.

The doomed city and the eternal city refer more to how we see future possibilities. Each of these may possibly be realised. The image of the doomed city may well motivate us towards the eternal city — as it did for Abraham — as it did for Augustine. If we wish the eternal city to become the reality we must journey towards it in faith and hope. Even as we journey we can sense the reality of that city. The signs of its coming shine through from time to time, even with our experience of the secular global city. They are to be found wherever people act, not out of self-interest but out of concern for others — not just within their own family, not just within their own nation, but out of concern for all their fellow humans of whatever colour, class, creed or political persuasion. In the eternal city there are no such divisions.

Nationalism belongs to the earthly city. The eternal city knows no national boundaries. Let me take a simple example. If loyalty and concern for others can be fostered in our young people by the regular saluting of a flag (and about this I have real doubt), then it is not the national flag of New Zealand, but the United Nations flag to which we should be encouraging loyal devotion. The coming city of God is present in our cities only to the degree to which we citizens look beyond our own city limits, beyond our national limits, to the global city of mankind.

Some, of course, would like the eternal city to be much more substantial than an image, a symbol of what is yet to be realised. They would either like to be able to point to it in this world or else have it proved to them in Holy Writ that it already exists in another world. There are no such guarantees. The eternal city remains in the class of future possibilities. Whether we realise it or not it has become a matter of human responsibility. We humans tread a razor edge, between the doomed city and the eternal city. It can be seen only by faith. It can be reached only as we shoulder our human responsibilities and move steadily towards it in obedience and hope. We can visualise it with the eye of faith. We can sense its presence. But it remains intangible — a hope for the future.

It was this city of which Samuel Johnson wrote. He was not the Dr Johnson of London fame, but an American of the same name from the last century. He was a man of quite radical theology for his day, a modest and deeply spiritual man but an active social reformer and vigorous anti-slavery protester. He was deeply learned in the religions of the East. He wrote a book on the oriental religions and how they too relate to the universal religion.

One should see all of that in his famous hymn:

City of God, how broad and far,
Outspread thy walls sublime,
The true thy chartered freemen are
Of every age and clime.

In vain the surge's angry shock,
In vain the drifting sands,
Unharmed upon the eternal Rock,
The eternal city stands.

With him and countless others who have joined the company of Abraham, we too are called to look ahead and move forward to the city which has foundations whose builder and maker is God. That is the city of which Augustine said, 'It has truth for its King, love for its law and eternity for its measure.'

Sacrifice in a Secular World

1. Why Sacrifice?

Sacrifice is a word which is today frequently on our lips. Not only preachers call their congregations to be sacrificial givers. Politicians explain to us that, in the interests of the future of our economy, various sections must be prepared to make sacrifices. In daily speech, if we stop to think about it, we shall find that we are frequently using the word to refer to some act of selfdenial. A test cricketer may say, 'I'm not prepared to sacrifice my family for sport.'

Have you ever paused to observe the oddity of our using such a distinctively religious word, when the age in which we live is increasingly secular? Many other words and concepts from traditional religion are rapidly falling into disuse. Even such a basic word as 'God' is rarely heard today outside the precincts of religious buildings. Yet there was a time, not so long ago in Western society, when the word 'God' was on everybody's lips many times a day and in all sorts of contexts. Now in the course of a day's activities it is unlikely we shall mention the name of God once.

If the name of God is being retired from everyday public discourse because of the process of secularisation, why has the same thing not happened to 'sacrifice'? For let there be no mistake: 'sacrifice' is a very religious word. The etymology of this word, which we have inherited from Latin, shows that it literally means 'to do a sacred thing', in fact 'to make something sacred'. Sacrifice was such a religious word that it was regarded as the key to all religious activities. Sacrifice was the religious act *par excellence*, the supreme manifestation of religious devotion.

When politicians call on us to make sacrifices, however, it is quite clear they are not expecting us to prepare a burnt offering on an altar. The word has evidently been changing in usage. But we need to ask: Why has the word changed its meaning? Why has the word been retained at all? What connection is there between what the word used to mean and what it means today?

Our modern use of the term 'sacrifice' makes it look very mundane and innocuous. Once we start to examine what it used to mean we may be in for something of a shock. The corresponding word for sacrifice in both Greek and Hebrew literally means 'slaughter'. That is why even the *Oxford Dictionary* to this day offers as the first definition of the word 'sacrifice', the slaughter of animal or person... as an offering to a deity'.

This immediately confronts us with a quite paradoxical situation. We may regard the age in which we live as rather irreligious. Yet no matter what our personal religious convictions may be, the idea of slaughtering even an animal, let alone a human, as an offering to God on an altar, fills us all with revulsion. What our distant ancestors regarded as the most holy religious act, we have come to regard as immoral, as irreligious. Yet the language which described it we have retained!

To understand why this is so we must try for a moment to put ourselves back in the cultural situation of our ancient ancestors. Although we cannot say for certain that human and animal sacrifice was ever universal in all primitive cultures, it was certainly widespread. It long played a dominant role in the religious tradition out of which Judaism, Christianity and Islam eventually emerged. In the oldest parts of the Bible there are even isolated examples of *human* sacrifice. Eventually this was resorted to only in times of extreme emergency. In pre-biblical times however, human sacrifice was not at all uncommon. It had been a common practice to offer the first-born child as a sacrifice to God, just as it long remained the practice to sacrifice the first lamb of the spring season. This is thought to be the origin of the lamb which was sacrificed and eaten at the Jewish Passover.

That ancient practice of sacrificing the first-born is actually still found in the Bible as a divine command: 'All the first-born are mine, said the Lord, I have consecrated for my own all the first-born in Israel, both of humankind and of beast; they shall be mine.' These words lie buried in the Bible and most Christians prefer to ignore them.

Already in the evolving religion of ancient Israel itself there was a growing revulsion against human sacrifice. It became the practice, on the birth of the first child, to slaughter a sheep or goat as a substitute for the child. It was said to be the act of redeeming the child. This is how the Bible states it: 'When the Lord brings you into the land of the Canaanites, you shall set apart to the Lord all that first opens the womb. Sacrifice to the Lord all the males that first open the womb, but all the first-born of your sons, redeem with a lamb'.

Some of you may find this language vaguely familiar, not because you are conversant with the ancient practice of sacrifice

but because the terminology was taken over to explain in a
religious way the death of Jesus. He was called the Lamb of God.
He was given the title of Redeemer, for his death was seen as a
sacrifice which brought to others divine forgiveness and new life.
This sacrificial terminology has remained in Christian hymns and
liturgical practices right down to the present day, even though the
more gruesome aspects of their primitive origin have long since
been forgotten or ignored.

It sometimes comes as a shock to us to realise that while *human*
sacrifice ceased to be practised by the ancient Israelites, the sacrifice of *animals* on the altar at the Jerusalem temple continued as a
regular Jewish practice until after the rise of Christianity. It seems
almost certain that Jesus himself witnessed these sacrifices. Though
he is said to have driven the money-changers out of the Temple,
there is no record of his having expressed any criticism of the
sacrifices which took place there. The first generation of Christians, being Jewish, continued to frequent the Temple and be
present at the priestly sacrifices.

It was not due to any Christian pressure that animal sacrifice
came to an end among the Jews. It was because the Roman armies
destroyed the city and Temple in 70 A.D. and prevented the
Temple from being rebuilt. The cessation of animal sacrifice was
for political and secular reasons rather than religious ones. Today
that magnificent Muslim building known as the Dome of the
Rock stands on the site of the former Jewish Temple. Should, at
some future time, that site ever return to the hands of the Jewish
people, the strictly orthodox Jews would be faced with a dilemma.
For on the most rigid interpretation of Jewish law those ancient
sacrifices should be reinstated.

I do not believe this will ever occur. For just as Christians came
to believe that the time for animal sacrifice had been superseded
(indeed the New Testament book known as Hebrews was largely
written to explain why) so also Judaism learned how to live
without the animal sacrifices. Both Christians and more liberal
Jews owe this solution to a viewpoint on sacrifice which began to
surface in Judaism some 800 to 600 years before the Christian era.
And it is to these people, the prophets of Israel, that we must look
to understand the radical changes which took place in the practice
of sacrifice and its continuing significance.

These prophets began to attack the practice of animal sacrifice
in the most provocative and iconoclastic ways. Listen to how the
prophet Isaiah interpreted what was going on in the mind of God:

What to me is the multitude of your sacrifices?

> I am fed up to the back teeth with the burnt offerings of rams
> and the fat of well-fed beasts.
> I take no delight at all in the blood of bulls,
> or of lambs or billy-goats.
> Don't bring these vain offerings to me any more.
> I'm sick to death of receiving them.

Just as the primitive human sacrifices had already been replaced by animal sacrifices, so the ancient prophets made a strong plea for a further radical change. The sacrifice of living creatures should now be replaced by a new and bloodless form of sacrifice. What was to be the new mode? The prophet Micah put it this way:

> Should I come to the altar of God with burnt offerings?
> Shall I sacrifice my first-born to atone for my sins?
> Of course not! He has shown you, O man, what is good.
> What does the Lord require of you
> but to do justice, and to love kindness
> and to walk humbly with your God?

Like all true prophets, the Israelites were ahead of their time. Their plea was rejected. The animal sacrifices *were* continued. People found it impossible to abandon the old and tried ways.

Yet slowly the words of the prophets began to take root. The concept of sacrifice came to be raised to a higher level. It was translated into moral or ethical demands. The focus of attention in all sacrificial acts began to shift from the slaughter of animals to moral and social reform, such as the establishment of social justice, the elimination of oppression, and the caring of defenceless people, particularly orphans, widows and the socially handicapped. These moral duties became a new form of performing outwardly the supreme sacred act.

As well, sacrifice began to take an inward, spiritual form. This is how a later psalmist put it:

> O Lord you take no delight in sacrifice.
> Were I to give a burnt offering you would not be pleased.
> The sacrifice acceptable to God is a broken spirit.
> A broken and a contrite heart, you will not despise.

For over 1900 years of Jewish and Christian religious practice, animal sacrifice has been replaced by the moral and spiritual forms of sacrifice. Yet the language of sacrifice has remained. This has been particularly so in Christian usage. Christian hymns and theology have been permeated with the language of sacrifice. During the Middle Ages the most solemn act of Christian worship—the Mass—became conceived as a sacrifice on an altar. In this ritual the death of Jesus on the cross was portrayed and re-presented as a sacrifice which was thought to bring new life to the worshippers. The elements of bread and wine were believed by a divine miracle to be transformed into the actual flesh and blood of Jesus, the sacrificial victim. The very word 'host' so dominant in Roman Catholic practice, is derived from the Latin word *hostia*, which means 'victim' or 'sacrificed animal'. For nearly 1000 years the most serious penalty one could receive was to be excommuni-cated, i.e. to be cut off from the spiritual benefits which flowed from that sacrifice.

Over a period of 3000 years, the outward forms of sacrifice changed, first from human sacrifice to animal sacrifice and then from animal sacrifice to symbolic ritual. Sacrifice slowly became moralised and spiritualised. But the terminology remained. Chris-tian worship is literally bloodless—yet to this day the Christian Eucharist speaks of eating the flesh and drinking the blood of the sacrificed Jesus. To appreciate why, we must ask what it was which motivated our ancient ancestors to slaughter animals, and even humans, as their supreme act of devotion.

In looking for the answer to this question, we stumble on another strange thing. As I have said, sacrifice was a widespread practice. There are two religious traditions in particular in which we have inherited full and detailed instructions of how it should be done. One is the Hindu tradition. Their explicit instructions for the proper conduct of sacrifice are preserved in their sacred books, the Vedas. The other tradition is that of ancient Israel and it is preserved in the Jewish and Christian Bibles, where it takes up some 50 chapters.

But the strange thing is this. In spite of the most detailed instructions of *what* to do, there is neither in the Vedas nor in the Bible any hint of *why* it should be done. The spiritual purpose which sacrifice fulfilled was apparently self-evident to the ancients. There was no need to argue a case in its favour. This suggests that the widespread practice of human and animal sacrifice evolved out of a deepseated and unconscious urge. They found themselves doing it without being consciously aware of any rational theory of why they were doing it.

Modern scholars have tried to penetrate into the subconscious mind and search for those urges which made the ancients feel that sacrifices were spiritually effective. One theory, for example, suggests that a sacrifice was essentially a gift to the deity. After all, we humans both celebrate and strengthen our personal rela-tionships with one another by exchanging gifts at appropriate times. Would it not be natural to show gratitude to God by bringing an offering to his altar? We can take the analogy further. A husband who feels guilty towards his wife for some failure on his part may send her a surprise gift of flowers. If the misdemeanour has been really serious he may go so far as to buy her a new car! Would it not be natural for the worshipper, then, to atone for his or her sins by offering a really costly gift?

There is no doubt some truth in this gift theory but it still does not explain why the blood and flesh of a slaughtered victim seemed to be called for. Another theory suggests, therefore, that a sacrifice was essentially a common meal shared by the deity with his worshippers through the priests. In the ancient Semitic world every slaughter of an animal was treated as a sacrifice and the consumption of flesh for human nourishment was a sacred and relatively uncommon experience.

It may even point back to a more primitive period in which the gods were thought to be dependent on humans for their regular sustenance. In that context the sacrifices were seen to be the very food of the gods, prepared and offered by their menial servants, the human race, in return for various divine favours. The Babylonian version of the Great Flood myth reflects this view. It notes that while the flood waters covered the Earth no sacrifices could be offered to the gods. So the first thing the Babylonian Noah did, as the waters receded, was to make a sacrifice. And so, the myth says, the gods gathered round like flies. They were simply starving for nourishment. Of course all that sounds very comic to us.

Once again there is some truth in seeing the sacrifice as a common meal in which worshippers and their God are all present. This has been a significant factor in the Jewish Passover and in the Christian Eucharist or Holy Communion. Moreover, in the transition from medieval times to modernity, the emphasis on Christ as the victim has been replaced by the emphasis on Christ as the bread of the world, broken to be shared by the worshippers.

But even the 'communion-meal' theory leaves an essential aspect of the sacrifice still unexplained. Why did there have to be a taking of life? The New Testament puts it very succinctly: 'Under the Jewish law almost everything is purified with blood and without the shedding of blood there is no forgiveness of sins'.

There emerged a third theory of the origin of sacrifice which may be called the 'life-releasing' theory. This rests on the obvious relationship between life and blood. If we suffer a serious loss of blood, life ebbs away. The ancients very understandably identified life with blood. 'The life of every creature is in its blood', says the Bible. Because of that ancient conviction, to this very day the strict Jew will eat only Kosher meat, flesh from which the blood has been drained away at the time of slaughter. In the same way the Muslim world insists on the Halal method of slaughtering its animals for food. (For the same reason Jehovah's Witnesses forbid the transfusion of blood from one person to another.) Blood was thought to be the very life or soul of a person.

But what came to be forbidden to humans was in fact the most appropriate offering to God. To sacrifice a human or animal was to return the blood, or life, to God, the giver of life. The slaughter of living creatures came to be seen as not only the costliest but the most sacred religious practice. The life released from the victim was believed in some way to bring spiritual benefit to the worshipper. The ancients sensed here the mysterious relationship between death and life. Not only does life come to an end in death; paradoxically, death also releases new life. 'He died that we may live,' Christians have been in the habit of saying about Jesus. But the very same thought keeps coming out in more secular contexts. On many a war memorial throughout our country you will find such words as, 'They paid the supreme sacrifice'. The implication is that the freedom and life we enjoy has been made possible by their death. So we call their death a sacrifice.

There is widespread agreement in the scholarly world today that none of these theories of the origin of sacrifice contains the whole answer. There is a certain amount of truth in each of them — the gift theory, the common-meal theory, the life-releasing theory. But the urge to sacrifice goes psychologically and religiously deeper than all of them. That is why, through the ages, people have continued to make sacrifices without being able to offer rational reasons for doing so. That is why, in spite of the diversity of forms of sacrifice, and in spite of the radical reforms which it has undergone, we still use the language of sacrifice. Thus when we call upon people to make personal sacrifices for the greater good of all, we have some confidence that it will strike a responsive chord in the depths of the human heart.

It is no doubt somewhat debatable whether or not we humans are all religiously programmed in such a way that the concept of sacrifice will always have the capacity to strike home to us because it touches something very deep in our human condition. Let me tell a little story which illustrates how, in fact, that may be so.

I first heard this story when I was quite young, being brought up in the aftermath of World War I. A few Australian soldiers had been cut off from their unit in the battlefields of France. They were sheltering in a shell hole. They were in no man's land, caught in the crossfire between the two opposing front lines. Shells were continuing to explode all around them. At any moment, it seemed, one was likely to land right on top of them. There were never any atheists in a shell hole, it used to be said. In this extremely critical predicament they looked to each other for someone to take the lead in praying for divine help. 'You can pray, Tom.' But Tom couldn't even remember a prayer from his Sunday School days. Another tried to say the Lord's prayer but petered out after the second phrase. At last, in desperation, one said, 'Ere, give us yer tin hat, Bill. I'm going to take up a collection. We've gotter do something religious!' This was not a true story, of course, but a joke, in which we used to laugh about the ridiculous incongruity of taking up a church collection in a shell hole.

But at another level this story may serve as a parable about something which is deep in the human psyche. In matters of life and death one must take extreme measures. All religious beliefs and practices originate out of life-and-death situations. One must do something to reach out to ultimate reality—the reality we traditionally call God. In the ancient world it caused men to reach out by slaughtering animals, and even fellow humans, without knowing why they did it. In that Australian digger we may see the same existential urge at work as, unconsciously, he grasps for that last remnant of the sacrificial act still present in the Protestantism of his boyhood.

You may have been wondering if what I have been saying about ancient sacrifices is very relevant to the kind of world we live in today. I have tried to show that though the mode of sacrifice has changed, the language and concept have continued. If it is true, as I have suggested, that this is because the urge to make a sacrifice, to do this holy thing, arises in times of emergency out of the depths of the human condition, then any attempt to understand the nature of sacrifice is very relevant indeed.

An increasing number of people are coming to view the surface of this planet as a kind of global shell hole in which we are going to be forced to cower while the superpowers direct their nuclear missiles at each other. In such a condition what holy act, what sacrifice shall we be urged to make? To find the enormous sums of money necessary to build these armaments, the superpowers have been forced already to sacrifice millions on this planet to die by starvation. Think not that human sacrifice was stamped out in the ancient world. More horrendous forms of it have occurred in our century than ever before. There are sacrifices and sacrifices. Some we are called to condemn. Some we are called to make. Let us now take a critical look at the forms which this ancient religious practice is taking in our day, in spite of the fact that we call it a secular age.

2. Sacrificing Possessions

'You shall love your neighbour as yourself.' Everybody in our society is familiar with that biblical commandment. It has always figured prominently in the Christian tradition. It finds constant expression in Christian worship and is frequently being expounded from Christian pulpits. Nearly everybody applauds the sentiment it expresses. Even those who have no longer any active association with the church regard this as the last remnant of the Christian life style with which they can identify.

The commandment to love one's neighbour occurs no less than eight times in the New Testament. It is mostly found on the lips of Jesus of Nazareth. Most Christians are under the impression this commandment is unique to Christianity and that it originated with Jesus. In actual fact he was simply quoting from the Jewish Bible, or what Christians now call the Old Testament. Moreover, this commandment is found in a section of the Old Testament where you might least have expected it.

Earlier I drew attention to the fact that a most detailed description of how animal and other sacrifices were to be offered in ancient Israel is preserved in the Old Testament. Tucked away in the very middle of this sacrificial code, and then almost only as the casual end of a longer sentence, is this now famous commandment. It is perhaps because this Levitical Code is the book of the Bible least read by Christians that they have so often been unaware that Jesus was actually quoting Scripture, when he placed the commandment, 'You shall love your neighbour as yourself' alongside the already famous Jewish Shema, 'You shall love the Lord your God with all your heart and soul.

But, you may ask, what has the love of one's neighbour got to do with sacrifice? My answer takes the form of another question: why is it that this simple commandment, which has shown such capacity to stir human imagination, first came to the surface in a complex set of directions on the ritual of animal sacrifice? The answer is very illuminating.

I have already briefly described the origins of the sacrificial slaughter of animals—that widespread practice which the ancient Israelites inherited from their prehistoric ancestors and which they continued until the Romans destroyed their Temple in the year 70 of our common era. Long before that, however, the prophets of Israel had raised loud protest against this ritualistic slaughter.

They denounced it in scathing terms. They urged its abolition. They called for its replacement with a practical programme for the promotion of social justice. Indeed modern biblical scholars have sometimes seen these prophets as the ancient forerunners of the modern secular age in which religious rituals of an other-worldly character have a rapidly diminishing place.

As everybody knows, the sacrifices were not abolished but continued for another 700 years. Yet the prophetic words did not altogether fall on deaf ears. The priests of succeeding generations began to take notice of the prophetic protest. Some fifty years after the first protest a now unknown school of priests sketched out a blueprint for a new kind of society which took into account the prophetic concern for social justice. This blueprint is preserved in the Book of Deuteronomy. It reads like long sermons put into the mouth of Moses, for its unknown authors wanted to claim the authority of Moses for what they were setting out as their ideal society. The traditional sacrifices and religious festivals still find a prominent place there—but a new element appears. Here we have, for the first time, a piece of social legislation which looks like a modern trade union requirement. It insists that every worker, right down to the slave and the toiling animal, must be given one full day's rest in every seven. It goes further. Caring consideration of a special kind must at all times be extended to the orphan, the widow and the resident alien. These were the people who lacked the protection normally provided by one's family. The whole community was now called upon to see that these unfortunate people were not disadvantaged. Nowhere else in the world of that day was there to be found such a far-reaching expression of human concern, which completely ignored distinctions of class, sex and race.

A century later came another burst of creative priestly activity. The priests and other chief citizens of Judah were now in Babylonia, where they had been forcibly deported. They were facing the possibility of national extinction and were making a desperate bid to preserve their identity and their cultural heritage. The priests were committing to writing, in systematic form, all the ancient practices they had been taught by the generations before them. This is how that sacrificial code of fifty chapters came into its present form. But the priests did more than just preserve the ancient traditions. They took the words of the prophets to heart and they tried to redirect the thrust of the sacrifices. Right in the middle of their sacrificial code is a special section, today often called the Holiness Code. It consists of Leviticus 17–24. It is a complete unit in itself, and sets out what the priests felt to be the chief matter of concern if the Jews were to be true to their calling as the holy people of God and avoid national extinction.

The Holiness Code *also* starts off with the 'how' and the 'how not' to sacrifice animals, but it then leads into quite different concerns. 'You shall not oppress your neighbour or hold back from him the wages which are rightfully his.' 'You shall not pervert justice, either by favouring the poor or deferring to the rich.' 'You must not go spreading slander or take sides against your neighbour on a capital charge.' 'You must not hate your neighbour or bear a grudge against him, let alone take vengeance on him. Indeed you must love your neighbour as yourself.'

At least three different words are used for neighbour. Sometimes it is 'brother'. Sometimes it is 'friend' or 'companion'. Sometimes another word is used which means something like 'one of the people', 'a person of your own community'. This last word is used nine times and almost nowhere else in the Bible. This may reflect the priests' growing community concern.

Thus, first in the book of Deuteronomy and then in the Holiness Code of sacrifice, the Israelite priests began to shift the focus of attention from the ritual of the sacrificial slaughter to the moral duties of good citizenship . . . to the need to develop a community spirit, which would have the effect of providing justice for everybody.

Let us pause to see the radical character of the changes first initiated by the Israelite prophets, for the modern world owes a great deal more to them than it ever realises. The primitive sacrifices, so harshly condemned by the prophets, had long been believed to be the way by which humans established good relations with the gods above and won their favours. The activities now being urged by the prophets, as the alternative, aimed at establishing good relations among humans. The prophets took the first steps in replacing the vertical look with the horizontal look. And that, in a nutshell, is the essence of the process of secularisation which characterises the modern secular age. The word 'secular' properly means, not 'irreligious,' but 'this-worldly'.

Earlier I pointed out that our word 'sacrifice' properly means 'the doing of a sacred or holy thing'. It cannot be overemphasised that (in the social and religious revolution initiated by the prophets) the promotion of social justice — the establishment of an harmonious human community — became the new way of doing the most holy thing possible. It is the form which sacrifice takes in a secular age, an age where our highest interests are this-worldly.

This revolutionary shift continued with Jesus of Nazareth, who followed in the footsteps of the prophets before him. For example, he is reported to have said, 'If you are bringing your gift to the altar and you suddenly remember that your brother has a grievance against you, put down your gift and go and be reconciled to your brother. Only then are you ready to come and offer your gift.'

Again and again in his recorded teaching, Jesus of Nazareth emphasised that a person's relationship with God can never be divorced from one's relationship with one's fellow humans. They are like two sides of the same coin. That is why Jesus linked together the two Old Testament commandments 'Love the Lord your God with all your heart' and 'Love your neighbour as yourself'. They were like two sides of the one commandment. And we have seen they were both composed by priests who had been influenced by the ancient prophets.

Some of the parables of Jesus are in similar vein. One of them portrayed the divine king as saying, 'Inasmuch as you have shown your care for one of the least of my subjects, you have done this act for me.' In other words, to make sacrifices of time, money or love, for one's fellow humans is the same thing as to make sacrifices to God.

We can now see why the word 'sacrifice' came to develop a new meaning as a result of the radical changes which were taking place in the Judeo-Christian tradition over a long period of time. It originally meant a slaughter of an animal as an offering to the gods above. It came to mean—and this is the second definition now offered by the *Oxford Dictionary*—the 'giving up of a valued thing for the sake of another.'

It is this meaning of the word which is uppermost in our minds when we use it in daily speech. Yet, when we lose sight of where the idea of sacrifice came from, something essential to its meaning easily and quickly becomes lost. When that happens the word becomes debased and is only the empty shell of its former self. Again and again in human history basic principles do get lost and then we have to backtrack for a bit to recover them. We need to recover the sacred character of sacrifice, the sacred component involved in surrendering some possession for the sake of another person. We need to learn again what a demanding, challenging and costly thing all genuine sacrifice is, whether it be ancient or modern.

The reason why the making of a sacrifice is a necessary prerequisite to the establishment of greater social justice is very simple. Social injustice arises out of gross inequality in the possession and use of the planet's natural resources. There are two chief ways in which the great gulf between the haves and the have-nots can be bridged. The first is by the use of force. This means either conflict between nations or internal violent revolution within a nation. In the modern era, wars have usually widened the gulf rather than lessened it, for the haves more often than not have the military might to win the conflict, and actually increase what they possess or control. For similar reasons it has even become more difficult to overturn an unjust order by means of violent revolution for it seems to be easier for those in power to hold revolutionary forces at bay. Thus injustice only becomes compounded.

The other way to overcome social injustice does not use force — but it is no easier. It is the way of sacrifice, the way in which the haves voluntarily sacrifice some of their personal possessions in the interests of the larger good. Unless this way is to remain an impractical and impossible ideal there are two very important components of it about which we must be absolutely clear. Both of them were present in the ancient form of sacrifice. Both of them remain essential for genuine sacrifice in a secular age.

The first is that genuine sacrifice is always costly. Token giving is not sacrificial. Giving away something which one does not want or which one will not really miss is not a sacrifice. The ancients knew that. A warning was carefully laid down in the ancient ritual for animal sacrifice. How tempting it would have been for a person about to offer a sacrifice to look through the flock for the scraggiest animal, perhaps a lame beast which had no future. No! It was laid down that the animal to be sacrificed was to be without blemish, a perfect specimen, the best in the flock; not the worst. The word used meant 'whole', 'complete', 'perfect'. Sacrifice of such a kind was costly to the owner.

Something of that feeling clings to us still when we make gifts to our friends. We feel embarrassed if the gift we offer turns out to be cracked, or stained, or second-hand, or even if the recipient later finds we got it in a sale for half-price. Although we often say that it is the thought that counts rather than the commercial value, nevertheless quality remains an issue. If this be the case even with gifts, how much more is it essential for a genuine sacrifice? Costliness is of the very essence of sacrifice. The more it hurts us, the more it is a real sacrifice.

The other essential ingredient of genuine sacrifice is that we give it voluntarily. It is not a sacrifice if it be forced from us against our will. This fact, too, came to be emphasised in the ancient biblical code of sacrifice. Indeed a special word came to be used. It is usually translated 'free will-offering' because it comes from a verb meaning 'to be willing', 'to be generous', to 'do something voluntarily'. What is even more interesting is that this particular term for sacrifice only begins to appear in those sections of the priestly heritage which reflect the influence of the Israelite prophets—the book of Deuteronomy and the Holiness Code. Thus already it was being recognised that any worthwhile act, either in the worship of God or for the benefit of one's fellows, must be a voluntary one.

Today, one of the ways in which we try to promote greater social justice in our community is through the social welfare programmes which are paid for out of our taxes. We may sometimes want to congratulate ourselves for (at least through our taxes) doing something worthwhile for those whose need is greater than our own. But that does not mean that our taxes may be seen as a sacrifice. It may certainly hurt us to pay our taxes. We may be acutely aware of their costliness to us. But most of us have to admit that, if we were left to pay our taxes on a voluntary basis, we would contribute a good deal less than we do to the welfare schemes of the total community. It is partly because of our past unwillingness to make the required degree of sacrifice that in the end they are squeezed out of us by legal constraints. What we contribute under these conditions, costly though it may be, is no longer a sacrifice. It is only as we give our possessions to the greater good in a way which is both costly and voluntary that they are genuinely sacrificial.

If social justice is to be advanced, both within a nation and between the rich and poor nations, it is essential that we recover the spirit of sacrifice. The way we at present do it through taxes is often costly but rarely voluntary. The way we do it by contributing to voluntary agencies is admittedly voluntary but most often it lacks the element of costliness. In both areas we fall short of the full requirements of a genuine sacrifice.

The possessions we are being challenged to sacrifice are not always of a material kind which can be given a commercial value. They may for example be rights or privileges which we jealously claim and will defend to the hilt. So let me look briefly at some of the areas where currently we are being challenged to sacrifice our possessions in the interests of social justice.

Just before doing so it is important to realise that we have already come some distance since those ancient prophets first made their plea, viz. that instead of putting our efforts into providing more burnt offerings on the altar we should cause justice to roll down like waters and righteousness like an ever-flowing stream. Progress may have been slow—but it has been very real. Some clamourers for social justice too quickly forget this and speak as if living conditions for the disadvantaged are as bad as they can possibly be. That is not so in this country and it is counter-productive to further improvement not to recognise it. It is only after we have acknowledged this that we are in a balanced position to survey what yet has to be done. Indeed, if we persist in fighting the same old battles as if nothing has been achieved at all it may well result in the loss of what has been gained.

Industrial relations is a case in point. In the last 100 years, through the strenuous efforts of the trade unions, tradespeople and unskilled workers have come to receive a much fairer share of the national cake than used to be their lot. But there comes a limit to the material gains one can expect to make. The time has come for industrial relations to be raised to a new level, where cooperation replaces confrontation, where people in all types of activity learn how to show restraint in their economic demands, whether it be salaries, wages or prices. Voluntary economic restraint is simply another term for sacrificing possessions.

In actual fact, instead of claiming that each of us is getting too small a share of the national cake, the truth may be that all of us are enjoying far too large a share of the international cake. The most urgent examples of social injustice are not to be found within a country like New Zealand. They are to be found in the great inequalities between nations, manifested in the degrading conditions of human existence in so many countries of the so-called Third World.

Recognising this deplorable state of affairs, the United Nations quite some time ago called upon the affluent nations to sacrifice one per cent of their gross national product as international aid. Only rarely has New Zealand managed to contribute even half of this amount. Yet such is our standard of living that we could sacrifice ten per cent of our GNP and we would still not go hungry.

But while we New Zealanders have enough and to spare, about a thousand million people live on the breadline or below. Literally millions of people are today starving to death, and not only in Ethiopia. This is what is meant by social injustice, and we are a party to it! This is not simply because we shut a blind eye and do not care sufficiently. It is because our affluence is at their expense. We of the affluent nations are less than a third of the world's population but we possess or control more than two thirds of the world's resources. The gap between the rich and poor nations is widening. As we get richer the poor get poorer. This is why patronising hand-outs on our part will not solve the problem. As well as percentage offerings of our GNP we shall need to sacrifice possessions and rights which we have long regarded as legally ours. And if we are not willing to see the writing on the wall and opt now for the way of sacrifice, the time may come when these possessions shall be forcibly taken from us. The mills of God grind slowly, it is said, but they grind exceeding small.

When I was ten years of age, living in Victoria, I was given a book for my birthday. It was called *Our New Possession*. It was a description of Papua, that German colony in New Guinea which had recently been given to Australia, following World War I, just as Western Samoa came to be possessed by New Zealand. In those days I was puffed up with pride with this new possession. It was still the days of the British Empire on which the sun never set. Not only has that Empire disappeared in the half-century since then, but something more has changed. If a superpower today marches into another territory and claims it as its new possession, it can no longer announce it as proudly as it did in the nineteenth century. It is required to justify its action to the outraged moral conscience of the world — as in Vietnam, Abyssinia, Nicaragua, Namibia and Cambodia. And the social conscience of the world is going to win.

Today it is no longer considered morally right to take possessions from others. Tomorrow it will no longer be right to hold on to possessions which exceed one's fair share of the Earth's resources. In order that we may advance to that time of greater social justice, in which the love of one's fellow human is not simply an ideal but a reality — and advance to it is a peaceful and orderly way — we must recover the ancient significance of sacrifice and learn how to sacrifice our possessions for the common good.

3. Sacrificing People

Sacrifice, as we have seen, is a very ancient and widespread practice but, from at least two to three thousand years ago, the human conscience began to develop a sensitivity about blood sacrifices. They came to be questioned and eventually condemned. This happened not only in the Israelite origins of our own cultural tradition, as a result of their condemnation by the ancient prophets. It also occurred in India, another ancient culture in which blood sacrifice was both dominant and central.

But in the Indian tradition the questioning was more tentative and consequently less effective. Blood sacrifice became explicitly condemned only by the Buddhists and the Jains. Asoka, who ruled much of India in the third century before the Christian era, and who was the only Buddhist king to do so, declared a royal edict. It stands inscribed in rock to this day: 'No animal may be slaughtered for sacrifice'. It did not stop there. The Buddhists, along with the Jains, developed the doctrine of *ahimsa*, or non-violence. They fostered an attitude of respect for, and kinship with, all living or sentient beings from humans down to the humblest creature. Not only animal sacrifice but tribal warfare and the ill-treatment of animals was outlawed. As Buddhism spread through the Orient, it is said to have exerted a remarkable humanising influence on the entire history of Asia. Respect for life became one of the chief virtues.

The Jains took this virtue to an almost ridiculous extreme. The first of the five vows taken by the Jain monk was this: 'I renounce the killing of all living things.' It became the practice for the Jain monk to carry a broom to sweep the path on which he was about to tread, lest he inadvertently kill an insect by standing on it.

Buddhism did not go to such extremes but the respect for human life which it fostered not only had the effect of softening the earlier warlike character of Tibetans and Mongolians but it meant that Buddhist societies, on the whole, have had a better record of peace and non-violence than either the Christian or Muslim societies. Moreover, Buddhist respect for the life of fellow creatures tended to cause them to become vegetarian, though this never became an absolute.

Eventually Buddhism almost disappeared from India, the land of its origin, but only because some of its chief emphases were reabsorbed into the evolving Hindu tradition. Thus the doctrine of *ahimsa* became permanently embedded in Hinduism. In our own century Mahatma Gandhi became the most impressive and effective exponent of this doctrine.

Thus, it was not only in the Judeo-Christian tradition that blood sacrifices came to be questioned and ultimately condemned. The human species is such that it has shown the capacity to develop sensitivity to the point where it can no longer tolerate the taking of life, even if this might appear to be for the very highest of motives, namely the worship of the gods.

This does not mean there is no room for further development of our sensitivity. Far from it. Later I will point to the most serious examples in the modern world where we are being challenged. Here let me simply cite the way in which we practise blood sports and take them for granted. The few who protest are often treated as cranks and extremists, like the Jains. I have read that, as recently as hundred years ago in the Australian outback, it was not uncommon for the Aboriginals to be hunted and shot by European settlers as a kind of sport suitable for boring Sunday afternoons. That would not be tolerated today. We find it hard to believe that it ever occurred. Perhaps in the same way the time will come when wild-game hunting, duck-shooting and similar sports will be more than the sensitivity of our descendants will be able to tolerate.

For similar reasons, the time is coming when vegetarianism may well come to replace the eating of flesh. Certainly the eating of *human* flesh fills us all with revulsion, even though it was practised in this country and in Polynesia less than two hundred years ago. Up until that time in those cultures it was not only accepted as right and proper, but the eating of human flesh was believed to be a way of absorbing hidden spiritual values. In other words it had a religious dimension. It reflected those ancient times in which the flesh of the animal sacrifice was shared as a sacred communion meal. The way in which this is symbolically, and even verbally, preserved to this day in the highest act of Christian worship is altogether quite remarkable.

I mention these things only that we may be reminded that we are much closer to the phenomenon of animal sacrifice, and even human sacrifice, than we usually realise. We may take some pride in the degree of human sensitivity which we have already developed, but there is no room for any easy optimism. What we call civilisation sometimes appears to be only a thin and fragile veneer hiding a strong residue of our primitive past, in what we may call our unconscious corporate psyche.

In the late fifteenth century there was a dramatic encounter between an ancient type of civilisation and what was fast becoming modern civilisation. It occurred in Central America, with the Spanish invasion. Today there is considerable criticism of the Conquistadors because of the way they destroyed the Aztec civilisation, partly by force, but even more by the diseases such as smallpox, which they inadvertently brought with them.

But however much we may want to admire the Aztec building achievements and certain aspects of their culture, none of us would deplore the fact that the Spanish brought to an end the ritual of human sacrifice which was such a central feature of their religious practices. In the last rebuilding of their great temple in 1487, it has been reckoned, as a conservative estimate, that no less than 20,000 people were sacrificed in the space of four days. This may have been partly due to the fact that a series of military expeditions had led to the build-up of an immense concentration of prisoners of war. These could have constituted a threat to their captors if steps were not taken to reduce their numbers. On the other hand, one of the reasons for making war on their neighbours in the first place was to provide a continuous supply of living human hearts to be sacrificed to the sun-god in the appropriate ritual. According to the Aztec view of reality, all life depended on the sun. In order to keep the sun in the sky it had to be fed a diet of living human hearts. In their view there seems to have been nothing crude or cruel about this ritual, as there is for us. They believed they were bestowing a religious honour on the sacrificial victims, for they were destined to become stars in the sky. To us, of course, such religious ritual not only appears to be magical hocus-pocus, but it displays a lamentable lack of sensitivity in the treatment of fellow humans.

Although such practices cannot be condemned too strongly, we must nevertheless try to appreciate the religious motivations which lay behind them. I shall try to do this by going back to the one or two examples of human sacrifice which have survived in the biblical tradition, for here we are on more familiar ground.

Take, for example, the well-known story of how Abraham was called by God to sacrifice his only son Isaac. Of course, in this case a ram was eventually sacrificed in place of Isaac and modern readers of the Bible heave a sigh of relief. Even the biblical story-teller shows some sensitivity and tries to make excuses for God. Right at the very beginning he says God was only testing Abraham and implies that God did not really intend the sacrifice to take place. In today's intellectual climate we cannot morally defend even a God who puts people through this kind of test, let alone one who calls for human sacrifice.

To understand this ancient biblical story, however, we must not jump in and pass judgment too quickly. In one sense the phenomenon of human sacrifice is only incidental to this story. The real point of this narrative is to portray, in the most vivid form possible, what it means to be committed in obedient faith to the divine will. Abraham finds himself in a most frightening dilemma. Is he to obey God, even though it means sacrificing his son? Is he to save his son, even though it means flying in the face of God?

The kind of dilemma so starkly portrayed here is by no means absent from our world, particularly where the lives of others are dependent on the decisions we make. We sometimes speak of this dilemma as a choice between two evils. But where the lesser of these two evils involves the death of at least one person, it can never be taken easily. Now if we were really to believe in God in the way in which Abraham did, and in the way Abraham's story-teller did, then the choice Abraham made, viz. to proceed as divinely commanded, was the only possible choice.

That is why this particular biblical story fascinated Soren Kierkegaard, that tragic Danish thinker of the early 19th century, who is often termed the 'father of existentialism'. One of his best and shortest books, *Fear and Trembling*, is a series of penetrating reflections on this story of Abraham. Kierkegaard calls the theme of this story 'the teleological suspension of ethics'. It poses this question: Are there not times when we face critical decisions which call for the suspension of ethics? It occurs on those rare occasions when the highest end we seek to reach (we may call it the doing of the will of God) conflicts with the highest known ethical demand. Then that ethical demand must be temporarily suspended. It must take second place to the call of God. That is ultimate. And that, according to Kierkegaard, is the very stuff of which religious faith is made. It is an act of obedience by personal decision which is prepared to transcend, if necessary, conventional morality.

Of course, to appreciate to the full what Kierkegaard was getting at, we need to remember that he lived at a time when the most influential philosophers of his day, Immanuel Kant and Johann Fichte, appeared to be reducing the eternal truth of religion to a set of ethical requirements. Kierkegaard was reacting against their reductionism and was doing his best to salvage religious devotion as something which is independent of, and beyond, any set of moral imperatives.

In our world today, an increasing number of people would probably agree with those philosophers of two hundred years ago, that the highest demands made upon us are moral ones; that the religious imperative is none other than the moral imperative. Our problem is trying to decide whether or not, with Kierkegaard, there is a religious imperative to be distinguished from the moral one in this. We cannot readily conceive, as the ancient biblical story-teller could, any situation in which the divine will of God would demand a human sacrifice, as it did of Abraham.

So let me take another biblical story of human sacrifice, much less well-known than that of Abraham. In this, the sacrifice did take place.

The prophet Samuel sent King Saul to quell the Amalekites. They are described as a marauding nomad people who kept making terrorist raids into Israelite territory. The prophet called Saul to a holy war. It was to be an ancient *jihad*, fought in the name of God. This meant that all prisoners taken and all booty captured belonged to God and had to be delivered to God as a great sacrifice. Hebrew had a special word for this kind of wholesale slaughter and destruction which makes it clear it was seen as an act of religious devotion. Saul was successful, but he did not follow the prescriptions. He spared the life of Agag, the King of the Amalekites. He also kept for Israelite use the best of the domestic animals they captured. Then Samuel arrived on the scene. He was furious. He denounced Saul as a man unworthy to be the Lord's anointed king because he had not fulfilled the requirements of holy war. Samuel called for the captured king to be brought to them. Then—the Bible tells us with brutal simplicity—'Samuel hewed Agag to pieces before the Lord'.

What is our reaction to this story? We are repelled by the action of the holy priest. Our sympathies are with Saul. At least he showed a little humanity. From our moral view he did the right thing in sparing Agag. But he did the *right* thing for the *wrong* reasons! From the point of view of *our* morality Samuel did a dreadful thing. But he did the *wrong* thing for the *right* reasons! This story helps us to distinguish between religious motivation and morality.

It serves to underline Kierkegaard's point. Morality varies from time to time and from culture to culture. There are no unchangeable moral laws. Moral laws are simply the conventions of behaviour universally accepted at a particular time. That is why there is something higher—the religious imperative. It is only by means of the religious imperative that the moral conventions can themselves be held up to judgment. It was the religious imperative which gave the ancient prophets the power to question the conventional morality of blood sacrifice. The religious imperative is the highest we know. In our tradition we commonly call it the will of God.

Because we live in a different moral context from the ancient biblical story-teller, we are better able to appreciate the very real dilemma he was portraying in Abraham by translating the situation into one of our own current problems. Let us consider the case of a newly-pregnant woman who has unintentionally conceived and in undesirable circumstances. Is she to have an abortion? Or is she to bring to birth a child which will face from the beginning more than the usual number of handicaps?

Let me make clear that I am not an anti-abortionist. I believe it begs the question to refer to the foetus as an 'unborn child'. It is only by the process of birth that we can at last speak of the existence of a child. The simplistic arguments and absolute dogmatism of many anti-abortionists hide the real issue.

But neither am I happy with some of the arguments and attitudes of the pro-abortion lobby. A foetus is not a child, but it is a child-in-the-making. The present occurrence in Western society of large-scale legal abortion does mean that there is only a very thin line between our society and those ancient societies which regularly disposed of unwanted children. They were prepared to do it immediately after birth. We are only prepared to do it soon after conception. The parallel should make us very uncomfortable.

Yet there is a line of difference, though a thin one. And there are circumstances in which a pregnant mother faces a dilemma very close to that of Abraham. In that dilemma a choice has to be made. It is a choice which is not for the community as a whole to make by imposing its prohibition. Only the individual can adequately make that choice. That was the point Kierkegaard kept making. The most that society can do is to emphasise the holy, sacred character of that choice, to give guidance and counsel, and to respect the sincerity and integrity of the person making the choice.

Our ongoing moral concern with the phenomenon of abortion is only the first of three examples I want to take to show that human sacrifice remains a tragic reality in the modern world. We delude ourselves if we think human sacrifice was a practice which belonged to the crude primitive cultures and that it has long since been stamped out. Easily the most shocking example of human sacrifice ever conceived and executed in all human history took place not in the ancient world, but in the twentieth century. It makes the Aztecs look complete amateurs. I refer to the Nazi extermination of their enemies and unwanted citizens in the gas ovens and concentration camps of Auschwitz, Belsen and so on. The Jews know it as the sacrifice of the Six Million — the approximate number of their fellow Jews who perished. But of course communists, homosexuals and others also lost their lives. A total of 13 million has been claimed. It is significant that the term Holocaust has come to be used for this gross act of inhumanity, for that term comes from the ancient sacrifices. It is the Greek equivalent of the biblical word for 'whole burnt offering'.

One of the most moving moments of my life was to visit — some twenty years ago — the Memorial of the Six Million, which had then been recently built on the outskirts of Jerusalem. It is a very simple but impressively designed monument. From afar it looks like a giant concrete slab. As one comes closer one sees that the walls beneath the slab are made of round stone boulders. They look like human bodies, heaped together, being crushed to death by an immense weight. One enters through giant doors into an almost empty space, dimly lit. As one becomes accustomed to the light, one sees on the floor a stylised map of Eastern Europe. There, are marked and named the death and concentration camps where the Holocaust took place.

Why did it ever occur? Today it is as hard for us to believe as the shooting of Aboriginals for sport. It simply shows the devilish wickedness of the Nazis, we say. Of course that's true, but it is not the whole truth. The Holocaust was only the frightful climax of a long, drawn-out process of anti-semitic hatred in which the whole Christian world has been involved.

That is why, in 1985, the fortieth anniversary of the cessation of the Holocaust, the Bishop of Salisbury called upon Christians to abrogate and disown the anti-semitic elements in the New Testament. Many Christians are not even aware that they are there — but they are. And out of them grew the Christian anti-semitism of the Middle Ages, which caused the Jews to be hounded and persecuted as God-killers. It was only because anti-semitism had a long history in European Christendom that the Nazis were able to seize upon it and use it to whip up emotional support for their programme.

The Jews became the scapegoat on which was heaped the blame for all the ills which had befallen the Christian Aryan race. Dealing with the 'Jewish problem' became the way to solve all problems. And the only way to deal with the Jewish problem was to exterminate the Jews, to offer them as a sacrifice to God (who was conceived as a pure Aryan). As this entered ever more deeply into Nazi ideology it became a fanatical obsession, a form of social psychosis. It is said that even in his last days in his bunker in Berlin, Hitler was still giving his attention to the way in which the Holocaust could be perfected. And even if he was to lose the war and soon to die, he would go down in history as the new saviour of mankind. That's madness for you!

Let us not think it is a madness in which we have clean hands, a madness in which we would never allow ourselves to become implicated. Many of the Germans who got caught up in the web of Nazi ideology were people just like you and me, people just like the millions who are today being sucked into a madness which is still gathering momentum. It is the madness by which we are constructing implements to destroy the world. It is significant that we have also given the name holocaust to the possible coming global disaster — the Nuclear Holocaust. If this ever happens, as pray God it may not, it will be a disaster which completely overshadows the Nazi Holocaust. It would be the sacrifice to end all sacrifices, the sacrifice of the human species and of planet Earth itself.

Now all agree this would be the final unthinkable disaster. Nobody wants it. But how plausible are the arguments being used to support the construction of the ever greater arsenals which will make that dreadful possibility come closer! We find it hard to counter the arguments of self-defence and deterrence, and to realise the utter madness of the direction in which we are going. Perhaps Sigmund Freud was right. Hidden in the unconscious psyche of us all is a death wish. If we cannot be immortal but must die, then, unconsciously, we shall see to it that the whole world dies with us.

Or perhaps, to understand this current madness, we should go back and search for the reasons why primitive man, for no clearly rational reasons, obeyed a deep psychological urge to sacrifice. Since those days we have thankfully become more sensitive to the human condition. Our moral values have changed. Yet we have not been able to rid ourselves of this deep urge to sacrifice.

For what all the plausible arguments about deterrents and self-defence amount to is this. Unless the arms race is simply a bit of bluff — which I believe it is not — then we are ready to justify an action in which we shall sacrifice millions of our so-called enemies in order that we may have one last chance to live, vain though it may be.

Because of what has already happened this century, because of what is happening, because of what yet may happen, we moderns are in no position to criticise primitive peoples for their practice of human sacrifice. We have already done it, and we contemplate yet doing it on a much grander scale. We may perfect it!

4. *Sacrificing Ourselves*

When we are sacrificing our possessions we are not only voluntarily surrendering something which is ours to give, but we are giving, as it were, something of ourselves. What we sacrifice is part of our extended self. For example, if we deny ourselves some pleasure in order to redirect our money, i.e. part of our livelihood, to such a venture as 'Operation Hope' — we are not only sacrificing our possessions, we are also sacrificing ourselves.

In the phenomenon of blood sacrifice it is quite different. When an animal is slaughtered on the altar — and even more so when a human is slain — in order that we may reap some spiritual benefit, it is not really us so much as the sacrificial victim who suffers the greater loss. In other words, it is not the sacrificer who is experiencing the sacrifice of self, but the person being sacrificed. That is made very clear to us in the case of Jephthah's daughter, much clearer to us than it was to the ancients. The life of this young woman was forfeited because her father had taken a vow to God. If God gave him the victory in battle over the Ammonites, then he would offer up to God as a burnt offering the first one to come out of his door to meet him on his return. Perhaps he expected a slave, who in that culture did not count. It turned out to be his daughter. He carried out his vow. But though he was the sacrificer it was not he but his daughter who showed self-sacrifice, willingly going to her death to fulfil the reckless vow of her foolish father.

It is only because of the many centuries of slow development in moral sensitivity that today we can draw such a clear distinction between sacrificing our possessions and sacrificing the lives of others. In ancient times no such distinction was made for the simple reason that animals and even human beings were regarded as the possessions of the sacrificer. They were part of one's extended self. Not only did a shepherd feel quite free to slaughter his sheep as required, but parents saw a young and unmarried son or daughter as a personal possession, over whom they had absolute rights.

That was even the case with the ancient story of Abraham and Isaac. Indeed we moderns approach that story with such different premises that we usually no longer interpret it in the way the ancient storyteller intended. We naturally assume it was because Abraham loved his son so deeply that he was reluctant to slay him sacrificially in obedience to the divine command. Abraham's fatherly concern is of course an element in the story. But there was another, even more important, reason why Abraham was reluctant. In the context in which this story is placed, Abraham had been told by God that he would become the father of a great nation. Since Abraham had already reached old age and was childless, he found that divine promise rather difficult to believe. But he did show faith and he set out for the new world. At last his son Isaac was born to him. But while his son was still a lad, God called him to sacrifice his son. It didn't make sense. It was not just the welfare of his son which concerned him. It was Abraham's own future which was being jeopardised. How could he become the father of a great nation if he sacrificed his son, particularly when because of his age, he had no hope of fathering any more? That was the dilemma, indeed the absurd paradox which he faced.

When we read this ancient story within its larger context we find it is not only an example of sacrificing another. It is also an example of sacrificing oneself, in this case Abraham's own eternal future. That is how the storyteller intended it and why he commended the faith of Abraham. Abraham did what was required of him in spite of the apparent absurdity. His obedient faith was divinely recognised. According to the culture of the day the story had a happy ending and Abraham became the father of a great nation. Indeed for Jew, Christian and Muslim, he became the perfect model of a man of faith. The lasting truth in this story of sacrifice is that Abraham was ready to sacrifice himself. That aspect of the story by which he was ready to sacrifice the life of another person is what we must today morally and spiritually renounce. It has for us become grossly immoral ever to sacrifice another for our own material or spiritual benefit.

Our ancient forbears were not yet in a position to analyse morally the ritual of blood sacrifice which they had inherited from the times of its primaeval evolution. But we *are* in a position to do so — to disentangle the component of self-sacrifice from the component of sacrificing another for our spiritual benefit. It is only in the former component — the sacrifice of oneself — that the permanent significance and value of sacrifice is to be found. Only the sacrifice of oneself can be commended as a moral value.

Why is it then, in an age when the idea of ritualistic human sacrifice fills us with horror, that we nevertheless find the human race prepared to perpetrate secular human sacrifice on such a grand scale? Perhaps we find some clues to the answer by referring to a peculiar Jewish ritual which came to be practised in the last few centuries before the Common Era.

On the annual day of Atonement — the holiest day of the Jewish year, and one which has remained so in Jewish circles right down to the present — it was the practice of the high priest, in the course of a more complex sacrificial ritual, to take a particular goat chosen by lot, to lay his hands upon it, and to confess over it all the iniquities of the whole people of Israel. It was as if all the national guilt was being quite literally transferred to the goat. Then the goat was led away into the eastern wilderness across the Jordan. The Biblical sacrificial code says, 'The goat shall carry away on his head to a solitary land all their iniquities.' It is because of this practice that we use the term 'scapegoat' to this day. Even in secular usage, we commonly apply the term to anyone upon whose shoulders somebody else tries to shift the blame for their own sins. Here is an ancient sacrificial practice which actually dramatises with unmistakable clarity this widespread human phenomenon. When we should be sacrificing *ourselves* to make atonement for our sins, we try to transfer the guilt (and the appropriate sacrificial act) to someone else. We make someone else pay the penalty.

Carl Jung, that great pioneer in the field of human psychology, offers us an explanation of why we so often unconsciously try to make others the scapegoats for our own faults. Indeed, if his analysis of the human psyche is correct, we may have here an important psychological reason as to why blood sacrifices evolved in the first place. Jung coined the term 'shadow' to refer to the darker side of what goes on in the unconscious depths of our psyche. We can think of it as the residue in us of our pre-human animal origins. The shadow is a powerful motivating and even creative force, but it is quite uncontrolled by any moral considerations. We all have a shadow but very often we are unwilling to recognise it. The more strongly we reject our shadow (according to Jung) the more inclined we are to project it on to someone else. It is an unconscious mechanism by which we try to protect our ego-identity from the inroads of moral criticism. (For more on Jung's views, see the final essay in this book.)

To openly confess that we ourselves are guilty of some attitude or behaviour of which we strongly disapprove may be more than we can mentally cope with. It would require swallowing our pride, and a sacrifice of our ego, which requires a good deal of personal maturity. Instead of pursuing that course, we refuse to recognise the failing in ourselves and we project it on to someone else. Then we are free to condemn it for all we are worth. Mentally, verbally, and occasionally even literally, we slaughter or sacrifice that person. So whenever we feel strongly antagonistic towards a person or a group, without being able to supply very convincing reasons for our hostility, and we refuse to listen to rational argument, the likelihood is that that person or group has some characteristics which we unconsciously know to be in ourselves. We refuse to recognise them, so we project our shadow on to somebody else. Let us look at some examples.

The prospect of homosexual law reform brought about a very emotional national debate. Psychologists have been warning us for some time that the heterosexuals who become most irrationally opposed to homosexual activity are those who are inwardly unsure of their own sexual orientation and who already experience some ambivalence. Those heterosexuals, on the other hand, who are able to discuss the pros and cons of such legislation in a calm and rational way, are quite confident of their sexual orientation and do not feel threatened by it. In a society where homosexuality has long met with strong social disapproval and prohibition, there is very strong motivation for refusing to recognise in oneself any signs of variance from what is supposedly the norm. As a compensatory form of self-protection many people become quite irrationally antagonistic towards the known homosexuals, on whom they now project their own shadow.

Whenever the projection of the psychic shadow takes place at the community level, there is even less rational restraint than at the individual level. It leads to persecution and even blood sacrifice, such as lynchings. Jung himself regarded the Nazi persecution of the Jews as the projection of the corporate shadow of the German people on a minority who could then be blamed for all the ills which had befallen the German nation. They had become the great scapegoat of that time — and it led to the Holocaust, a perverted form of sacrifice on a mass scale.

If Jung were alive today it is likely that he would interpret the confrontation between the two superpowers in the same way. Both are projecting their own corporate shadows on the other. Neither of them are willing to become in any way subject to the other. That means that each of them, secretly or unconsciously, wants to be in the international driving-seat. It would be too much to claim that publicly, so each accuses the other of wanting to rule the world. Each accuses the other of increasing the arms race. Each speaks of the urgent need to provide adequate self-defence, but each constructs massive weapons of destructive offence. The situation calls for radical self-sacrifice but all we hear is the readiness to sacrifice others for one's own material benefit.

In the human condition from time immemorial there has been strong resistance to the recognition of ourselves as we really are. We cannot face our own faults and weaknesses. We hate losing face. Our shadow we project on to others. While true self-knowledge does make us more ready to accept self-sacrifice, we are always being tempted to transfer that sacrifice to others. We want others to suffer the loss we ought to be sustaining ourselves. So we are prepared to sacrifice others that we may retain our pride, preserve our freedom or reach some kind of fulfilment.

Even when we come to recognise the supreme value to be found in self-sacrifice there is still one warning to be borne in mind. We must not go to the other extreme and take perverted delight in sacrificing ourselves willy-nilly. There is no value in self-sacrifice for its own sake. The value of self-sacrifice is to be found in the particular cause which is being promoted. It is important to remember that, as well as having a duty towards our fellow humans, we have a duty to ourselves.

This is particularly well brought out in the biblical commandment, 'You shall love your neighbour as yourself'. As this comes from the Old Testament, or Hebrew Bible, it is just as important for the Jew as it is to the Christian. Jewish scholars often point out that Christians frequently misread this commandment and interpret it as saying: 'You shall love your neighbour more than yourself.' It does not say that. It commands us to love our neighbours equally with ourselves. There is no virtue in denigrating ourselves. We should no more denigrate ourselves than we should denigrate others. Each of us also is a human person, whose spiritual and even material welfare we have the duty to promote.

The need for self-sacrifice arises when there are concerns and issues which must, by their very nature, take precedence over our own purely personal concerns. Perhaps this can be illustrated most clearly by looking at those examples where self-sacrifice may involve the surrendering of life itself.

Here, at the outset, we must say that this supreme form of self-sacrifice can be morally justified only in extreme circumstances. None of us has the right to end our lives for trivial reasons or unworthy causes. Those millions in the armed forces who died in World War II quite rightly had no intention of being killed, if they could possibly help it. Yet, generally speaking, they all judged the circumstances to be so grave and critical that it was necessary to take that risk. On our war memorials we quote the words of the Bible: 'Greater love has no man than this, that he lay down his life for his friends'. However much we deplore the rise of those circumstances and think of the war dead as a shattering human waste, we nevertheless rightly honour the memory of those who died and regard their actions as a form of self-sacrifice. Note, however, it was not sought for its own sake, and it was for a cause they judged to be worth it.

A somewhat different element enters in the case of those Buddhist monks and nuns who committed self-immolation in the streets of Saigon during the Vietnam war in the hope that it would promote the cause of peace. Here, however much we may wish to respect their decision and their courage, we may have reservations as to whether this kind of self-sacrifice is to be commended or not. This is largely because the actual death was self-imposed rather than being brought about by others.

Even the New Testament has a warning about this kind of self-immolation. Curiously enough it may well be because Buddhism had actually reached Greece by the time of Christian origins and a Buddhist had actually performed this ancient kind of self-sacrifice in the streets of Athens. Although we cannot be sure about this, there is a small amount of evidence to support it and, if so, this may lie behind the famous reference in St Paul's hymn on love: 'Though I give my body to be burned, and have not love, I achieve nothing'. That was a warning against unnecessary self-sacrifice.

It was a warning which Christians needed to heed in the early centuries. For during the period of the fierce persecutions of Christians by the Roman authorities, some overzealous Christians were tempted to seek out martyrdom, as if it were the supreme virtue, no matter how it came about. It is recorded that on one occasion, when the persecuting crowds were on the rampage in Alexandria, the great Christian scholar Origen was only prevented from bringing about his own martyrdom by his mother, who hid his clothes so that he could not venture outdoors.

To understand the significance and value of self-sacrifice we must steer a middle course between two extremes. At one extreme we reject all forms of self-sacrifice and we end up by sacrificing others. At the other extreme we seek self-sacrifice for its own sake and so do ourselves an unjust and unwarranted harm. Self-sacrifice — whether it is of our pride, possessions or very existence — becomes a supreme virtue when we do not shrink from it in circumstances where it becomes a necessity because of a higher good. In these circumstances it must always be left to those most closely involved to make the final decision as to whether the higher good warrants whatever it is they are being challenged to sacrifice. That is why it is never for us to tell others what they must sacrifice and when to do it. When Captain Oates walked out into the blizzard knowing he would never return to his companions in the tent, he wanted to give them one last chance to return to base in safety, unencumbered by the burden he felt he had become to them. The world, ever since, has honoured his act of self-sacrifice.

In the season of Lent the Christian world honours what it has long taken to be the prototype of all self-sacrifice — the death of Jesus of Nazareth by crucifixion at the hands of the Roman authorities. It is significant that the cross became the chief symbol of Christianity. It spells out vividly the enduring significance of sacrifice — the sacrifice of self. One of the New Testament documents, the Letter to the Hebrews, sets out to expound the death of Jesus as a sacrifice — a sacrifice to end all ritual sacrifice.

A tremendous amount of Christian thought through the centuries has been devoted to the sacrificial significance of Jesus's death. Much of it is no longer relevant. Some of it even has to be abrogated. Christians, after all, are no more immune than other humans to the common refusal to accept self-sacrifice. The death of Jesus on the cross often came to be interpreted as the one great sacrifice which now relieved Christians of the necessity of sacrificing themselves. Here the projection mechanism was at work again. It is true that Christians have universally acknowledged themselves to be sinners. But the tragic consequences of our sinful failures — the penalty to be paid for them — we have too often simply projected on to the man on the cross. The sacrifice of self which we are being continually challenged to make we have transferred to the Christ figure. That is far from being the whole of the New Testament message.

It is true that Jesus of Nazareth did not shrink from the sacrifice he was called to make, even though he did not seek it for its own sake. It is true that he set forth the supreme example of self-sacrifice. But, according to the Gospel teachings, he also said that if we would be his followers we too must take up a cross — our own cross. His act of self-sacrifice does not relieve us of the necessity all through life, to sacrifice ourselves. No modern Christian demonstrated this more clearly than Dietrich Bonhoeffer.

In this essay on the theme of sacrifice I have tried to show that there are very good reasons why this concept from ancient and even primitive religion has left a permanent deposit in our common secular language. I have tried to show, in the space available, what a rich concept it is, and how multifaceted it is both in thought and in practice. There are many aspects of ancient and traditional sacrifice which we must not only condemn but also do our best to avoid. Because of the nature of the human condition, they have a way of reappearing even when we assume them to be obsolete. But there are also aspects of sacrifice which are enduring. Chief of these is the challenge to sacrifice ourselves whenever the circumstances warrant it.

If we are to become whole and mature persons we need to acknowledge ourselves for what we really are and that means sacrificing our pride. If we are to build healthy human relationships in family, in industry, in civic and national affairs, we must sacrifice purely personal interests (such as material goods) in order to promote the common good. In international affairs we may have to sacrifice national pride, and even our national income, in the interests of promoting international peace and well-being. The permanent value of sacrifice is that it is a continual challenge to each of us personally. If we respond, it can lead to new hope, to greater social justice, to peace and to ultimate wholeness. This indeed is the heart of the Christian message.

Encounter with Evil

1. The Problem of Evil

We have all been aware of good and evil for as long as we can remember. Our earliest training in acceptable human behaviour was based upon these polar opposites. 'Be a good child' we were continually being exhorted. And we were punished for behaviour which our elders judged to be naughty.

Fairy tales were often the first introduction into our awareness of a mysterious world beyond the narrow confines of our family home. In them the continual struggle between the forces of good and evil was impressed upon us through the visible shapes they took in fairy godmothers and wicked goblins. As we grew older the forces of good and evil took on more human shape. We read exciting stories in which the baddies were always finally brought to justice by the goodies. In the cowboy films of the early cinema, just to prevent young minds from being confused, the goodies always seemed to wear white hats and the baddies black hats.

Only with growth to adult maturity do we come to realise that our earlier simplistic division of people into good and evil is not really true to life. There is usually some good in the most evil of people (we even speak of honour among thieves); while we are sometimes distressed to discover that someone we have admired as a hero, or venerated as a saint, has hidden weaknesses we never suspected were there. This is one of the ways in which evil first becomes a problem to us. Evil is not nearly so easy to recognise and track down as it seemed in our fairy tale days. Instead of being surrounded by white and black, we mostly find various shades of grey.

Yet this still leaves us in no doubt about the reality of evil, particularly when we encounter it on the grand scale — though admittedly for most of us in the favoured country of New Zealand, this is more often at a distance than close at hand. I vividly remember what a great personal shock it was for me when, in about 1933, I saw for the first time a film set against the background of World War I. I found it difficult to believe that humans, such as I knew, could really act like this to one another — and this in spite of the fact that, since I had been born in 1918, talk of what went on in the trenches of France had been in my ears from the beginning. Nowadays through television, both in news items and in documentaries, we cannot escape seeing with our own eyes the evil which goes on all the time — large-scale famines, devastating wars, the Jewish Holocaust, the threat of a nuclear holocaust — while nearer to home we hear of armed hold-ups, increasing incidence of rape, murder and other forms of violence. Of the existence of evil we are absolutely in no doubt — but why is it so?

In asking this question we are voicing the problem of evil at a deeper level. Why does evil exist in a world in which — in so many respects — there is so much that is good, making human life worthwhile and full of fascinating interest? This aspect of the problem of evil surfaced as soon as our human forbears began to reflect on the nature of human experience. The problem has been wrestled with for millennia, generation after generation. Yet with the best will in the world we do not seem to be any nearer to a solution, particularly with regard to our ability to overcome and eliminate evil. This continuing human failure only serves to accentuate the nature of the problem which evil poses. It would be a sign of arrogant over-confidence for us to expect to solve this problem when everybody else has failed, but it is a considerable step forward simply to clarify our minds about the problem. The more we understand the nature of the evil we encounter, the better equipped we are to face evil with hope of gaining the victory over it.

First of all we must examine how we commonly use the word 'evil'. What are the particular things, events, behaviour etc. which we categorise as evil? It has been customary, and it is certainly useful, to discern three distinct forms of evil: (1) metaphysical or supernatural forces of evil, (2) natural evil and (3) moral evil.

The metaphysical forms of evil were often regarded in earlier ages as easily the most terrifying, especially as they were frequently regarded as the actual cause of the other two forms of evil. For example, evil spiritual forces were often held to be responsible for such things as famines and plagues, just as they were conceived as frequently taking possession of otherwise innocent people and turning them into evil creatures. The New Testament refers to these spiritual forces as 'principalities and powers'. The New English Bible translates a well-known verse this way: 'For our fight is not against human foes but against cosmic powers, against the authorities and potentates of this dark world, against the superhuman forces of evil in the heavens' (Ephesians 6:12).

In Christian mythology these dark cosmic powers came to be known as Satan and his fallen angels. All through the Middle Ages their supposed unseen but powerful presence had a powerful effect. Martin Luther was certain on one occasion that he had a personal encounter with the Devil. And since the New Testament actually described an encounter between Jesus Christ and the Devil, the authority of Scripture alone was sufficient to cause Christian consciousness to be quite certain of the objective reality of the Devil right down to the late 19th century. For conservative Christians metaphysical evil in the form of the Devil still plays a dominant role in their view of the world. Even Karl Rahner, a rather radical Roman Catholic theologian, could write only a decade ago: 'The existence of the devil cannot be denied'.

Yet that is just what most modern people of the Western world, including many practising Christians, do in fact deny. Devil-talk may well be a very apt and striking way of describing the dark side of human experience, but for a growing number in the last hundred years it has become no more than that—a metaphorical way of speaking. Even C. S. Lewis, who made such entertaining literary use of the devil concept in his famous *Screwtape Letters*, was not really defending the real being (or what philosophers call the ontological reality) of Satan. In the modern, highly secularised, view of the universe which has replaced the dualistic (or two-world) view so prevalent in the Middle Ages, not only the Devil but all other metaphysical forms of evil have been evaporating from the way we view reality.

This means that to continue our pursuit of the character of evil we must confine our attention to the other two categories. Let us now turn to natural evil. Here we think of such occurrences as earthquakes, droughts, plagues and disease. In former centuries it was bubonic plague which struck fear into the hearts of people; today it is cancer and Aids.

Let us examine these occurrences more closely. Why should we regard earthquakes as evil? Are they not simply natural phenomena which in themselves are neither good nor evil? If, through a telescope, we could observe them occurring on some other, uninhabited planet, we could take a purely objective interest in them. Then we could see that it would not be appropriate to categorise them as either good or evil. It is because of what the earthquake may do to *us* that we judge it to be evil. Any natural phenomenon which threatens our security or well-being is seen by us as an evil. It is we, and our attitude towards it, which makes it evil. Shakespeare had noted this, saying through Hamlet, 'For there is nothing either good or bad, but thinking makes it so'.

Thus, the evil we attach to certain natural phenomena is not inherent in them, but derives from the judgment we make of them, because we view them as a threat to our security. This humanly subjective component in all so-called natural evils can be illustrated by how we humans interpret the practice by which one species preys on another. We have even been inclined to find this repulsive, speaking of 'Nature red in tooth and claw'. But is this not because of our tendency to identify immediately with the unfortunate prey, if we happen to observe the lioness pouncing upon the antelope and tearing it to pieces for food? It is certainly an evil misfortune from the point of view of the antelope, but from the point of view of the pride of lions it is an event of good fortune.

On the other hand, when we humans take the role of the hunter we do not appear to find any evil at all in killing various types of animals to provide our food. What is even more serious is the fact that whereas animals prey upon other species only for the purpose of supplying themselves with food, we humans have even made a sport out of the sheer excitement of stalking and killing our quarry. If the taking of life is to be regarded as evil, then human-kind might well qualify for being the cruellest of all living species in relation to others.

Sensitivity to the taking of life has varied from one cultural tradition to another. We have always felt fully justified in taking the life of non-human creatures. Not only do most of us regularly eat the flesh of specified animals, birds and fish but up until last century, some tribal communities saw nothing wrong in eating human flesh. New Zealand takes some pride in the fact that we deliberately breed animals in large numbers so that while they are still young and tender we can slaughter them for food. It is even claimed to be the basis of our economy. India, by contrast, would rather suffer from a poor economy than take the drastic step of slaughtering the cows which wander freely through its villages and which contribute to its poverty. The Jains and the traditional Hindus view with horror what they take to be the evil of our flesh-eating practices. I mention these contrasts simply to illustrate the fact that, in the category of natural evils, what one species sees as evil another experiences as good and what one human tradition regards as good another may regard as evil. Even in the category of natural evil there is something relative about the term evil for it is always related to the particular people who are making the judgments.

Yet there is one particular form of natural evil on which all humans are agreed — and perhaps even non-human animals would add their assent if only they could — and that is disease. All forms of life, plants as well as animals, are subject to diseases which hinder and distort growth, cause premature death and, in the case of humans and other animals, bring pain and suffering. Before we knew anything of microbiology the origin and nature of disease was a great mystery. It was easy to jump to the conclusion that it was certain evidence of the evil influence of the metaphysical powers I referred to earlier. That is why we have inherited, and still use, the term 'stroke' for the symptoms now seen to be caused by a cerebral haemorrhage. Even if disease was not attributed to the influence of a mysterious unseen world, it seemed at least to indicate that there is something radically wrong with this world.

As humans wrestled with this aspect of the problem of evil they arrived at different conclusions. The Buddha, for example, concluded that pain and suffering permeate the whole of reality, and that there is nothing in life or in death which is not marked by it. He despaired of ever finding out why this is so. The Enlightenment which finally came to him, and which he wished to share with others, took the form of Four Noble Truths. The first is simply to acknowledge how suffering dominates all existence. The second is to recognise that suffering originates in human desire (the craving for possessions, for sensuous pleasures, for everlasting life or for extinction are all equally bad). The only solution to the problem of suffering is to renounce (or be liberated from) craving; that is the third Truth. The fourth Truth outlines the Eight-step Path which leads to Nirvana, a state in which all suffering has been eliminated because the flame of craving has been snuffed out like a candle.

Our own cultural tradition saw it rather differently. Disease, frustration, pain and suffering were all felt to be real enough but they pointed to the fact that this world is not as it was divinely intended to be. It is a fallen world. That is why we are plagued by disease. That is why women suffer pain in childbirth, natural process though it is. That is why our agricultural efforts are for ever being frustrated by weeds and plant diseases. The Genesis myth of origins not only explains disease and suffering as evidence of the fallen character of this world but, in effect, traces these natural evils back to moral evil in that it was the moral evil in the human heart which brought them all about.

The advent of modern biological sciences enables us to look at the problem from quite a new angle. We now know that permeating the world of life forms visible to the human eye there is another living world—the world of microbiology. Indeed there has been a noticeable correlation between our recognition of the micro-world of life and the evaporation from modern consciousness of the super-world of spiritual life forms. In some ways biological science enables us to give a rational explanation of at least some of the evil we associate with physical disease. If we choose to subject our bodily organs to treatment for which they were never designed — continually filling our lungs with smoke, for example — it should not surprise us if they begin to malfunction. Various forms of cancer can, in non-medical terms, be described as the malfunctioning of natural cellular processes. We are also now learning that our bodies are marvellously equipped with immune systems to protect us from physical disease, but an unbalanced diet may prevent them from functioning as they ought. Thus some diseases which we suffer, either physically or mentally, may be of our own making, through ignorance or through wilfulness.

Yet this approach does not wholly solve the problem. Many years ago our then three-year-old daughter posed what I thought was a very intelligent theological question — 'Why did God make mosquitoes?' We can extend it further — Why did God make streptococci and other bacilli, whose very existence depends on living off us humans as parasites, even to the point of destroying us? Perhaps we are no more able to answer that question than the Buddha and simply have to accept the fact that this is the way it is. Just why there is life at all is quite a mystery, which is why it has been widely attributed to a divine creator. Part of this mystery is the fact that life exists on this planet in a staggering variety of forms, at many levels of existence, from the virus right up to the human being.

What we are learning today about life is that, not only have complex forms evolved out of simpler forms, but at any one time all forms of life — both plant and animal — live in an amazing network of relationships. We are still coming to grips with the ecology of the biosphere of this planet. Among the almost infinite variety of species there is both interdependence and competition for survival. The necessity to make an effort to survive seems to have been a factor in the process of evolution. It is even conceivable that the micro-forms of life which still attack us as disease have actually, in the long run, played a positive role in the evolution of the human organism to its present state. This may not wholly solve the problem of natural evil — but it does help us to approach the problem in quite a new way. Moreover it continues to highlight the subjective component in the problem of evil. It is *our* problem, a problem which arises because of the way we view reality from the pressing angle of our own survival and well-being.

This is why death itself has so often been regarded as an evil, and the last enemy of humankind which needs to be conquered. There has been a great reluctance by humans to accept the phenomenon of death as having any rightful place in their view of the ideal world. The Christian tradition did not hesitate to attribute the fact of human death to the sin of Adam. 'It was a man who brought death into the world,' said Paul. (1 Corinthians 15:21) Modern scholars have questioned whether this Pauline (and subsequent Christian) interpretation of the Genesis myth is actually legitimate. It is claimed that the general Old Testament view was to accept human mortality as very much part of the divinely-intended order of creation. If this is so, it was much closer to what is becoming a widely accepted view today, namely that death is an essential part of life. There cannot be life as we know it unless there is also birth and death, the beginning and the end of the changing process of development that we call life. If we come to view death in this more positive way then it is only *premature* death which is to be judged as evil and not the phenomenon of death in itself. It is only because of this phenomenon that the evolution of life has been possible. In other words, our life has been made possible because the countless generations of our forbears have died and our own future death opens the way for subsequent generations to live. Moreover, when the life of an individual has reached more than the average span (the 'four score' years or more) then death can actually be welcomed, as in the spirit of St Francis: 'And thou, most kind and gentle death, waiting to hush our latest breath'.

Let us now turn to the third type of evil — moral evil. Here we are thinking not of the way non-human phenomena threaten human existence, but of the way we injure one another either in ignorance or by intention. The human or subjective factor in evil now takes centre stage. It is sometimes claimed that we human beings are the only animal species who destroy one another — at least on the scale it has been done. Thus the human species is even a menace to itself. In spite of our supposed moral superiority over other species, we not only kill our fellow humans but on occasions have tried to annihilate whole races. In the present arms race we are building arsenals which could bring about the total annihilation of all planetary life. There's moral evil for you on the grand scale!

What is the reason for 'man's inhumanity to man'? The traditional answer given in our own cultural past is very clear. We live in a fallen world, and we humans (more than all other creatures) are fallen creatures. Moreover, we — through our distant ancestors — brought about this unhappy state of affairs by our own most grievous fault. Although we recognise today that this answer to the problem of moral evil was expressed in dress inherited from ancient mythology, there still remains in it more than a grain of truth—for moral evil, once it takes root in human culture, has a way of reproducing itself over and over again.

Does this mean that there is something permanently wrong with human nature? The Christian tradition has long taught that there is—it is known as the doctrine of sin. This declares that we are creatures who, however hard we try, can never escape from the moral distortion of our will which causes us to do evil in spite of ourselves. The human experience on which this doctrine was based was succinctly put by St Paul: 'The good which I want to do, I do not do, but the evil I do not want is what I do.' (Romans 7: 19). This experience has been echoed by many people through the ages. The problem of moral evil then is twofold: we not only observe other people perpetrating evil in cruel and inhumane acts, but we so often find ourselves involved in an inner struggle—as if the evil we encounter has got right inside us, overpowered us, and taken possession of us.

So far I have been mainly attempting to describe the three categories into which the evil we encounter may be distributed—supernatural evil, natural evil and moral (or humanly based) evil. What has emerged in the study of these to this point is the human or subject component in all the experiences where, traditionally, people believed they were encountering evil. The effect of this is to cause us to focus our attention chiefly on moral evil. This indeed is what the Christian doctrine of sin was always attempting to do. Yet (we shall later see why) the non-human forms of evil, which we have called natural evil and supernatural evil, often took precedence in human consciousness.

We must delve into the nature of moral evil a great deal more. But before doing so, we must turn to another aspect of the problem of evil. Evil has long constituted a theoretical problem from a philosophical and theological angle and it is this which people often have in mind when we refer to the 'problem of evil'. This problem has been felt much more acutely in Western culture than elsewhere. As I have said, in Buddhism it was suffering rather than evil which became the focal point.

The reason why the existence of evil became such a problem in the West is that it has always been extremely difficult to reconcile the existence of evil with belief in a God who is both all-powerful and all-loving (i.e. perfectly good). This kind of affirmation about God leads to a dilemma: either God is perfectly good but has been unable to prevent evil from entering and spoiling the good world he has made, or else he was perfectly able to create the perfectly good world but chose not to do so, in which case his goodness is in question.

Ever since the eighteenth century the problem of reconciling the existence of evil with belief in a good and almighty creator has been called 'theodicy', after the title of a book by the German philosopher Leibniz, who set out to 'justify the ways of God to men'. The problem itself, of course, is a great deal older. Let us look briefly at some of the attempts to solve it.

One way to solve this philosophical problem of evil is simply to deny that evil exists. This solution has been adopted in some forms of Hindu thought and also in Christian Science. The existence of evil is said to be an illusion of the mind, due to our ignorance and to misguided interpretation of life in this world. If we only come to apprehend reality correctly then we shall find that evil, pain and suffering all disappear. Most people do not find this solution very convincing.

Another way is to deny that God or the gods are perfectly good. The nearest the Judeo-Christian tradition ever came to affirming God as the author of evil is in Isaiah 45: 7 where the prophetic oracle records God as saying, 'I form light and create darkness, I form peace and create evil'. This thought was never developed in Christianity though it was quite acceptable in Judaism and Islam, both of which have always been more militantly *mono*theistic. In *poly*theistic cultures, on the other hand, the problem of theodicy never arose because the gods were conceived as performing acts both good and evil. Some gods were more evil than good and this readily explained why we humans suffer from forces beyond our control.

This is most clearly to be seen in any religious faith which moves in the direction of a supernatural dualism. Here ultimate reality is conceived not as *one* but as *two*, one good and the other evil. The world is then seen as a kind of cosmic battlefield in which these two are engaged in perpetual conflict. We humans are not only caught up in the crossfire but we are being continually urged to take sides. The best examples of such dualism are ancient Zoroastrianism and its derivatives, such as Manichaeism.

Such dualism is, of course, quite irreconcilable with monotheism and it has consequently never received any official recognition in Christianity. Yet it did come to influence Christian thought indirectly, not least because the very influential Augustine was a Manichaeist for some years before his conversion to Christianity. During the Middle Ages popular Christian thought became very dualistic and this left its deposit in conservative Christianity, both

Catholic and Protestant, to this day. Such Christians have seen themselves caught up in a conflict between God and Satan. The goodness of God was safeguarded by being able to place the blame for all evil, including even human sin, on to the shoulders of Satan. This in turn endangered monotheism, which affirms there is only one divine source of supernatural power. Monotheism was safeguarded, it was thought, by declaring Satan to be a heavenly being created by God to be good, who had wilfully chosen to rebel.

This mythical attempt to solve the problem of evil was largely a projection into a supernatural spiritual world of what had earlier, and with biblical support, been expressed in the mythology of this world. The Fall of Adam was taken one stage further back and translated into the Fall of Satan and his angels. But whether one traces the origin of evil back to the sin of Adam or to the rebellion of Satan, in an attempt to defend the perfect goodness of God, it still does not altogether let God off the hook. It may disguise the issue but it still leaves a basic question unanswered — if God is all-powerful and all-loving, why did he not create the world in such a way that neither human beings nor Satan would ever rebel, even though they were free to do so?

It is not surprising, therefore, that just when medieval mythology was beginning to lose its power to convince, the problem of evil once again began to be experienced very acutely. This time, to preserve the goodness of God, it was the divine power which came to be examined. Leibniz argued that though God was almighty, he was still restricted to what is logically possible. For example, not even God can cause two and two to add up to five or call black white. God can only create a world which is logically possible and this means that the things we call evil are logically necessary to creation. What God did was not to create the perfect and ideal world but 'the best of all possible worlds'.

Since the time of Leibniz the theoretical problem of evil has descended from the rare atmosphere in which philosophers live to the down-to-earth level of popular thought. Here we find that it is the common encounter with evil which, almost more than anything else, has led increasing numbers to question not only whether God is either good or almighty — but whether God exists at all.

In politics, in business, in industry, in sport and even in family life, it is increasingly the case today that apart from an occasional nod in the direction of God, we conduct our daily affairs on the basic premise that God is not a relevant factor. This may be regarded by many as the final solution to the problem of evil as it was understood theoretically, but it still leaves us with the practical problem of knowing what to do about the evil we encounter. What is more, the less we have any theoretical explanation of why evil exists, the more confused we become, to the point where we not only disagree as to what is good and what is evil but we grow insensitive as to whether the difference really matters. In that sad state of affairs all that matters is whether we get our own way. Then ethics gives way to what we may call 'pragmatics', the most efficient and practical way of achieving our own ends.

In international affairs, in economic issues, in industrial disputes and even in family problems, our common life together appears to be dominated more and more by how to protect our own interests, no matter by what method so long as it works. When ethics thus becomes displaced by 'pragmatics', it means that, in effect, we are attempting to solve the problem of evil by denying the relevance of good and evil.

Let me take you back to an insight contained in the biblical myth of human origins, which has too often been lost sight of, even by Christians. Life in the Garden of Eden was perfect and idyllic. No evil or frustration was experienced there. The one tree whose fruit was forbidden was called 'the tree of the knowledge of good and evil'. God warned Adam and Eve that on the very day they ate from that tree they would die. Along came the serpent and said, 'You will not die, but you will become like God, knowing good and evil.' Now when Adam and Eve subsequently ate of the tree they did not die. God had told a lie and the serpent had told the truth. What had happened was that they now had first-hand experience or knowledge of good and evil, and had become like God. Prior to the mythical Fall they had known no evil — but neither had they known good. Life simply was life. That is the way it still is for all the non-human forms of life on this planet. They may experience pain, but good and evil are beyond their experience. Only human beings know good and evil and, in doing so, they have become like God.

This means, very paradoxically, that what has been traditionally called 'The Fall', might just as truly have been called 'The Rise', for it portrays in the symbolism of myth the way our ancient pre-human ancestors rose into the human condition. (Incidentally, the Bible never refers to this myth as 'The Fall'. That term comes from Christian theologians.) The first person, so far as I am aware, to recognise this fascinating insight in the ancient myth was the German philosopher Hegel (1770–1831).

What this means is that the most important distinguishing mark about us humans, viz. that which makes us like God, is our capacity to recognise good and evil for what they are. If we lose that faculty, if we no longer care about the distinction between good and evil, we cease to be human and we descend again into subhuman forms of existence.

2. *The Origin of Evil*

Good and evil belong together, both in concept and in experience. You cannot have one without the other. Each is dependent in part on the other for its meaning. We may go further and say that whenever we humans grow indifferent to the reality of evil, it is usually balanced by an equal indifference to good. We become, not *im*moral but *a*moral. We lack a fully developed moral sense proper to our humanity.

On the other hand, good and evil are such polar opposites that any relationship between them can only be of a logical character. The question then arises as to what independent reality each of them may possess. Philosophers refer to this as an ontological problem. Do good and evil exist as independent realities or forces? Now there is little doubt that in most cultures, throughout most of human history, good and evil were conceived as objective realities. This was always the case where the human view had a definite place for metaphysical forms of evil.

The clearest example of this is to be found in ancient Zoroastrianism, where the ultimate cosmic forces were actually given such names as 'Good Spirit' and 'Evil Spirit', where a heavenly being called 'Good Thought' was opposed by 'The Lie' and so on. Good and evil qualities recognised in the human condition were thus objectified, projected mentally out into an unseen spiritual world, and conceived as possessing independent being of their own.

Something similar occurred in Christian thought, at least at the popular level. But there, instead of being the creation of a prophetic mind, as in the case of Zoroastrianism, it came about by slower evolution. Good and evil qualities and forces were objectified as guardian angels and devils, respectively. Even though it had started off as monotheism (the one God being called Ahura Mazda, the Lord of Light), Zoroastrianism gradually developed into a dualism of opposing forces, equally strong. So also did the strict monotheism of Christianity become seriously threatened by the objectification of evil into the person of Satan and his fellow devils.

Christian thinkers fought hard against that growing dualism. They insisted that Satan was not eternal as God was. Satan was a creature, who had taken a wrong turning as humans have. Thus evil itself is not from the beginning and has no independent reality of its own as good presumably has. Now this was an attempt to work out in mythical or symbolic language what Christian philosophers attempted to express in philosophical language. Here the work of Augustine was easily the most important and influential.

It is no accident that Augustine spent so much time wrestling with the problem of evil for, before he became a Christian, he was for a number of years a Manichaeist. Manichaeism (as we have seen) was dualistic, like the Zoroastrianism from which it was partly derived. As a Manichaeist, Augustine had been convinced that evil was just as real and objective as good, with which it was in conflict. How could this be reconciled with the belief in one God who is exclusively good?

The problem really tormented Augustine, partly because his personal involvement with evil had left such a mark on him. In his famous *Confessions* he goes back to what may strike us as a rather trivial and amusing incident. As a boy he and some friends had stolen pears from a neighbour's orchard. Stealing was clearly wrong. Why had he done it? Not because he was hungry. Actually the pears turned out to be of poor quality anyway. No, he had done it for the sheer joy of doing something wicked.

Augustine found this to be a puzzling paradox. Evil was a powerful force, even in the smallest child, and yet evil can be utterly trivial. If Augustine had got pleasure from nothing but the theft itself, he got pleasure from nothing at all. Evil is nothing in itself but the absence of the good. If this is true, the polarity of good and evil may be likened to the polarity of light and darkness. Darkness is not a thing in itself; it has no ontological reality. It is simply the absence of light; and light does have a reality. Light is a form of energy and can be measured. Similarly it may be compared with heat and cold. When we are young we are inclined to think that cold has just as much reality as heat, and it comes as quite a surprise to find that cold is simply the absence of heat. That is why there is no highest possible temperature. But there is an absolute lowest temperature — absolute zero — the complete absence of heat.

Evil, then, according to Augustine, had no substance or reality of its own for it was simply the complete absence of good. It was not an entirely new idea. The ancient philosopher, Plotinus, whom Augustine much admired, had said that evil is nothing. But Augustine took it further, concluding that even searching for the cause of evil was itself a vain and evil thing. Evil is nowhere to be found, in that sense, for evil is a no-thing.

The paradox of evil is that, true as this may be, it does not make our human experience of evil any the less real. Augustine expressed this paradox in a clever play on Latin words. The theory that evil is nothing but the absence of good is known as *privatio boni*. So Augustine said *deprivatio boni* leads to *depravatio hominis*. That is, when we become deprived (or lacking in good) we become depraved.

Something like this argument is often heard in our community today when increased violence and other forms of lawlessness are blamed on unemployment and lack of opportunity to live a good and wholesome life. In other words, we encounter evil when the things which make life good and worthwhile are taken away from us.

Now there is a certain amount of truth in this but it is not the whole story. To regard good as being a real and positive force, ultimately residing in God himself—and evil as no more than the absence of good—does let God off the hook (in that evil is not something God created) and it does avoid postulating a cosmic dualism of good and evil forces. But it still does not adequately explain why we human beings are so frequently lacking in good intentions, good attitudes and good deeds. Here Augustine naturally thought of his own experience, when in his pre-Christian days he had for years lived with a mistress and, try as hard as he could, he was not able to gain the mastery over his sexual inclinations. Augustine concluded that his nature was a distorted form of what it was divinely intended to be and this prevented him from actually carrying out the good intentions of his mind. There was (he thought) a distortion in all human nature, stretching right back to our first parents, and it had been transmitted to each new generation by the act of procreation itself. Thus all evil, i.e. absence of good in human nature, could all be traced back to the original sin. This became a basic plank in Christian doctrine, both Catholic and Protestant.

It is curious to observe that, though the myth of Adam and Eve is a Jewish story, from the first book of Moses, Jewish thinkers have never interpreted it the way Christians have done. There is no doctrine of the Fall and original sin in the Jewish tradition. For that matter the Adam and Eve story is never referred to again in the whole of the Old Testament. This is not because Jews were unaware of the problem of evil. The way they deal with the problem may strike many people, even Christians, as more convincing. The rabbinical teaching is that we humans are always being pulled in two directions. We are subject to the *yetzer-ha-tov*, the 'good inclination', which pulls us in the direction of the good. We are also subject to the *yetzer ha-ra*, 'the evil inclination', which pulls us towards evil. In some people one gains the upper hand and in some the other, but in all both inclinations are at work. Moreover the fact that they are both there is not in itself a bad thing, for what really makes the good so very good is that, if it is achieved, it is gained only after a struggle. Otherwise, good would be only a colourless, dull and unsatisfying sort of thing, like the winning of a race in which there were no other competitors. This kind of approach means that 'the evil inclination', while it can so easily lead a person into wrongdoing, is really essential to life, providing life with its driving power.

Now whereas it has been Christian teaching that original sin has rendered us powerless against the evil within us, and hence in need of a Saviour who will deliver us, the Jewish view has been that, though we are engaged in a constant struggle within ourselves, it is still possible for us to keep the evil inclination under control. Moreover the rabbis taught that the struggle against the evil inclination is never-ending in this life and that this is essential for growth to full human maturity. It may come as surprise at first to hear the human capacity for evil referred to in such positive and appreciative terms. But it all goes back to the fact that good and evil are essentially related. They are both equally real or unreal. It is not adequate simply to regard evil as the absence of the good. It becomes simply one more way, (of which there have been so many in human history) of our trying to shut our eyes to the reality of evil.

The advent of depth psychology this century has thrown tremendous light on what goes on in the human mind or psyche and perhaps helps us to understand, better than anything else, the struggle that goes on within each of us between the good inclination and the evil inclination. Carl Jung, in particular, has not only helped us to grow in self-understanding but has explained the origin and nature of evil in a fresh and positive way.

Depth psychology has enabled us to say with some confidence that the human psyche is much more complex than the stream of consciousness in each of us. Consciousness is simply that part of the psyche of which we are actually aware. But, like an iceberg, most of which is submerged under water, there exists beneath consciousness a much vaster area of the psyche we now call the unconscious. There is activity going on in it all the time, of which we are unaware.

Carl Jung used the term 'ego' to refer to the centre of consciousness. It is what we are referring to when we say 'I'. As we grow from infancy the ego develops an ever clearer and more distinctive identity. It is shaped by the 'ego ideals', i.e. the standards to which our parents, our peers, and society generally expect us to conform. But the ego is not the whole of the psyche. Jung coined the term 'shadow' for that part of our unconscious which comes into conflict with our ego. Because of the ego ideal, the shadow is that part of our total psyche which becomes unwanted and rejected. It is the dark side of us which we do not want to own. If our ego ideal is urging us to be loving, forgiving and sexually chaste, then our shadow consists of that part of us which wants to get angry, vindictive and enjoy sexual licence.

There are two very important things to note about the shadow. The first is that the shadow is not in itself evil though it can easily lead to evil. The unconscious operations of the psyche are quite amoral. Judgments of good and evil do not apply there but belong to human consciousness. Moreover the shadow can play an important creative role in personality development. It is there to prompt the growing ego to ask questions, to be critical of the ideals being imposed upon the ego from external sources. Otherwise the ego simply becomes a colourless puppet. So when little children appear to be wilfully naughty, when adolescents kick over the traces and rebel against parents and society, it is the shadow at work prodding them to become the independent, unique selves they have the capacity to become. In the ancient myth of Adam and Eve, the shadow was symbolised as the crafty serpent. He led them to ask questions and to take the step which led them towards full humanity, which involves the knowledge of good and evil.

The second important thing about the shadow is that, when we refuse to recognise this darker, more complex content of our psyche, a psychological mechanism comes into operation. Unconsciously we project our shadow on to people or spiritual forces external to us. Once we have done that we are free to condemn without any threat to our own supposed innocence. We heap upon persons outside, the blame for all the evil we encounter. They become for us the very embodiment of evil. We in turn become dogmatic, self-righteous and fanatical. Those with strongly puritanical ego ideals become fiercely judgmental in their condemnation of those who do not conform to their standards. Religious groups project their collective shadows on to other religious groups which differ from them in matters of doctrine etc. By means of this mechanism of projection we protect ourselves from the niggling questions which our shadow might otherwise prompt us to ask.

It is not only in relation to other humans that the projection mechanism works. In an age when it seemed much more self-evident than it may be today that we are surrounded by an invisible spiritual world, the shadow was commonly also projected there. There is the real significance and ultimate origin of the figure of Satan. This projection did not take place through any one person or at any one time. It was a slow cultural development to which large numbers contributed. When the figure of Satan first appeared in Jewish thought he was the crown prosecutor in the heavenly court (See Job 1–2). By New Testament times (and probably due to the influence of Persian dualism), Satan had assumed a more evil role. In the Christian mythology which evolved in post-biblical times Satan was not only identified with the serpent in the Garden of Eden story but became interpreted quite explicitly as the embodiment of evil. Yet what is Satan but the projection into the spiritual world of our own collective shadow?

One of the better aspects of the practice of projecting our human shadow on to a supposed spiritual realm is that it lessened the tendency to project our shadows on to one another. It could be claimed that from the time when the unseen metaphysical world began to decline in human consciousness confrontation between human groups has been increasing. This can be illustrated from a distinctive element in the thought of Karl Marx. For Marx was greatly influenced by the philosopher Ludwig Feuerbach (1804–72), who long before the rise of depth psychology explained the traditional metaphysical world in terms of the projection of human ideas and feelings.

Feuerbach's ideas brought to Marx and Engels a great sense of release. But what did Marx then do? The great cosmic conflict traditionally thought to have been taking place between the spiritual forces of good and evil, Marx now transferred to the human scene. He interpreted the human encounter with evil in terms of the class struggle. 'The history of all hitherto existing society is the history of class struggles,' the Communist Manifesto begins. Marx identified good with the slave, the serf, the common people, the oppressed, the proletariat. And the evil he identified with the aristocracy, the landowners, the capitalists. This analysis of human history hangs heavily upon us to this day and is embraced by large numbers who would see themselves as anti-Marxists. The particular truth which lies behind Marx's analysis is rather this: in every class struggle, in every industrial dispute, in every religious controversy, in every ideological clash, in every international conflict, we are all too frequently projecting our own shadow on our adversaries and trying to lay on them the blame for all the evil we encounter. The Nazis projected their collective shadow on the Jews. For them the problem of evil had become 'the Jewish problem'. The United States projects its shadow on the communist world. Russia projects its shadow on the capitalist world. Here in New Zealand trade unions project their shadow on the employers and the employers do likewise on the unions. And so it goes on. Each of us finds others to be the origin of the evil we encounter.

Evil does have a human origin. That is true. Our search for the origin of evil keeps bringing us back to this conclusion. Yet it is a conclusion we are always trying to avoid by pointing the finger elsewhere—to other people, to Satan, even to God. To avoid personal responsibility we may try to assert that evil has no reality. Evil is real and it originates in each of us. That is the lasting truth in the traditional Christian doctrine of the sinful character of the human condition.

We are still left with paradoxes. The fact that we can know and experience good and evil is part of the glory of the human condition. It makes us like God. We have the capacity to create both good and evil—and we do. Yet the human capacity for evil derives from the shadow side of our psyche, which, if recognised and understood can be both creative and fruitful. A year or two before he died Carl Jung said in a BBC interview with John Freeman, 'Man himself is the origin of all coming evil.' (For more on Jung and his views, see the final essay in this book.)

3. The Power of Evil

In our cultural past it was common to speak of the power of evil. In the light of what has been said already about 'our encounter with evil', we should perhaps now question whether this is altogether an appropriate phrase or, if it is, what precisely is meant by it. It is very easy to understand why the phrase arose. Evil was frequently conceived as an unseen spiritual power, ready at any time to take advantage of any weakening of our defences. Often this power was personalised as Satan. It was just such a power that St Paul was thinking of when he spoke of 'principalities and powers, the superhuman forces of evil'. And since, in the ancient languages, our words 'power' and 'spirit' were expressed by the same word, the 'power of evil' and 'evil spirit' were synonymous.

We have seen that these metaphysical forms of evil were only one of the three types under which our encounter with evil has been customarily analysed. In the past, not only were the metaphysical or spiritual powers the most to be feared, but they were frequently regarded as the unseen cause of the other two i.e.

natural evil and moral evil. Earthquakes, famines and droughts were interpreted as 'acts of God', deliberately caused by him as a way of administering divine judgment. Similarly wilfully wicked behaviour displayed by a person who was normally kind and gentle was explained by saying that some Satanic power had taken possession of him or her. Indeed in the early biblical tradition, the ancient Israelites did not shrink from conceiving God as the author of both good and evil. As a consequence they could say, for example, that the Lord withdrew his own spirit (or power) from the ancient Israelite Saul and replaced it with an evil spirit.

Reflection on the nature of evil, within the context of the modern world has had the effect of turning the traditional view on its head. Whereas metaphysical evil powers were regarded as the cause of natural evil and moral evil, these metaphysical powers themselves are now to be seen as the mental projection of something lying in the human condition itself—something Jung called the shadow in our own unconscious. Thus metaphysical evil has been traced back to its place of origin—the human psyche. Whatever might properly be meant by the power of evil has to be understood in relation to something human. Metaphysical evil has no other reality than that.

But before we turn to examine this further we need to say a final word about natural evil. Earthquakes, plagues, bacterial diseases and now Aids are all natural phenomena. In themselves they are neither good nor evil. It is we who judge them to be evil because of the way they threaten our well-being. It was very natural for the primitive human mind to attribute sinister intent to natural phenomena which proved threatening, caused bodily harm or brought death. We can still see the same psychological mechanism working in a little child who accidentally knocks into the corner of a table or trips on a step. There is the instinctive temptation to hit the offending object and say, 'You naughty table!' Indeed we ourselves often, quite irrationally, feel similar annoyance when some very simple thing frustrates us, such as getting an electric flex in a tangle. We feel it is deliberately trying to make things difficult. What we feel has been well expressed in what has been called Murphy's Law—'If anything can go wrong, it will'. At the time, it makes us feel the world is against us . . . that we are in an encounter with a personal will antagonistic to our own.

In such instinctive responses we are simply once again projecting our own feelings and judgments into the natural events external to us. Once we recognise this we can concede there is nothing inherently evil in any natural phenomenon, not even in the virus infection or bacillus which may destroy us. It is rather that we judge to be evil anything which threatens the life and well-being of either ourselves or our fellow creatures.

Yet the fact that we make such judgments, even though we may occasionally make them incorrectly, is extremely important. As I have said already, our capacity to discern between good and evil sets us apart from all other creatures we know, and makes us like God. The very fact that we come to regard some natural phenomenon as evil means that we can envisage a different scenario where evil is replaced by good. Once again it is a case of good and evil always being felt together. It is the vision of something better which helps us to recognise the evil: it is the experience of the evil which motivates us to seek that which is better. The Christian vision of the Kingdom of God, the Marxist vision of the classless society, the Maoist vision of the New China were all motivated by the recognition that certain conditions of life were open to great improvement. But if we are going to speak of the power of evil, we find it is no longer an appropriate term to be used of any natural phenomenon which we judge to be evil. We must turn back to ourselves, humankind. We not only have the capacity to judge between good and evil; we are in fact the origin of all evil. If evil has power then it must be a form of human power.

Albert Einstein put it this way: 'The real problem is in the hearts and minds of men. It is not a problem of physics but of ethics. It is easier to denature plutonium than to denature the evil spirit of man.'

This should not be taken to mean that the human will is characterised only by the will to evil or even that the will to evil is always stronger than the will to good. Yet that unfortunately has been the most dominant emphasis in the traditional Christian teaching about the human origin of evil. The tradition has run from Paul to Augustine, right through to the Protestant reformers. This doctrine emphatically proclaimed that the human heart is desperately wicked, for by original sin it has lost the freedom to do good and has retained only the freedom to do evil. This means that it is only by divine grace that we ever achieve any good whatsoever. Thus it is not we who ever do good, but God who does it through us.

Such a doctrine must now be judged to be lopsided and out of balance. It is true that Paul can readily be quoted in support of the traditional doctrine, but there is much else in the Bible, including the recorded teaching of Jesus, which is in sharp conflict with it. Indeed the one-sidedness of the doctrine has caused much harm over the centuries. What the rabbis taught and what Jesus taught, is much closer to the reality of the human condition. In each of us there is the inclination to the good and the inclination to the evil. What takes place in us is the inner struggle between the two. This teaching restores the balance in our human experience of good and evil. It recognises the dignity, as well as the shame, which may be associated with the human condition.

If we are going to speak of the power of evil in the human heart, we also must speak of the power of good. And we need to acknowledge that both powers reside within us humans. The unfortunate effect of the traditional teaching was that any good which humans ever managed to achieve was not actually credited to them but to God, leaving the humans simply to bear responsibility for whatever evil they had unfortunately done. This was very powerfully pointed out in the early nineteenth century by Ludwig Feuerbach in his very perceptive analysis called *The Essence of Christianity*. Feuerbach asserted that in the Christian tradition there was an inverse correlation between the perfection attributed to God and the imperfection of humankind. The holier God was conceived to be, the more sinful and blameworthy humans felt themselves to be. They were denuded of any power to do good, and this was given to God alone.

Nearly a hundred and fifty years after Feuerbach we are able to observe another correlation. As conviction about God as an objective deity has been receding in human consciousness, the natural human capacity for good is coming to be acknowledged more and more, even though it still has to be balanced by the capacity for evil. Perhaps the place where this is most noticeable is in the education of the young. The traditional doctrine of human sinfulness led consistently to negative attitudes in the moral training of the young.

It is noticeable that these persist among more conservative Christians to this day. Children tended to be approached as potential evildoers. They were almost *expected* to break out into bouts of naughtiness. Firm punishment was thought to be required to keep this capacity for evil firmly under control. 'Spare the rod and spoil the child' ran the maxim. In the more severe instances of these negative attitudes the original sin, supposed to exist in the child, was treated like an evil spirit which had to be beaten out or at least permanently tamed.

In modern educational practice these negative attitudes have been replaced by more positive ones. Instead of focusing attention on the evil inclination, it is the inclination to the good which is being continually encouraged to develop. It is rewarded with praise and the growing child is helped to appreciate the reasons for this by having the benefits pointed out, both for others and for themselves. This does not mean that the results are always 100 per cent successful. Encouragement for the natural inclination to do the good does not automatically eliminate the inclination to do the evil. This gives the opportunity for defenders of the traditional approach to declare that modern moral education is a failure and we should return to the old methods. Liberalism, modernism, humanism are today frequently blamed for every manifestation of evil in society. Such criticism cannot be simply ignored but it must be looked at critically and in context. I believe the positive attitudes to moral education, focusing attention on the innate inclination to the good does result in greater personal maturity and in more social harmony than the negative methods which have been abandoned.

But even if it is preferable to focus on the positive rather than the negative aspects of the human condition, i.e. on the human capacity for good rather than the human capacity for evil, it still remains necessary to acknowledge them both. These two were once set forth symbolically and dramatically in a famous piece of early science fiction. It is a hundred years since Robert Louis Stevenson wrote his novel, *The Strange Case of Dr Jekyll and Mr Hyde*. It is useful to remember that this was before the age of depth psychology, though the first steps towards the science of psychology were already being taken. Dr Jekyll was a GP, fascinated by the mixture of good and evil in his own nature. He wondered what would happen if these two elements could be separated from each other and clothed in two different personalities residing alternately in the same body. He discovered a drug which enabled him to create a personality which absorbed all of his inclinations to evil and none of his inclinations to good. It transformed him into Mr Hyde, a person who was even repulsive in appearance as well as being wholly evil in mind and will—a fact which soon led him to commit murder.

Most of us know within ourselves something of that inclination to evil, even though with us, fortunately, it is still being held in check by other factors, not the least being the natural inclination to good. The result is that our evil inclinations can have their energy dissipated in daydreams or verbal outbursts, such as, 'I'll *kill* you for that'.

What Dr Jekyll found in his experiment was that once this inclination to evil is given free rein, there is really no limit to the lengths to which it might go. Indeed the unfettered perpetration of evil takes on the character of an expanding snowball speeding on its downward path. This is what the early stories in the Book of Genesis were intended to convey to us very vividly by the way they were assembled together. Adam and Eve simply disobeyed a divine command. But their son Cain became a murderer, killing his brother Abel. Only two chapters, and some nine generations later, we are told that the wickedness of humankind had grown so great that their thoughts and inclinations were continually evil like those of Mr Hyde. God was sorry he had ever created humankind. Indeed he decided to blot them out with a Great Flood and start afresh. Of course it is all told in the medium of myth but the meaning is clear enough. Remove the inclination to good along with any other restraining influences and humankind can become possessed by evil, the Devil incarnate.

There have been times in human history when something rather like that has taken place. The Nazi plan to exterminate the Jews was wholly fiendish, without one single redeeming feature to support it. And such was the power of that evil that most of those actually participating in it had become blinded.

Yet most of the examples of gross human evil, past and present, are not as unambiguously evil as that. They do appear to have one or two redeeming features, however pitifully inadequate. The reason for that is, that unlike the case of Mr Hyde, the inclination to the good is rarely completely absent but acts as some kind of restraining force. This forces the evil inclination to do its work in a much more subtle way. This, alas, may have the effect of making the evil much more dangerous, for it means now that the evil is being planned and carried out ostensibly in the name of good.

Let us take the activities of the Spanish Inquisition, for example. No one wishes to defend them today. But at the time, they were not only defended, but they were being organised, by those who saw themselves as the holiest people in the land. What they did was for the highest conceivable good — the glory of God. Moreover the men of the Inquisition sincerely believed that those who suffered from their instruments of torture actually benefited from what was done to them, so far as their eternal destiny was concerned. The burning of a heretic at the stake was called an *auto-da-fe*, which literally means in Portuguese 'act of the faith'.

This is no isolated example. Because we can now view it from a distance, we can see it more objectively. There are any number of similar examples from our own age, but because we are nearer to them in time and sometimes even involved in them, they appear to us to be that much more ambiguous. Let me name but one or two examples.

When China, after the Maoist revolution, entered Tibet and began systematically to destroy so much of Tibet's Buddhist culture, they did it — they said — as an act of humanitarian emancipation. They believed they were freeing a people enslaved to landlords and weighed down by the dead hand of outmoded superstition. Our television even screened an Australian-made documentary giving moral support to this Chinese venture.

Even if we see things differently and deplore this brutal destruction of another culture, we people of European extraction now living in non-European lands are not in too safe a position to be overjudgmental. For what Europeans did from the sixteenth to the nineteenth century, as they moved about over the globe establishing colonies, was to bring to so-called native peoples what was unquestioningly assumed to be a superior culture. They were certainly not always as brutal, but they did use force. They were often iconoclastic, openly suppressing what they saw as superstitious elements in the indigenous culture. This is the message which the revival of Maori culture in New Zealand is saying to the Pakeha. In Maori eyes the European is seen as an oppressor and the arrival of the European culture is being judged an evil they could have done without. The point I want to make is that Europeans have always assumed that what they brought was in the Maori interest. There was never any intention to do evil.

These few examples lead me to three important points to be made about the way the human inclination to evil operates. The first is this. Only on rare occasions is evil done in a completely unfettered or Mr Hyde-like way. Even if it is consciously known to be evil, there is usually in the evildoer's mind some form of justification. Those who have too little for example, may feel justified in stealing from those who have too much — it's a rough sort of social justice.

The second point is that the more blatant forms of evil are often perpetrated in the name of good. It is as if evil can suddenly gather more power and momentum when it assumes the mantle of goodness. We could put it this way. Under normal conditions psychic energy is distributed between the good inclination and the evil inclination and is used up in the struggle between the two, but when the two unite — thus eliminating the inner conflict — then all the energy or power of the human will is available to the evil inclination, operating under the banner of the good. The crusading do-gooders who are so absolutely sure they know what is best for other people may do some good; but they may also, unwittingly, be a powerful force for evil.

The third point is that a great deal of evil is done neither deliberately nor under cover of the good but out of sheer ignorance. This point is especially pertinent in our day for the very word 'power' in the phrase 'power of evil' has taken on a new connotation. The capacity for humans to perpetrate evil has been greatly multiplied during this century, not because we have ourselves grown more wicked, but because we now have such vaster quantities of power at our disposal.

First came the knowledge explosion, bringing us rich benefits. Then followed the technology explosion, again bringing us rich benefits. First we harnessed coal, then oil, then nuclear energy. With this energy we have been changing the face of the earth, and all for the benefit of humankind. We in the affluent countries have been enjoying these benefits. But in the third world there is an increasing number who see themselves as now worse off than before these changes occurred. Few there are who ever willed it that way. It is in our ignorance of all the consequences of our newly found power that we have brought this about; as it has been in ignorance we have polluted the atmosphere, polluted our water supplies, killed our forests with acid rain, increased the desert by denuding the land of natural vegetation, caused the extinction of an increasing number of living species, rapidly used up the non-renewable resources of the planet, and — as if that were not enough — built such arsenals of nuclear weapons that with one faulty decision we could destroy it all.

We are all agreed about the iniquity of the Spanish Inquisition — but what of twentieth century humankind? Is some future generation (if it comes into existence) likely to look back on this century as that in which humankind went crazily blind, wastefully exhausting the newly found sources of power and soiling the human nest for all future generations? If then, we were to be brought before some mythical judgment seat we would no doubt plead that what we did, we did for the best. It was because of our ignorance it turned out otherwise.

The phrase 'power of evil' may no longer be applicable in the way it once was, but it has assumed a new and perhaps even more frightening meaning. When we talk about the power of evil we are referring to the power which resides collectively in the 5,000 million people on this planet. 'Man himself is the origin of all coming evil,' Jung said. We are indeed, and not least because it is so often in ignorance — and even in the name of good, that we exercise our power.

4. Can Evil be Eliminated?

The evil we encounter is very real. Even though we may have

cleared away a few of the supernatural mysteries which surrounded it in the past, this has done nothing to remove the reality of evil in human experience. Indeed it is possible that evil may even be more frightening in its manifestation in the contemporary world just because evil can be traced back to us humans ourselves — and human power has been greatly magnified this century, power which can be used either for good or for evil. Because we humans now possess such power, and the human future hangs so much upon it, what should we be doing about the problem of evil? Can evil be eliminated?

As with most basic questions, we usually cannot start from a completely neutral position. Our minds are already shaped by the traditions of the past. That is why we must look briefly at what the traditional answer has been in our cultural past. Put in its simplest form it can sound foreign to modern ears, and even a trifle shocking! It is this: We humans cannot do anything at all about conquering or eliminating evil for we are sinful, fallen creatures from whom has been removed any natural inclination to do any good. All we can do is simply multiply the amount of evil in the world.

That of course is only the first half of the traditional answer to the problem of evil. The second half is this: though we *humans* cannot do anything about the problem of evil, *God* can. And he has done so! Through the life, death, and resurrection of Jesus Christ he has overcome the sin and evil which entered the world as a consequence of the Fall. In Christianity the coming of Christ was interpreted as a cosmic event. Eventually Christians were led to number the years from his birth, as we do to this day. And the message Christians proclaimed was called the Gospel — Good News. It was the news that evil had been overcome and humans were now freed from its power to live a new kind of existence in a new world soon to appear.

Just how it was that this man Jesus, could have had such a cosmic effect as the conquering of evil, was expressed in picturesque imagery appropriate to the time. Much of this has continued in Christian hymns right up to the present.

Evil was in those days chiefly conceived, we have seen, as a metaphysical spiritual power, personified as Satan. The human race was depicted as being held in a state of enslavement to the Devil. God decided to rescue humankind by offering his Son to the Devil as a ransom. The Devil accepted the divine offer but then found he had been tricked, for when Christ was found to be perfect and blameless he could not be held behind the gates of Hell. It was considered quite ethical to trick the Devil seeing that is how he gained power over humankind in the first place. This ransom imagery is already present in the New Testament in such phrases as 'The Son of Man came to give his life as a ransom for many' (Mark 10: 45) and 'You were ransomed with the precious blood of Christ'. (Peter 1: 18–19) But it became more fully developed in the early centuries and was popular right up until the twelfth century. Pope Gregory the Great for example, said that Christ's humanity was the bait that caused the devil to bite on the hook of the Cross and thereby be snared. Peter Lombard, who wrote the standard text book of theology used through the Middle Ages compared the Cross to a mousetrap baited with the blood of Christ.

A variation of the ransom imagery depicted the vanquishing of evil as the result of a cosmic struggle which took place between Christ and the Devil—a struggle which the Devil lost by over-playing his hand. He brought about the death of Jesus, thinking him to be only a man when in fact, unbeknown to the Devil, he was really divine.

In whatever way the divine victory over evil was conceived, the death of Jesus on the Cross remained central. That is why the Cross became the chief symbol of Christianity, and Good Friday became the holiest day of the year. The Cross was more than a visual symbol. It was thought to embody and mediate victory over evil. People wore crosses, not for decoration, but to protect themselves from the power of evil. This is reflected in a wide-spread popular superstition practised to this day. When people express hope for a piece of good fortune and then knock the table with their hand and say 'touch wood' they are blindly following medieval Christian practice, in which any piece of wood touched in this ritual could stand for the wood of the Cross. It had the power to withstand Satan. Otherwise he might hear what they said and come and turn their hoped-for good fortune into something evil.

The important point in all this for our purposes is that ancient and medieval Christians interpreted the coming of Jesus Christ in terms of a divine victory over evil, a victory which humans could never have achieved for themselves. Even when, from the Middle Ages onwards, new imagery was used to describe the significance of Christ, imagery which dispensed with the figure of the Devil altogether, human deliverance from evil was still conceived as being wholly dependent on a divine act of cosmic proportions which had taken place at the beginning of the Christian era.

So strongly did Christian devotion come to be fastened on this divine act, that all purely human effort came to be devalued. It was held as vain and useless. We were said to be dependent at every turn on the grace of God. This has been the dominant message of Christian orthodoxy, clearly spelled out by Paul, Augustine, Aquinas and Luther. Yet if this be the whole truth, why did Jesus in the famous Sermon on the Mount exhort his hearers to be perfect as their heavenly Father is perfect? Surely those would be words of pitiful mockery if humans are as helpless to do good as Christian orthodoxy has affirmed?

So we find that besides this dominant message about the conquest of evil, there have been in Christianity, from time to time, other voices raised. Even in the New Testament we have the Letter of James which quite openly challenges the devaluation of human effort. There it is clearly stated that humans not only *can* but *are expected* to exert human effort to overcome evil in themselves. This book, of course, has never been popular among theologians and Luther positively despised it.

Easily the most crucial period when voices were raised against what was becoming the dominant Christian doctrine was at the beginning of the fifth century in a theological debate which went on for nearly two hundred years. The chief antagonists were Augustine and Pelagius. I have already mentioned Augustine. His views, for better or for worse, have come to dominate Christian thought more than those of any other single person. Pelagius was a British monk who arrived in Rome about the year 400. He was a man of considerable learning who himself lived a very austere life. He was scandalised by what he regarded as the loose living of so many Christians in Rome. He exhorted them to pull up their moral and spiritual socks and preached a spirituality which emphasised the capacity for the human will to respond. He often appealed to the Old Testament where, for example, Moses said, 'I have set before you this day life and good, death and evil. Therefore choose life... this commandment is not too hard for you.' (Deuteronomy 30: 11, 15) That is just where Augustine disagreed, contending that we can no more choose good of our own free will than we can lift up ourselves by our own shoelaces.

The battle lines became drawn. Pelagius and his followers said that God has given us free will in order that we may become fully adult, taking full responsibility for our actions and learning how to make good moral use of our freedom. Pelagius denied the doctrine of original sin, by which we all inherit the consequences of the sin of Adam. All children, he contended, are born in a state of innocence. The good and evil which each of us performs thereafter is entirely of our own making. Pelagius denied that we all die as a result of the sin of Adam; we die because death belongs to the created order of things. Augustine would not have it so. He not only declared that we are all born in a sinful state which prevents us from ever choosing the good of our own free will, but the only way we can ever become transformed to do the good is by the gift of divine grace, and this grace is mediated to us through the sacraments of the Church. Herein lies the key to the great power wielded by the ecclesiastical institution all through the Middle Ages and for a long time thereafter.

It came about because, of course, Augustine won the battle. Pelagius was declared to be heretical and he died in disgrace. In all theological controversies the antagonists are inclined to overstate their case. For a time there were many who thought that Augustine had overstated his case. They have been called the semi-Pelagians. Eventually even they were condemned. The Council of Orange in 529 settled the matter for all time, as it thought, declaring 'Man can do no good without God. God does great good in man without any action on man's part, but man does no good which God does not enable him to do'. Since that time any sign of a fresh emergence of Pelagianism has been roundly condemned by Christian thinkers even though it was to lead Christian theology into what has become an impossible position. For the implication of the traditional doctrine is that there can be no hope for the world in general, or for individuals in particular, outside membership of the Christian church. It implies moreover that nothing that non-Christians do can ever be good but only evil. It is hardly surprising that the whole system of Christian doctrine has been successively breaking down over the last 400 years under the sheer weight of the impossible conclusions it had reached.

Yet even today anything smacking of Pelagianism has been looked on with great suspicion by orthodox theologians though a good deal of it has begun to emerge in more popular Christian attitudes. It could be said that it is only in modern humanism that Pelagianism has finally triumphed and to do so it had to disengage itself completely from its Christian origins.

Why have I had to spend this amount of time, brief though this sketch has been, on understanding the traditional prescription for the conquest of evil? The reason is this. What was the chief asset of Christianity, what was proclaimed in the ancient world as Good News, has become in the context of the modern world a liability. It is in fact bad news. For it tells us, as we encounter the evil originating in ourselves, that we can do nothing about it, nor can we do anything about the accelerating potential for evil in the world at large. Only God can handle evil. Now that may be good news for those who still conceive of God as one who will ultimately step in to prevent the multiplication of evil from getting out of hand. But to those who find themselves forced to conceive God in very different terms today, it is in fact bad news.

What is good news in our day as we contemplate what can be done about the evil in ourselves and in the world is this. We do not need to wait in helplessness for the arrival of some almighty Godot who never seems to turn up (to borrow the thrust of Samuel Becket's play). We do not need to wait helpless in the face of evil. We can do something. That is the good news which has been discovered by so many people in the last two hundred years as they have worked to achieve a long series of emancipations. First it was the oppressed working classes who began to throw off their chains, when Christian orthodoxy, I feel ashamed to say, was warning them to keep to their divinely ordained place in order of society. Then it was the women who discovered they could actually do something about the way, all through the centuries, men had denied them the rights and privileges they jealously retained for the male. Once again I regret to say it has been the ecclesiastical institutions which have been dragging the chain in granting total equality to the sexes. While this has been going on there has been the struggle for the emancipation of colonial and subject nations from Western imperialism, and the emancipation of the coloured races from the domineering and chauvinistic attitudes of the white races. Of course there have been problems, and social conditions are as yet far from ideal, but they are a great deal better than they would have been if those who had acted for social reform had not done so.

And it is possible for us actually to do something about the evil we encounter just because there is also in us an inclination to good. This does not mean it will always be wholly successful, but it is there. Moreover it is not confined to the saints, to the good, and certainly not to the Christians. It is there in all humans, however hidden it may have become. And because it is there, we can have some hope for the future.

Let me take a particular example which has had quite a success record (even though it is certainly not 100 per cent). That is Alcoholics Anonymous. This group fastens on a particular evil, which is freely acknowledged to have originated in themselves personally and about which they desperately want to do something. The new member of AA is led through a number of steps and is encouraged to believe he or she can achieve victory over his or her alcoholism. Not only do the other AA members identify with this person by sharing their own stories, but they continually provide the newcomer with sacrificial support. Together they nurture the will to reform already present in the new prospect.

To understand better how this inclination to the good operates and under what conditions, we could usefully start with a very early type of Christian summons 'Repent and believe the Gospel'. I want to reinterpret these words in a kind of Jungian way. First of all we should note that the Greek word *metanoia* translated 'repent', does not mean 'be filled with penitent remorse' as the English translation suggests. It really means 'undergo a change of mind', 'take a new view of things', 'change direction'. Indeed, the Jewish equivalent *teshuva* quite literally means 'turn about face'. That is exactly what the Prodigal did, when he came to his senses after wasting his fortune in a distant country. Incidentally have you ever noticed how Jewish that well-known parable is and how inconsistent it is with Christian orthodoxy? The Prodigal did not wait until his father came to ransom him. There is no hint here that he was powerless to do anything about the evil situation he had got himself into. All by his own efforts he sorted it out, changed direction and took positive action. It was because there still remained in him the capacity to recognise the good and the ability to choose it. So we may legitimately interpret that original Christian summons something like this: 'If you are really concerned to seek a better future for yourselves and for the world, then here is good news. You can change direction and do something about it.'

Norman Vincent Peale called this *The Power of Positive Thinking*. Of course it goes without saying that Peale has been severely criticised by orthodox theologians as a theological lightweight who has really abandoned the heart of the Christian Gospel. What he was drawing attention to in his own particular way was the power of good which is to be found in every person just as much as the power of evil.

Because of our traditional concentration on the power of evil à la Augustine, we have underestimated the power of good à la Pelagius. Let me give a simple example. A man who had an alcohol problem for some years met an old friend who expressed surprise and pleasure that he had recently become a reformed person. 'Well,' explained the man, 'it was my wife who did it. Whenever I came home the worse for wear she always had strong coffee waiting for me. She put me to bed and the next morning she never referred to it. A man can only resist that treatment for so long. I just had to give it up.' The power of the good, of which love is the chief manifestation, is such that it can overcome evil. That is why those people in history who came to be recognised as the saints — good people — radiate a power which continues to influence others long after they are dead. The recognition of the good in them strikes a chord in us, causing the good in us to respond and to flourish, enabling us to control our evil inclinations.

There *is* a way to deal with evil and we have it in our power to do it. I would not say we can *eliminate* evil but we can deal with it *positively* so that it fails to flourish. And that way is to change our thinking habits, to think positively, to look for, to recognise and to encourage the good wherever it is to be found in others and in ourselves.

Let me contrast two scenarios of urgent relevance to us all — how it is and how it might have been. It is generally agreed that the whole world says it wants peace and relief from the threat of a nuclear holocaust. First Russia openly declared it will not be the first to use a nuclear missile. No other nuclear power followed suit. Then Mikhail Gorbachev announced a six-month moratorium on nuclear testing. How does the West respond to these peace initiatives? 'No good thing ever came out of Russia. This is clearly a communist trick to lull us into a false sense of security while they secretly prepare to take over the world.'

But what would have been the scenario if the Western powers had accepted these gestures of goodwill at face value and responded in kind? We could now be experiencing an arms de-escalation of massive proportions, and be already planning to redirect the enormous resources tied up in arms production to projects much more fruitful for the welfare of the human race.

That it has not been so cannot wholly be laid to the blame of President Reagan for he knows he has the support of the majority of his countrymen and of the rest of the Western world, including many in New Zealand.

The difference between these two scenarios is the difference between negative thinking and positive thinking, between looking for the evil in people and looking for the good.

When one looks for the good in this way one is often criticised for being naive and unrealistic. So one would be, if one became blind to everything else. That is why I want to conclude by returning to the topic of evil to remind you of its place in the balanced picture which does represent reality. The polarity of good and evil belongs to human existence. The experience of the good is only made possible by the presence of evil, either actualized or potential. We can never eliminate evil, nor should we want to, for good also would disappear. To attempt to destroy evil completely would be to destroy our very humanity. On the other hand to give free rein to the evil within us leads to the same result. What we have to learn to do is to come to terms with evil, to harness the creative power in evil to serve good ends. To do this we must grow in self-knowledge. We need openly to acknowledge in our complex psyches what Jung called our shadow. When we accept ourselves for what we are, we then stop projecting our shadow on to our various antagonists. This frees us to see the good in them and to recognise that the same struggle between good and evil which we experience within is also going on in them.

Does what I have been saying about evil, and the way to deal with it, mean that the events traditionally celebrated at Easter have now become obsolete and redundant? Not necessarily. The significance of Easter came to be interpreted in myth just as the ancient story of origins was narrated in myth. Myth is a form of symbolism which needs to be reinterpreted for every age.

What the figure of Christ hanging on the cross visually presents to us in stark symbolic form is the total picture of human tragedy brought about by the evil within us. In the figure of Jesus on the Cross we have the symbol of what evil can do to goodness, if unrestrained. But if that were the whole story, if it were true that evil finally triumphs we never would have heard of that man Jesus. In spite of what men did to him it was he who triumphed, or rather it was the goodness in him which triumphed. And that is expressed, in mythical language, in the affirmation that he rose from the dead. And that Easter ring of triumph in turn symbolises what goodness can do in its encounter with evil, not only among Christians, but among people of all cultures, all classes, all faiths and all ideologies. Easter is the celebration of the triumph of universal goodness in that encounter with evil which goes on perpetually within us, so long as we share with God that knowledge of good and evil which, more than anything else, has raised us to the dignity of the human condition.

Jung, the Unconscious and God

Religious experience is traditionally understood to have arisen out of the interplay of a person's own consciousness and the influence brought to bear upon it by an invisible spiritual world existing outside of it, but occasionally invading it. Human imagination saw this world to be inhabited by spiritual beings or forces of various kinds. The intercourse between a person and this spiritual world could take various forms. It might take the form of voices (heard by no-one else), or of visions (seen by no-one else), or of emotions (felt by no-one else), as when John Wesley felt his heart strangely warmed. One of the most frequent media of this communication was believed to be in the almost universal phenomenon of dreaming.

In ways such as these it may be said that human beings have long been aware of experiencing an inner life which was not under their own conscious control. But it was believed to have originated in a source wholly outside of oneself. This was largely due to the fact that people commonly identified their real selves, their souls, with consciousness alone. In many primal societies it was common to interpret dreams as experiences which were just as real as those of waking hours. It was the same conscious 'I' which seemed to be observing the phenomena in the dream. The reason for the strangeness of the events and the surroundings was open to a simple explanation — the soul had temporarily left the body and was visiting some of the mysterious areas of the spiritual world. By the same token this constituted first-hand evidence of the reality of such a spiritual world.

From time to time in western thought it had been mooted that consciousness might not be the sum total of the human thought processes and the term 'subsconscious' was coined as early as the sixteenth century by a strange but able scholar called Paracelsus (1493–1541). There are some quite curious parallels between him and Carl Jung. Both studied at the University of Basle. Both showed the influence of Plato. Both developed medical practice on the basis of empirical evidence found in the study of nature rather than on scholastic speculation. Paracelsus developed a mystical philosophy in which he held that just as we know nature only to the extent that we are ourselves a part of nature, so we know God only in so far as we are, i.e. participate in, divinity.

But it fell to Sigmund Freud (1856–1939) to demonstrate fairly convincingly that the human psyche is much more complex than traditionally thought. Consciousness, far from being the whole of the psyche, is but a small component. It is like the tip of an iceberg, most of which is hidden beneath the surface. So it is with the content of the psyche now referred to as the unconscious, or subconscious. For example, you go to introduce a well-known friend and suddenly you cannot remember his name. When such a thing slips out of consciousness and refuses to be recalled, it has no more ceased to exist in the memory bank of your psyche than the motorcar ceases to exist just because it disappears around a corner.

The existence of a large and complex content to the human psyche, of which we are not personally conscious and which consequently we previously knew nothing at all about, has had the effect of putting into question the traditional interpretations of so-called religious experiences. It has made possible an entirely different interpretation of the widespread phenomenon of dreams, visions, inner voices and the like. They could all have originated, not in some imagined spiritual world external to us, but in the mysterious inner world of our own subconscious. This discovery of the unconscious, along with other factors, led Freud to come to a completely negative judgment about the validity of all religious experience. One of his books on the subject of religion he called *The Future of an Illusion*.

Carl Jung (1875–1961) came to an entirely different understanding about religion, as we shall see. But at this point it is important to appreciate how much they shared in common. To the end of his days Jung acknowledged his debt to Freud, who must be universally acknowledged as the pioneer explorer of the unconscious. Freud, Jung and all depth-psychologists agree on the existence of the unconscious. They further agree that, within limits, it can be explored: and one of the chief avenues into it is by the study of dreams. Both Freud and Jung created a number of terms to describe psychic processes which have become part of our everyday vocabulary. To Jung, for example, we owe the terms 'introvert', 'extrovert', 'archetype' and 'collective unconscious'.

For several years Freud and Jung worked in close collaboration, Freud in Vienna and Jung in Zurich. At the end of 1912 a serious break occurred in their relationship, which was very painful to both of them. It was an important factor in leading Jung into a personal psychiatric crisis. It lasted two or three years and he later described it as his own journey into the inner world of the psyche. It was an important threshold in his own life, and only on this side of the great divide did Jung begin to develop his own very distinctive model of the human psyche.

Perhaps the seeds of it came out of his growing conflict with Freud. He believed from the beginning that Freud had greatly overplayed the significance of the sexual drive and the oedipus complex. Jung could not agree that this was at the root of all psychoneuroses. Then he noted that Freud became quite compulsive and dogmatic when questioned on the matter. Jung reports that in 1910 Freud said to him, 'Jung, you must promise never to abandon the sexual theory. We must make a dogma of it, an unmistakeable bulwark.' 'A bulwark against what?', asked Jung. And he was told, 'Against the black tide of occultism!'

Jung began to observe a strange and very unscientific process at work in Freud. He wrote in *Memories, Dreams, Reflections* (p. 151) 'Freud, who had always made much of his irreligiosity had now constructed a dogma: or rather in the place of a jealous god whom he had lost, he had substituted another compelling image, that of sexuality . . . the sexual libido took over the role of a hidden or concealed god'.

This led Jung to see that Freud was far too dogmatic in his conclusions and very dictatorial in his relationships. On the verge of the break Jung wrote him a letter saying, 'I am objective enough to see your little trick. You go sniffing out all the symptomatic actions in your vicinity, thus reducing everyone to the level of sons and daughters who blushingly admit the existence of their faults. Meanwhile you remain on top as the father, sitting pretty . . . .'

Jung claimed that he always remained more scientific than Freud. Freud based his conclusions on too narrow a collection of empirical evidence, his clinical work with pathological middle-class Viennese. Jung eventually travelled the world and studied psychic phenomena in as many different cultures, contemporary and ancient, as he could.

Moreover, Jung was always more tentative. To the end of his days he was growing in his understanding. In so far as there is a Jungian approach he left it open-ended, free to develop still further.

Now, whereas Freud saw the unconscious as the depository of past experiences and the source of certain basic drives, all of which were having a damaging effect on psychic health, Jung held the unconscious in awe. He viewed it in wonder and delight. He saw the collective unconscious in particular as a creative seedbed. On it all consciousness ultimately rests. From it there comes into consciousness all creative art, inspiration, poetry and religion.

Thus they came to quite opposing views on religion. One must allow also for the difference in their upbringing. Freud was undoubtedly influenced by the rationalism, positivism and anti-religious prejudice, so strong among intellectuals in late nineteenth century Europe. Jung had a religious upbringing. Although he soon shed conventional religion, he retained the feel for mystery, and spiritual aspiration, which it both encouraged and reflected.

Moreover, Jung reflected, in his own psychic growth and religious pilgrimage, the dramatic living out in one highly intelligent person of what was happening on a large scale to western culture as a whole with the emergence of modernity. Up until roughly some two centuries ago church rituals and beliefs had played a very important role in promoting psychic health. In Catholicism, for example, the deeply seated psychic change which takes place during the adolescent transition from childhood dependence to adult independence was psychologically aided by the church rituals in that the mother image was enlarged and transferred from the natural mother to Mother Church and the father image similarly transferred from the natural father to the Holy Father.

As Jung interpreted it, Protestantism had already done considerable damage to the psychological (and hence spiritual) benefits of classical Christianity at its best by demolishing much of the visual and dramatic imagery and replacing it with an over-intellectualised and didactic emphasis on doctrine. In the last 200 years, however, modern secularisation had further uprooted western people from the rich cultural process which had nourished the human spirit and promoted psychic health. Their predicament was like that of a plant which begins to wither when its roots are removed from the life-giving soil on which it depends. Jung had experienced this himself when he disengaged himself not only from his father's authority but also from his father's religion. In part, then, it was Jung's own search for a satisfying replacement for the now outmoded tradition of his father which led him in the direction of his analytical psychology.

For such reasons Jung could write near the end of his life, 'Among all my patients over thirty-five there has not been one whose problem in the last resort was not that of finding a religious outlook on life. Everyone of them fell ill because he had lost what the religions of every age have given to their followers and none has been really healed who did not regain his religious outlook. This has nothing to do with any particular creed or church.' Thus Jung placed a very high positive value on having a religious outlook on life, in the broadest sense of that term.

The need for faith of a religious quality Jung believed to be just as real as hunger and the fear of death; he regarded it as the strongest and most original of all the spiritual activities of humankind. He noted that some people deny themselves sex for the sake of religious commitment while others, like Gandhi, have denied themselves food for spiritual purposes. Jung deplored the fact that modernity was bringing about the erosion of the traditional religious systems which had kept humans in a reasonable state of psychic health; it was opening up a dangerous spiritual vacuum. Whereas Freud saw religion as a social neurosis; Jung saw the lack of religion as the cause of neuroses.

This did not mean that for Jung there could be any simple return to the religious traditions of the past. He himself abandoned traditional Christianity, finding that it no longer performed its proper religious function. Yet he believed that it was still possible to draw much from it, and not only from the Christian tradition but from all the great paths of faith. He wanted to leave the door open for the Christian message because of its essential importance for western humankind but he insisted that it had to be reappropriated in a new way in accordance with the general character of the contemporary spirit.

Jung came to believe that, just as the 'collective unconscious' which his researches had uncovered had in the past been the creative seedbed for the classical religious traditions, so it was the key to the recovery of genuine religious experience in the present. He did not think any the less of it just because it was an inner spiritual world and not the external spiritual world it had been taken to be. The inner world of the collective unconscious was for Jung a very real world, a world of mystery, creativity and unlimited potential, to which each person has access and on which each depends for the achievement of wholeness and fulfilment.

In his writings Jung expounds his basic concepts again and again, exemplifying them copiously from dreams. But he was not a systematiser; his writings are discursive. It has been left to others both to develop his ideas further and to put them into some sort of system. They do not all do it in exactly the same way. In what follows I shall draw on the work of others, as well, of course, as on the writings of Jung himself. But it must also be conceded that this is a personal interpretation of Jung and does not claim to be a final or absolute one.

Jung's Model of the Psyche

Psyche is the Greek word (to be roughly translated as 'soul' or 'mind') which is embodied in our word 'psychology' (i.e. the study of the psyche). Freud had already shown that there is much more to the psyche than the stream of consciousness and that which can be readily recalled into it from the memory bank. The psyche refers to the totality of the human being's thinking and feeling processes. It may be regarded as the dynamic process which constitutes each personal identity over and above the purely physical form and the physiological processes. In one sense the psyche is quite non-physical and yet it is undoubtedly bound up with the neurology of the brain, which serves as its physical base of operation.

Because the psyche is a dynamic process it may be likened to physical energy (and psychic energy is often called *libido*). The psyche is a kind of non-physical organism directing the flow of psychic energy. As a rough analogy we may think of the magnetic field which surrounds a magnet. The iron filings experiment which most of us did at school shows how the magnetic energy of the magnet has the power to cause the filings to assume a pattern when they are subjected to kinetic energy, even though there is no physical contact between the filings and the magnet. Another rough analogy is the computer programme. This is a code of directions which is itself non-physical, even though it may be stored in a physical object. Nevertheless it is referred to as software in contrast with the hardware of the computer itself. The psyche, then, is not so much a 'thing' as a code, a pattern of inner relationships. The chief difference between the psyche and the computer programme preserved on a floppy disk is that the psyche is alive, changing, developing and growing in the same way as a physical organism grows.

Jung never asserted that he knew exactly what the psyche is. Even late in life he said, 'I only know that there is a psychical realm in which and from which certain manifestations start.' He likened the psyche to the invisible inside of a mountain from which flows forth a quite large spring of water. He said that all that the modern psychologist could do was to produce, in the symbols of a scientific model, a description of the psychic process, knowing at the same time that the real nature of the psyche transcends us just as much as does the mystery of life or of matter. Jung never claimed to have explained the mystery of the psyche and it is with this proviso that we must approach his distinctive model of it.

Like Freud, Jung recognized that it is very misleading to identify the psyche with consciousness alone; there exists beneath the threshold of consciousness an even vaster segment of the psyche, now referred to as the unconscious. Because our conscious efforts are unable to penetrate it, it remains a mysterious unknown. The unconscious, however, is not inactive. It is quite unlike the life which is preserved inert in a deeply frozen state. The unconscious is a veritable powerhouse of psychic energy which operates ceaselessly. Consciousness is being regularly interrupted by periods of sleep. The unconscious never sleeps.

The most convincing evidence of the existence of the unconscious is the phenomenon of dreaming. Yet since we can recall into consciousness at least some of our dreams, this suggests that even dreams may occur in that area of unconscious which is closest to consciousness. Freud sometimes used the term 'preconscious' to refer to that part of psyche which forms a band between consciousness and the unconscious proper, which contains all memory data capable of being recalled. In the unconscious proper are such things as the repressed memories of unpleasant experiences and of unresolved problems. They continue to play a role in motivating our behaviour without our being aware of their influence.

Where did the content of the unconscious, which supposedly exerts its influence upon us without our realising it, originate? Apart from basic drives, such as sex and hunger, which are instinctive urges which have a physiological base, the content of the unconscious originated in the person's experience of the outside world. Although it is now hidden beneath the level of consciousness it was at one time or another present in the conscious area of the psyche. To put it very simply, Freud believed, with Locke, that the content of the psyche originates in the psyche's experience of the external world, but once the psyche has felt that impact it never really loses touch with it. Either it is stored in our memory bank, to be recalled into consciousness from time to time, or else it becomes buried more deeply in our unconscious. We say we have forgotten the experience but the psyche retains it. Those experiences in particular which caused us special concern or emotional strain when they were in our consciousness leave the deepest imprint in the storehouse we call the unconscious. They continue to influence us, making their presence felt in dreams and nightmares. The phenomenon of dreaming remains the one chief avenue of communication between the unconscious and consciousness; this is why Freud called the analysis of dreams the royal road into the unconscious.

All of Freud's model of the psyche was accepted by Jung with one exception. He came to the conclusion, after studying the personal dreams and the mythology of several quite diverse cultures, that the content of the psyche could not be adequately explained on the theory that it had all passed through consciousness. There was also another source, an innate one, shared by all human beings. So just as Freud had discovered in the psyche a hidden lower story below consciousness, Jung's model added a basement which is even lower. This basement he called the Collective Unconscious, and Freud's unconscious he now renamed the Personal Unconscious. The content of the Collective Unconscious Jung called the Archetypes.

The Collective Unconscious and the Archetypes

The Personal Unconscious contains the forgotten, repressed and subliminally perceived psychic material which has been deposited there out of a person's own experience and which, at some previous time, has passed through the conscious level of the psyche. The Personal Unconscious has been accumulating since birth (and perhaps even from the pre-natal period) and is unique to each person.

Jung became convinced that there exists in each of us from the beginning a second psychic system which, far from being unique and personal, is universal. It is the same in all humans and may even have something in common with the psychic structure of the higher animals. This second psychic system Jung called the Collective Unconscious. 'The collective unconscious,' he wrote, 'contains the whole spiritual heritage of mankind's evolution born anew in the brain structure of every individual' (*The Structure of the Psyche*, p. 158). If this is true it would presumably mean that the Collective Unconscious is transmitted to us in the genetic code but our knowledge of that had not developed when Jung was doing his main work. He simply maintained that just as we inherited, at conception, the capacity to develop the shape and physiology of the human body which has been evolving over millions of years, so also the brain has the capacity to develop a basic psychic system which has been evolving over a very long time. It contains, as it were, our racial psychic past.

This does not mean that the human infant is born with inherited knowledge or ideas which will later rise into consciousness. In this respect Jung is to be sharply distinguished from Plato. What we inherit are aptitudes. This means that we are predisposed to respond to our experience of the external world in mental images which are much the same as those of our ancestors, irrespective of the particular culture into which we are born, and which will undoubtedly fashion the content of our Personal Unconscious.

The existence of the Collective Unconscious cannot be demonstrated empirically because it remains even more hidden than the Personal Unconscious which is open to partial investigation through dreams and hypnosis. Why then did Jung postulate the existence of the Collective Unconscious, seeing that he placed such emphasis on grounding theory in empirical data? Jung arrived at his theory on the basis of his transcultural studies. He found that the symbols, images and motifs which appear in dreams and myths are basically the same in all human cultures past and present. To be more precise, dreams could be divided into two broad classes. There are common dreams which originate in the Personal Unconscious as a result of the individual problems and anxieties a person may have. But there are also great dreams (we shall presently see why they may be called archetypal dreams) which may occur at natural turning-points in one's life, such as puberty, mid-life crisis, approaching old age, etc. It is these latter dreams which show universality. Even then the visual appearance of the figures in the dream may be drawn from one's culture or personal experience but the role played by the figures is basically the same in all cultures. Jung concluded that every human psyche has the capacity or tendency to throw up the same basic dream motifs.

We may illustrate this question of aptitudes with an analogy from the modern science of linguistics. It is maintained by some that the human infant learns language much faster than would be possible if all learning had to be explained in terms of the input of external stimuli. The particular language a child learns is, of course, that of the environment into which it is born and hence called its 'mother's tongue'. Yet without ever having been taught the grammatical structure of that language the child can very soon compose grammatically constructed sentences which the child has never previously heard. There is a deep structure to all languages for which the human child has an innate capacity. It is as if our brain is already programmed for the development of language in the way that the brain of a chimpanzee is not. This human predisposition for language is analogous to the innate aptitudes which Jung believed he had discovered.

Freud, of course, completely rejected Jung's concept of the Collective Unconscious. But Jung pointed out that it was somewhat illogical for him to do so seeing that, even in his own view, he regarded the unconscious as being motivated by innate drives, such as the sexual drive, as well as by repressed memories. In

Jung's view Freud was already acknowledging some innate component in the psyche which is common to all humans. Jung believed he was simply coming to a clearer understanding of this innate structure, which Freud had grossly oversimplified by explaining the psychic process too exclusively in terms of the sexual drive and the oedipus complex.

Jung drew a clear distinction between the physically based instincts such as sex and hunger, and the psychic propensities he called archetypes, and yet he saw a clear parallel between them. In his view the archetypes are to the psyche what the instincts are to the physical body. He thought of instincts as 'modes of existence' in that they do much to determine our behaviour, and these we share with the higher animals. The archetypes he saw as 'modes of apprehension', in that they predispose the way in which we mentally apprehend our experience of the external world.

Just as the instincts have evolved and strengthened over a long period due to their survival value, so have the psychic predispositions. The bird inherits the instinct to build the nest in the way appropriate to its species, the migrating fish inherits the capacity to find its way back to the spawning ground of its species and the human psyche inherits the capacity to reproduce the images and motifs which have proved useful in the past for interpreting experience.

Thus, the Collective Unconscious is as old as the human species. It is timeless, the universal basement of the psyche of every human. On this base there develops the Personal Unconscious, which is only as old as our individual existence. Consciousness is something which is younger again, particularly in the form of a self-conscious identity which emerges only as we grow to adulthood. Jung described the way in which, at the age of eleven, he seemed quite suddenly one day to come out of a mist and consciously realise his own identity. No doubt others have had a similar dramatic experience.

The innate propensities which form the structure of the Collective Unconscious were first of all called by Jung 'primordial images'. But as his thinking progressed he chose the term 'archetypes'. This term he found in the work of the mystical theologian known as Dionysius the Areopagite (c. 500 AD) but it had earlier been used by the Jewish philosopher Philo (c. 40 BC–20 AD), who had in turn been influenced by Plato. In Greek the term *archetupos* means, a prototype, an original pattern or even an originating model. Jung also found that Augustine had used a similar term, *Ideae principales*, to refer to the principal ideas which, in his view, were not created by any individual but were received from the eternal mind of God. In this respect Augustine closely followed the Platonic view of eternal ideas.

Because of the difficulty of saying anything definite about the Collective Unconscious seeing that it remains so hidden from investigation, Jung eventually came to distinguish between the *archetype per se*, which must be presumed to be present in the innate psychic structure even though there is no way of demonstrating it, and what may be called the *actualised archetype*. This refers to the form in which the archetype eventually makes itself visible in dreams, myths and art forms, once the archetype per se has enfleshed itself, i.e. actualised itself, in the psychic material deposited in the Personal Unconscious. The archetype of the Shadow, God or the wise old man, for example, will appear in visual forms which owe something to a particular culture.

When we come to name the particular archetypes, however, Jung's theory becomes a little more confusing. Jung seems to speak as if there is almost an endless supply of archetypes. Indeed he said in one place that there are as many archetypes as there are typical situations in life. Further, he includes in his category of archetypes not only such symbolic figures as the demon, the wise old man, God, the trickster, the hero etc, but concepts like birth, rebirth, death and even natural objects like the sun, moon, fire, the wind and so on. And when Jung's disciples try to bring some order into the clarification of archetypes they do not always say the same thing. Some of the archetypal images are much more convincing than others and of these we shall look at four — the ego, the persona, the shadow and the animus/anima. These all appear to play an important role in the way the psyche itself operates and an appreciation of their function can lead us to a higher level of self-understanding.

The ego is the term Jung uses to refer to the centre of the field of consciousness. Because consciousness is far from being the whole of the psyche, the centre of consciousness or ego must not be confused with the centre of the psyche. The latter is the self and we shall look at that later. The ego appears to possess a high degree of continuity and identity and it is because of the ego that we feel that we are the same person day after day. A little reflection soon reveals to us, however, that this is not wholly true. The ego is also subject to change. We no longer think and view the world in the way we did as children. In fact the ego changes a little from day to day, as a result of every new experience which enters our field of consciousness. Thus there is no permanent and unchangeable ego. The ego is simply the centre of an ever-changing field of consciousness. The feeling of continuity, however, which the ego gives to us, is very important for growth to personal maturity and from the point of view of evolutionary theory it has great survival value. The ego supplies our consciousness with a strong sense of identity and this in turn increases our courage, determination and decisiveness. If we have a poorly developed ego we can be indecisive, inclined to drift as external forces direct us, and be inclined to be puzzled as to who we are and who we ought to try to become. In normal psychic growth we have the innate propensity to develop a clear ego identity and that is why we can speak of the ego as an archetype which has risen up from the Collective Unconscious.

The ego exercises an organising role at the conscious level of the psyche. It has the function of mediating between the outer world and the inner world of the psyche. It acts as a kind of gatekeeper or controller. It can switch attention and is very highly selective with regard to the wealth of sense data (from the outside world) and thought data (from the inside world) with which it is presented. If a person is a thinking type and has a highly developed ego, he or she has great powers of intellectual concentration and can readily shut out external sense data and even thoughts which are not relevant to the line of enquiry being followed. If a person is a feeling type and similarly endowed with a strong ego identity, he or she is quick to note the needs of others within the field of vision.

The ego is the self-conscious 'I', the 'I' that each of us conceives ourselves to be. This includes experiences, memories and thoughts which are very personal and known only to ourselves. For the ego to develop self-confidence and retain a clear sense of identity, it must always remain somewhat private. It is like a tender plant which needs protection. This protective shelter is provided by the archetype for which Jung chose the name 'persona'. This Latin word referred to the mask worn by the actor on the ancient Roman stage in order to make clear to the audience the character role being played. Incidentally it was this very same word which the ancient Latin-speaking theologians chose in order to construct their model of the divine reality. To expound the doctrine of the Trinity as one God in three persons (meaning our modern sense of the word 'person') is a gross distortion of what the ancient theologians intended. They wished to affirm the unity of God but allow for the fact that in their religious experience God had become recognised through different masks — the Father Creator, the Redeemer Son and the empowering Spirit.

The persona is the mask of the psyche which we choose to present to the world. It is our public face. In part it is a deliberate construction of how we would like to be seen by others. It filters out personal traits and thoughts we want to keep private and it accentuates those we would like to be known for. It is constructed in part to meet the expectations, and win the approval, of those to whom we wish to relate, such as parents, teachers, children, lovers, bosses. The clothes we choose to wear are a visible symbol of our persona.

Not only does our persona change in the course of our personal development but it is usually sufficiently flexible to adapt to the different social contexts in which we find ourselves. For example we may choose to present an authoritative or dependable persona in the presence of our offspring, an affectionate and somewhat indulgent persona when alone with our spouse, an efficient and business-like persona when confronting the boss and a jolly good fellow persona with our golfing companions.

While there is considerable social advantage in possessing a multiple or flexible persona, it can become detrimental to psychic growth if the personas vary too much from each other. Then it becomes obvious to others that a person is deliberately playing a part. If there is too great a gulf between the persona and the ego, one gives the impression of insincerity. If a particular persona proves socially successful the ego may try to adopt it permanently; then the ego runs the risk of becoming shallow and empty, and the persona represents only the shell of what ought to be a real or mature person. The tension between the ego and the deliberately chosen persona can be a real hazard for the professional actor.

Jung sometimes spoke of the persona as deriving ultimately from an archetype. The reason is that the persona, by virtue of the way it provides protection for the ego, does have real survival value. It is not surprising if it should have become part of the genetic structure of the embryonic psyche transmitted in the collective unconscious.

An archetype in the structure of the psyche which Jung regarded as being particularly important to understand is what he came to term the shadow. This contains more of one's basic animal nature than any other part of the psyche. It may be regarded as the primitive pre-human component which is still alive and active in us however civilised we may appear on the surface. Morality and civilised rationality mean nothing to the shadow and because it contains the residue of all the primeval urges of our race it can be very dangerous if it is not given adequate recognition.

The shadow may be regarded as the counterpart of the ego. As the ego is the centre of the conscious level of the psyche, so the shadow is the centre of the unconscious. As the structure of the psyche developed in the evolution of the human species towards our present civilised state the previously uncentred psyche developed these two subcentres. As the self-conscious ego formed its own identity in relation of society, it was necessary to hold in check some part of its animal nature. The psychic energy or libido now becomes divided between the ego and the shadow and there is tension between the two. It leads to an inner struggle in the psyche and, because the shadow is hidden from consciousness within the unconscious, the ego is often puzzled by the evidence of this struggle. Dr Jekyll and Mr Hyde in Stevenson's famous classic dramatically portrays this inner conflict through the medium of science fiction.

We have a very good example of this psychic struggle in the well-known words of St Paul (Romans 7: 15–20):

> I do not understand my own actions. For I do the very thing I hate ... So then it is no longer I (*the ego*) that do it, but sin (*the shadow*) which dwells within me. For I know that nothing good dwells in me, that is, in my flesh (*the shadow*). I can will what is right, but I cannot do it. For I do not do the good I want, but the evil I do not want is what I do. Now if I do what I do not want, it is no longer I (*the ego*) that do it, but sin (*the shadow*) which dwells within me.

This personal confession of Paul, supplemented by further Christian reflection including in particular that of St. Augustine, led to the particular emphasis which orthodox Christianity has always placed on the doctrine of sin.

Paul's explanation of his internal struggle stemmed in turn from the rabbinical teaching of the Jewish tradition (where there never developed a doctrine of the Fall and of original sin as in Christianity). The rabbis taught that as humans we are continually being pulled in two directions. We are subject to the *yetzer ha-tov* (the good inclination) which urges us to do the good and we are at the same time subject to the *yetzer ha-ra* (the evil inclination) which pulls us in the direction of what we know to be evil. These two inclinations correspond fairly closely to Jung's concepts of the ego and the shadow.

The shadow, however, should not be regarded as essentially evil. It is amoral rather than immoral. It represents psychic urges which cannot be easily accommodated into the behavioural restraints expected by the society to which the ego must respond. For psychic health it is important to acknowledge the existence of one's shadow. If it is ignored or, worse still, suppressed, very undesirable results may ensue. For example, the mechanism of psychological projection may come into operation by which, unconsciously, one projects one's shadow externally on to someone else. We tend to feel an otherwise irrational animosity towards those people who manifest the same weaknesses as we possess but which we do not wish to acknowledge. Jung contended that this can occur on a collective level and that in the rise of Nazism the German people unconsciously projected their collective shadow on to the Jewish people.

In the Jewish understanding of the human psyche, as outlined above, the inclination to evil (or shadow) was acknowledged to be part of the human condition. In the Christian tradition, by contrast, there was a strong tendency to reject the shadow. It was done first by developing the doctrine of original sin by which the responsibility for the inclination to evil was shifted from oneself and placed on the shoulders of our primeval parents. In the further development of Christian mythology the collective shadow of the human species was projected on to the figure of Satan. This enabled the Christian to retain, at least in his or her own eyes, a certain degree of moral integrity by thinking, 'It was not I who did it but Satan who caused me to do it'.

If we are to grow to psychic maturity, however, it is essential for us to acknowledge and confront the shadow that each of us carries within us. The less we do this the blacker and denser it becomes; the more we do it the more the ego and shadow can complement each other in an harmonious and creative relationship. For example, because we tend to project our shadow on to others when we suppress it, this leads us into personal conflict with them. If we acknowledge our shadow, we may then come to see that what we find wrong with others is something we must face in ourselves. By acknowledging our shadow our relationships with others are improved and we have gained some maturity in self-understanding.

The physical organs which determine our sex as human beings are either wholly male or wholly female and only in very abnormal cases is there any ambiguity. With the psyche, however, there is no such clear and unambiguous distinction, as the phenomena of transvestites and homosexuality illustrate. The sexual character of the psyche seems rather to range over a spectrum between the male and female poles. While the psyche is predominantly nearer to one pole than the other (and usually to the pole corresponding to the physiological sexual distinction), some elements of the contrasexual pole are also present. To refer to these Jung coined the terms 'anima' and 'animus', anima in the male and animus in the female. Each of us, he suggested, also possesses the soul image of the opposite sex. Where a man does not acknowledge his anima or feminine self he rejects emotion (big boys don't cry!) and as a result may become hard and somewhat impersonal. But if his ego is lacking in clear identity, his anima (though in the unconscious) may take over, leading him into a feminine type of behaviour. In a similar way, suggests Dr Jolan Jacobi, a disciple of Jung and herself a woman, 'The animus-possessed woman is opinionative, argumentative, a female know-all who reacts in a masculine way'.

But can we be really as sure as Jung was that we know what it means to behave in a masculine way or in a feminine way? The feminist movement has radically questioned the common stereotypes assumed by Jung with the suggestion that they may be due to cultural conditioning rather than to factors innate in the psyche. It may well be that when we have had time to work through the current feminist critique of sexist attitudes and stereotypes we shall arrive at a clearer understanding of qualities and tendencies which may be legitimately referred to as either female or male. It is unlikely that the feminist critique will have the effect of obliterating all differences in the human psyche, which derive from one's sex. Because the sexes have different roles to play in the regenerative and early nurturing processes on which the perpetuation of the species depends, it is logical to expect that these differences will show themselves in both instinctive behaviour (shared with other animal species) and in psychic characteristics.

Jung saw the anima-animus archetype performing an important function in establishing the deep personal relationships which are essential for healthy psychic growth. He suggested that in early infancy, when the umbilical cord is being replaced by spiritual bonding, it is the projection of the anima archetype on the mother which (unconsciously) enables the infant to 'recognise' the mother and respond in trust. But if this is so, should the female infant be drawn more to the male parent than to the mother? Perhaps there are some differences in infant behaviour here, which Freud fastened on for his famous oedipus complex.

After puberty, however, the anima-animus archetype performs another function in personal relationships. It is this which leads to the almost universal experience of falling in love. This archetype is one's contrasexual component because it is one's mirror image which most perfectly complements one's ego or conscious self. Falling in love with oneself (narcissism) is a distortion of the normal phenomenon of falling in love, where one is attracted to the qualities which one admires but lacks. In one sense they are embryonically there in the anima/animus. But this becomes pro-

jected on the person of the opposite sex who most clearly corres-
ponds to one's own mirror image. It has long been recognized
that some aspects of psychic wholeness can most readily be
achieved, not in personal isolation but in personal relationship,
and particularly in two people of the opposite sex.

All the archetypes (including others there has been no space to
mention) have a role to play in the promotion of psychic health or
wholeness. The most important one, that of the self, we shall look
at later; it is the one which holds all the others in some kind of
complementary balance and its chief functioning period is in the
latter half of life.

Dreams and Visions

Jung always gave credit to Freud for being the first modern to
recognise the importance of dreams and to rescue them from the
hands of the soothsayers. He regarded Freud's *The Interpretation of
Dreams* as his most important work. But Jung gradually developed his own quite distinctive approach. Freud was somewhat
negative in his understanding of both the unconscious and the
phenomenon of dreaming. Freud saw dreams as distorted wish-
fulfilments and regarded the dreaming process as a mechanism for
preserving sleep from the interruptions which repressed psychic
forces might bring. Jung disagreed, claiming that it was just as
true to say that dreams disturb sleep.

Jung always approached the unconscious and the phenomenon
of dreaming in a very positive way. He treated the dream as the
utterance of the unconscious; it was the attempt of the unconscious to communicate something of importance to the conscious
ego. Every dream had its own particular message to convey,
provided it could be adequately interpreted. Jung would have
agreed with the Jewish sage who said, 'A dream unexamined is
like a letter left unopened.' Further, Jung regarded the vision and
fantasy as belonging to the same genus as dreams. There is of
course a slightly higher level of consciousness present in vision
and fantasy, but conscious control still remains absent so that the
creative forces of the unconscious are being allowed freedom to
enter into consciousness relatively unhindered.

The chief function of the dream, according to Jung, is to
compensate for what has been occurring during conscious experience and thus restore equilibrium to the psyche when certain
forces have thrown it out of balance and left it in a disturbed or
fragmented state. Jung claimed that the psyche, just like the
physical body itself, is a self-regulating system of checks and
balances. For example, unprincipled scoundrels may have dreams

of a moralising kind while purtains frequently have immoral dreams of quite lurid quality. Whereas Freud was always searching for the hidden causes (e.g. repressed unpleasant memories) Jung was searching for what the dream was attempting to communicate. He saw each dream as the dreamer's own possession and the dreamer more than anybody else potentially held the key to its interpretation.

Dreams and visions are both examples of a creative flash of insight originating in the unconscious where there has been deposited, as it were, a kind of superior wisdom which has accumulated over many generations. In so far as dreams may be conveying a message about the immediate future (as they were often claimed to be doing in the biblical tradition) they are not saying, 'X, Y and Z will occur and you can do nothing about it'. Rather they are saying, 'If you do not take any notice of what these messages are saying to you, then X, Y and Z are likely to follow'.

To understand the message of the dream it has to be interpreted, i.e. decoded. The reason why the unconscious communicates through symbolic visions and events is that human language is a highly abstract medium of relatively recent emergence and dreams probably long predated it. Only in the modern world are we beginning to develop a conscious appreciation of the role of symbol even though symbolisation has been operating from time immemorial. The German word for 'symbol' is itself quite illuminating. It is *Sinnbild* and literally means a 'meaning-picture' from *Sinn* (meaning) and *Bild* (picture). The recognition that dreams are symbolic in character and need to be interpreted is clearly demonstrated in the biblical story of Joseph, which takes us back at least 2500 years and probably more.

Indeed the importance attached to dreams and visions in the biblical tradition is very open to a Jungian approach. In Ecclesiastes 5:3 we read 'The dream comes in a multitude of busy activities', which could be paraphrased as 'Excessive busyness leads to a night of dreams'. Even more well-known is the observation first found in Joel 2:28, 'Your old men shall dream dreams and your young men shall see visions'.

Dreams were always believed to convey an important message and, since God was thought to be the author of the dream, it consequently was interpreted as conveying a message from God. This is remarkably close to the Jungian approach as soon as one remembers that, for Jung, the collective unconscious houses the 'God' archetype. In the Israelite view, the God of Israel communicated through dreams; in the Jungian view, the archetypes of the collective unconscious communicate through dreams, particularly in times of intense personal crisis. Take for example the dream of Jacob at Bethel. Here is a man in real trouble, fleeing for his life from his brother's fury. Yet it was his own iniquitous behaviour which led to his brother's anger. Jacob is lonely, facing exile in a strange land and obviously at a turning point in his life. He dreams of a ladder stretching to heaven, with angels (themselves the messengers of God) going up and down. God himself appeared at the top of the ladder and delivered to him a message of hope and comfort for the future. In Jungian terms the 'God' archetype was restoring equilibrium to Jacob's disturbed psyche and reviving his faith and self-confidence.

The two books of the Bible which contain little else than dreams and visions, Daniel and Revelation, are now recognised as belonging to a type of ancient literature we call apocalyptic, which flourished among Jews and Christians in the period 200 B.C. to 200 A.D. They are famous (or notorious) for the rich and bizarre imagery which they contain. They are highly symbolic and describe creatures and events which humans have never seen except in dreams. How much the material in these books was consciously composed by their now unknown authors and how much it came unconsciously from the creative power of their unconscious, it is now impossible to say. The author of Revelation tells us he was 'in the spirit on the Lord's day', which may indicate he was in a state of spiritual ecstasy, after which he described the visions he saw.

There is one visionary experience which was so crucial for the development of early Christianity that it is told three times (Acts 9: 1–9, 22: 4–16, 26: 9–18) and referred to in his own words (Galatians 1: 11–17) by the person who experienced it. This is Saul's vision of Christ on the road to Damascus. We have a fairly clear idea of what was going on in Saul's psyche. Here was a devout and zealous Jew who was trying to stamp out what he took to be a dangerous and divisive movement growing up in the aftermath of the crucifixion of Jesus of Nazareth.

Consciously Saul was quite single-minded. But in his unconscious there were other forces at work, motivated by the concern for justice and truth which themselves stem from ageless archetypes. So his subconscious had a message of great import to him, to the effect that the policy on which he was so intent was itself faulty and one-sided. He had become blind to the implications of what he was doing and deaf to the intimations of the archetype of the 'wise old man'. So his unconscious broke through to him in a vision which spoke to him in symbols. He saw a flash of light which blinded him. Light has always been an important symbol of truth. We often say when a new idea enters our consciousness, 'Light dawned!' In his vision (which was neither seen nor heard by those accompanying him in the way it was by Saul) he saw the very Jesus whom he believed to be dead and was actually address-ed by him and charged with being a persecutor. Saul found himself temporarily blinded; his later recovery indicates that this condition had a psychological rather than a physical cause. A Jungian interpretation is that Saul's unconscious was communi-cating to his consciousness, in a quite dramatic way, that he had been spiritually blind in his persecution of Christians. It is impor-tant to note that Saul (later Paul) regarded this (visionary) en-counter with the 'Risen Christ' to be of the same order as those 'appearances' which had happened to Peter and others of the twelve disciples.

Let us now turn back to see in what way Jung's understanding of visions throws light on the origin of Christianity. All agree that Christianity arose quite suddenly after the crucifixion of Jesus with the emergence of the Easter faith, that is, the proclamation that Jesus, though crucified, had risen from the dead. What gave rise to the Easter faith? Of the two sets of reasons offered in the New Testament, the finding of his empty tomb and his sudden 'appearances' to his disciples, it is widely accepted by New Testament scholars that the latter represents the older and more reliable tradition and is the only one of which Paul, the earliest of the New Testament writers, reveals any knowledge.

To appreciate the nature of those 'appearances' it is best to start with the vision of the Transfiguration (Mark 9: 2–8, Matthew 17: 1–8, Luke 9: 28–36). The versions of Matthew and Luke are dependent on that of Mark, which is quite certainly the oldest. It is widely acknowledged today that Mark did not present his material in the original historical sequence, for it was no longer known by the time he was writing. Rather he collected the large number of stories about Jesus circulating among Christians, some of them historical and some of them legendary, and strung them together like beads on a necklace. He simply joined them together with phases like 'and after some days', 'and some time later', 'after that' and 'in those days'.

It is thus quite legitimate to separate the Transfiguration story from its present context and to suggest, as Rudolf Bultmann did, that it does not belong to the period of the Galilean ministry but to the post-resurrection experiences of the disciples. If this is so, a Jungian interpretation is particularly pertinent. We know the dis-ciples must have been deeply disturbed, indeed quite distraught, not only by the loss of their Master but by the shocking way in which it occurred. Going through their minds must have been such questions as: How could this man Jesus, in whom they had found such great spiritual worth, be allowed by God to end his life as an executed criminal? It did not make moral or spiritual sense.

In this state of psychological distress being experienced by the disciples, (and particularly Peter their leader) the unconscious psyche came to the rescue to overcome the trauma and restore equilibrium. It broke through into consciousness in a vision and spoke through symbols, drawing upon hopes, motifs and symbols already embedded there as a result of their Jewish culture and experience. In particular was the conviction that the two historical figures most honoured by devout Jews — Moses the law-giver and Elijah the most exciting and unpredictable prophet — were both believed to be alive and in the divine presence. In the biblical tradition Elijah had been taken up to heaven in a whirlwind and in a post-biblical legend Moses, though he had died and been buried, had also subsequently been taken up by God. Moreover, since at least the second century B.C. it had been held that all Jews, who died as martyrs defending their heritage, would also be raised to a new life and clothed with the garments of glory. In addition it appears that Jesus himself had taught them to look for the resurrection to come. These are just the most obvious samples of the psychic content which lay ready for the unconscious to use.

In the light of these comments let us now look at the Transfiguration narrative. After six days (itself a symbol for the sabbath and the preparation for a new segment of time) Peter, along with James and John found themselves being led up a high mountain (another symbol for breathtaking experiences in which one sees the world as God sees it). There they saw Jesus transformed, wearing robes so dazzling white that no human eye had seen such before, for these were of the kind divinely prepared for the martyrs at the resurrection. But Jesus was no ordinary martyr. Peter saw him in the company of Moses and Elijah, the two Jewish 'greats' who had already won complete divine approval. The vision was thus declaring that the death of Jesus had not been the meaningless disaster they had assumed it to be. Jesus had won the complete approval of God. He had achieved a paramount place in the divine scheme of things and was henceforth to be listened to as the very Son of God.

Another clue indicating the symbolic nature of this visionary experience is the response of Peter — 'Master, let us set up three tents, one for you, one for Moses and one for Elijah'. It is interesting that commentators have always had difficulty interpreting this. Even Mark, the first narrator, inserted, 'He was so afraid, he did not really know what to say'. Interpreted in Jungian terms, the unconscious was saying to Peter, 'You must give to Jesus the same honour you have always given to Moses and Elijah'.

If there is any validity to this way of interpreting the Transfiguration narrative then it means that Jungian analysis may throw light on how the Easter faith arose and that this was one of a series of visionary experiences in which the disciples, starting with Peter, encountered Jesus in a glorified state. If the mountain-top vision had been the first, it would help explain why in oral tradition it was unconsciously transferred back to the pre-crucifixion experiences. It is today generally accepted that the other 'appearances' of Jesus originally took place back in Galilee and only in the course of developing oral tradition did they come to be transferred to Jerusalem and associated with the empty tomb tradition.

Traditional Christians are likely to reject this Jungian account of Christian origins on the grounds that it not only conflicts with the biblical tradition taken at face value but, even more seriously, appears to explain away both its unique character and its divine origin. Jung would have disagreed on both counts. In his view visions must not be lightly dismissed. They are real experiences, communicating an important message from the inner world. (Jung records how, on waking from a dream, he himself had a vision of Jesus appearing in a glorified state.) Moreover, he approached the unconscious of the psyche with something of the same wonder and awe as Christians feel towards God.

Christians and other non-Muslims may more readily appreciate the significance of the Jungian interpretation of religious experience if we apply it to Muhammad. It is almost certain that the material preserved in the Qur'an was first uttered by Muhammad before it was committed to memory by his followers and subsequently written down. This material is expressed in such fine Arabic poetry that Muslims regard it to this day as proof that it originated with God and was delivered to Muhammad through the angel Gabriel as Muslim tradition has always claimed. Even non-Muslim Arabic linguists agree about the quality of the poetry. This raises a dilemma for non-Muslims. Either we should concede that it comes from God (in which case in all honesty we should become Muslims) or we must conclude that Muhammad not only composed it but knew that he had composed it (in which case he was guilty of a hoax in making out that he had received it through the agency of Gabriel). In actual fact such historical evidence as we possess about Muhammad suggests that he was a man of honesty and integrity who would not have stooped to such deception. A Jungian interpretation enables us to resolve this dilemma without forcing Muhammad into the role of a deceiver. It was not his ego who consciously composed this material; in a trance-like state he did hear these poems spoken to him but they originated in his own creative unconscious. The fact that he had these experiences is not wholly surprising for he was a very sensitive person who was already deeply troubled by the feuding among his people and the moral excesses which occurred at the religious ceremonies. Having secretly admired what he had observed in other religious traditions, particularly Judaism, his unconscious came to his aid to resolve his spiritual dilemma.

In a similar way a Jungian appreciation of the creative role of the unconscious may help to explain the origins of Mormonism and how Joseph Smith (another spiritually tortured soul from all accounts) came to write the Book of Mormon. We may conjecture that his unconscious dictated it to him, as it were, in a state so trance-like that he fully believed himself the explanation he was to give to others as to how he had received it.

In the light of Jungian analysis there is no longer any need to accuse religious seers and prophets of setting out consciously to deceive, though it may well be that after careful examination we may conclude in some cases they have misinterpreted their own experiences. The value of the Jungian approach is that it allows for the very real spiritual values, the creativity and the legitimate sense of mystery all present in religious experience and at the same time preserves for the conscious ego the role of critic so that by adequate criticism religious experience may be interpreted and used in the way which best achieves self-fulfilment.

Types of Personality

As Jung pondered the rifts which had occurred among the three pioneering colleagues of depth psychology — Freud, Adler and himself — he stumbled across what he came to call the psychology of type. He came to realise that all three of them were different psychological types, and this helped to explain why they saw things so differently. In his book *Psychological Types* (1921) he set out to deal with the various ways in which a person may relate to the world, to people and to things. He came to the conclusion, not only from clinical evidence but from a study of biography and literature, that 'every judgment made by an individual is conditioned by his personality type and that every point of view is necessarily relative'. (*Memories, Dreams and Reflections*, p. 207).

In his analysis of the various psychological types into which we humans fall, Jung first of all distinguished between the two opposing attitudes which the psyche may adopt and of which one is usually more dominant than the other. He referred to these basic attitudes as extrovert and introvert and his terminology has subsequently come into general use. In the extrovert attitude our attention is focused on the world outside of us; in the introvert attitude our attention is focused on our own thoughts and feelings. Our attention cannot be focused on both areas at the same time. In practice we are continually switching from one to the other. But one of these attitudes is normally more dominant and that determines our type.

The extrovert is a person whose psychic energy is directed more commonly outwards to things, to people, to objective data being received through the senses. The extrovert relates with great ease to the external world and can quickly become involved in sport, social activities, public issues and the political arena. By the same token, the extrovert may be ill at ease when challenged to spend time in meditative reflection and often depreciates the intellectual and spiritual activities in which others choose to engage.

By contrast the introvert turns very naturally and happily to the inner, subjective world, exploring his or her own feelings, thoughts and experiences. Introverts are glad to retreat from the 'madding crowd'. They feel most at ease in their own company. They often become bookworms. In more extreme cases they may withdraw, in an unbalanced way, from the world and live in a world of their own. Introverts are not attracted to team sports and other social activities.

The extrovert and the introvert, even though they are presented with the same object or situation, experience it in different ways. The extrovert tends to respond wholeheartedly and exclaim, for example, 'How wonderful!'. The introvert reflects on the impact made on him or her and confesses, 'That makes me very happy!'. In view of his compensatory theory of the role of dreams, Jung contended that the extrovert often becomes an introvert in dream life and the introvert becomes an extrovert.

In quite a different category from these two basic attitudes Jung concluded that the psyche engages in four basic functions which occur in two pairs of polar opposites. When asked why there are four and only four, he replied, 'I can only say that this number has shaped itself out of many years of experience.' He believed these four exhaust all the possibilities. One pair he called the Rational Functions: they are Thinking and Feeling. The other pair he called the Irrational Functions; they are Sensation and Intuition. In every person one function becomes dominant and then its polar opposite is the weakest of all and may be denied the opportunity to develop. One of the other pair of functions plays an auxiliary role, giving support to the major function.

The Thinking Function of the psyche is perhaps the easiest for us to grasp seeing that the psyche has popularly been known as the mind. Thinking has to do with recognising and using concepts, connecting ideas together, drawing logical inferences, developing arguments, making judgments about truth and falsehood. The raw material with which the Thinking Function works comes from two sources — the objective data supplied by the senses and the subjective data stored in the memory. (The latter has partly come from cultural conditioning and has been shaped in part by the archetypal images rising from the collective unconscious.) The extrovert depends more on objective data and the introvert more on the subjective. Jung concluded from observation that the Thinking Function is more commonly found to be dominant in males than in females.

The Feeling Function is also rational and is not to be confused with sensuality. It exercises an evaluative role. Whereas the Thinking Function enables one to discern the true from the false, it is the Feeling Function we draw upon for making moral, and aesthetic judgments, discerning, that is, between the right and the wrong, the pleasant and the unpleasant, the beautiful and the ugly. It is what people are referring to when they say they have arrived at a certain conviction because of a 'gut feeling'. The Feeling Function is particularly important in building human relationships. In making friendships and in falling in love, people are guided almost wholly by feeling and very rarely by logic. Jung, again on the basis of experience, concluded that the Feeling Function is more commonly found to be dominant in females than in males.

While the rational psychic functions have to do with making judgments of one kind or another, the irrational (or preferably non-rational) functions have to do with the way we comprehend the nature of reality. For those in whom the function of Sensation is dominant, reality is to be found in that which is tangible, visible, audible. There is distrust of theory and speculation, and any notion claiming to be based on intuition is quickly dismissed as groundless. For them the real world is solid, objective, materialistic.

Those in whom the Intuitive Function is dominant seek the reality behind the visible and the tangible. They are more interested in the possible than the actual. They are looking for the hidden relations which are operating. The Intuitive Function relies heavily on the unconscious and raises to consciousness ideas and inner connections which are not immediately perceivable and, if they can be arrived at all by a process of logical reasoning, it is by a route much slower than the flash of insight.

When we link the two possible dominant attitudes with the four possibilities for the major function, we arrive at eight combinations or basic personality types, which we may briefly describe and exemplify as follows:

1. The Extroverted Thinkers tend to be practical people, solvers of external problems. They are drawn to the pursuit of empirical science, economics, military strategy and careers involving management and rationalising of resources. We find examples in Aristotle, Adam Smith, Darwin, Einstein.

2. The Introverted Thinkers are interested in ideas for their own sake and pursue speculative trains of enquiry. They are prone to philosophise, either at the academic or popular level, and are often fascinated by the nature of the human condition. We find examples in Plato, Descartes, Kant, Nietzsche and many theologians. Jung saw himself in this category and recognised intuition as his second most important psychic function.

3. The Extroverted Feeling Types are interested in other people for their own sakes rather than for any light they throw on the human condition. They readily forget their own needs in order to see that the needs of others are met. They develop an acute moral sense, and are found in the vanguard of moral crusades. They are drawn to the serving professions, such as nursing. Florence Nightingale and Mother Teresa are good examples but so also were the Israelite prophets and perhaps this is where Jesus of Nazareth is to be placed.

4. The Introverted Feeling Types may go through agonies because of the world's starving millions, but because they internalise such problems and take the suffering upon themselves, they are often powerless to achieve more practical solutions. They often become silent and melancholy because they are unable to verbalise or express externally what they feel. They are drawn to intercessory prayer, to poetry and often to a solitary life. Gautama the Buddha may have been of this type and so also are ascetics.

5. The Extroverted Sensation Types are quite clearly the sports lovers, the practical, down-to-earth activists who enjoy life as it comes and do not concern themselves with whether life holds any ultimate meaning. They can be pleasure-loving and thrill-seeking but not necessarily in any crude sense. They see themselves as

realists and are drawn to an epicurean philosophy of 'Eat, drink and be merry for tomorrow we die'. Examples are so frequent, particularly among the New Zealand male, that we hardly need to specify them further.

6. The Introverted Sensation Types find the outer world uninteresting and unsatisfying and turn inwardly to seek fulfilment. They persist with the religious rituals long after other personality types have abandoned them. Through the ages they have been drawn to mysticism; perhaps the existence of this type explains why the mystical stream has surfaced in all the major religious traditions. This type is drawn to the use of psychedelic drugs on the one hand or to the supposed gifts of glossolalia on the other. Muhammad may well have belonged to this Type.

7. The Extroverted Intuitive people enter new relationships with great gusto but do not always prove dependable. They can move quickly from one new interest to another, especially if it is not immediately fruitful. They have visions of new worlds to conquer or to build. They are promoters of new causes. We may name as examples Alexander the Great, Julius Caesar, Napoleon, Hitler, Henry Ford and builders of today's economic empires.

8. The Introverted Intuitive people are dreamers and visionaries who draw from their inner resources. They tend to live in a world of their own and often feel out of place in their social environment and even their own historical age. They can turn out to be really creative in the visual arts, literature and music and are often not recognised until after their death. On the other hand they may simply be judged as cranks, both in their own day or later, because they were so out of touch with what others regarded as reality. Possible candidates for this category are the anonymous author of the Book of Revelation, William Blake, Franz Kafka and James K. Baxter.

These eight personality types may be doubled to sixteen by considering which of the other pair of functions becomes the auxiliary to the main function. The more one follows this procedure, however, the more artificial the analysis tends to become. It is a mistake to think that every person, on analysis, can be quickly and unambiguously placed in even one of eight types, let alone sixteen. The value of this typology is to use it as a guide to discern what may stand out in our own type of personality. The more we are able to do this the more we grow in self-understanding.

It is possible during the course of life to undergo personality change. Just because we appear to belong to a distinct personality type at one point in life does not mean that we are fixed in it for all time. To recognise which type we conform to most not only helps us to understand more clearly our moods, responses and feelings, but it helps us to pinpoint which psychic functions we are allowing to atrophy. All psychic functions are of equal value to human personality. All have a positive role to play, and in a well-balanced and mature psyche all should be encouraged to function as fully as possible even though one may still show a tendency to play the leading role. The acknowledgment of psychological types is an essential first step if we are to appreciate Jung's concept of individuation, the process by which each of us becomes the one unique and whole human person we have the potential to become.

Self-Realisation or the Process of Individuation

In an essay written only four years before his death, 'The Undiscovered Self' (included in *Civilization in Transition*), Jung analysed the plight of the individual in modern society. Because of the rise of modern science and technology and the move from village communities to immense metropolitan areas, an increasing number of people are being tempted to think of themselves as impersonal units, statistical fodder and individually insignificant. Modern authoritarian states are robbing the individual of dignity, personhood and self-confidence. Jung contended that modern humankind has become increasingly divorced from the ancient spiritual resources preserved in the unconscious. These have normally in the past become available through religious symbolism. The archetypes rising up from the collective unconscious normally function in their role of promoting psychic health by manifesting themselves in symbols — symbolic concepts and images and ritualistic practices.

The various great religious traditions of the past, according to Jung, had played an essential role in promoting and protecting human individuality and personhood. They had the capacity to promote psychic health or wholeness. He once referred to them as 'the world's great psychotherapeutic symbol systems'. In modern times, however, they had become over-rationalised, and crystallised into rigid dogmas and credal systems, and were very little different from the ideologies of communism and scientific materialism to which they were bitterly opposed. Jung believed the solution to the spiritual predicament of modern humankind in the mass was in his analytical psychology. It provided the true diagnosis and the only possible cure. This he expressed in what he called the process of individuation.

Individuation may be defined as the process of psychic growth by which a human being becomes the one fully developed, whole, unique individual person that this person alone has the potential to become. This does not of course mean becoming individualistic, egocentric or self-centred. It means becoming one's own true self.

It is in the psyche, much more than the physical body alone, that we find the essential person. Adequate psychic development means personal development. Psychic health means personal wholeness. It is not accidental that the word 'health' is etymologically derived from the root 'whole'. Health means wholeness. It is further to be noted that, in the Gospel stories of how Jesus is reported to have brought spiritual salvation to some of his contemporaries, we read quite simply that he made them whole. The human goal of achieving wholeness (in Jungian terms) is what was being expressed in the basic questions of traditional religion— 'What must I do to be saved?', 'What must I do to gain eternal life?', 'How do I find fulfilment?'.

The process of individuation, or the road to self-realisation, Jung found useful to divide into two successive periods in life. In the first half of life, up to middle age, the main need of the psyche and the main thrust of psychic energy is to become fully adjusted to external reality. This involves the finding of an ego identity, the formation of an adequate persona and the establishment of an harmonious relation between the individual and the demands of the environment, which of course includes human society. In the second half of life the main task of the psyche is to complete psychic wholeness by becoming fully adjusted to internal reality. This means understanding and accepting one's inner reality, the mysterious psychic world of the unconscious. The total process can be spoken of as growth in self-understanding. It could also, as we shall presently see, be termed growth in God-consciousness.

There is a sense in which every new-born child is in a state of wholeness but it is a state of undifferentiated wholeness. A seed is whole, but the roots, the trunk, the branches, the leaves, the flowers, the fruit, into which it will grow (and roughly in that order) are only potentially there. They are not as yet differentiated or individualised. In an analogous way the psyche of an infant is whole but is yet to develop into its individual components, thereby achieving a much richer quality of wholeness. Where this growth process does not occur evenly, each step at the appropriate time, then malfunctioning and fragmentation of the psyche may result. The psyche may be engaged in war with itself. We may speak of an inner conflict. The process of individuation is spontaneous and natural, analogous to physical growth. Just as diet and physical exercise assist the latter, so individuation may be aided by ideal conditions and impeded by adverse ones.

In the pre-natal and early infant stages there is no awareness of an ego to be distinguished from the environment. The ego is only latently present. This has been called the uroboric stage, from the symbol of the tail-eating serpent. It is possible that the sub-human animals remain for ever at this stage. Then comes the birth of consciousness and the first glimmerings of an emerging ego. As the child learns to speak it takes a little time to learn the use of 'I' in preference to the proper name by which the child has referred to itself hitherto.

The development of the ego, from those first glimmerings to the more fully developed self-consciousness usually occurring with the onset of puberty, takes quite some years. In the initial stages the mother normally plays a vital role, for the breaking of the umbilical cord at birth is replaced by spiritual bonding; and by loving care and verbal communication the mother, as it were, draws the embryonic ego into reality. Jung contended that the archetype of the great mother enables the child to respond; this archetype is unconsciously projected on to the actual mother and she is thus recognised for what she is.

In due course, however, the feminine tie grows weaker and is replaced by attachment to masculine authority. The archetype of the great father becomes dominant and in earlier times was ritualised in initiation rites. Thus the matriarchal stage is followed by a patriarchal stage. It is interesting to see how this process came to be reflected in Catholicism. One's spiritual birth and nurture take place in the bosom of Mother Church but as one moves towards responsible adulthood one is expected to give obedience to the father figure manifested in an all-male priesthood and particularly the Holy Father, the Pope. These stages in psychic growth may be re-enacting in the short span of a person's life the same basic stages of cultural life in the evolution of the human species, especially if it is true, as some feminists maintain, that the patriarchal culture of the last few thousand years was preceded by a matriarchal culture which, in turn, in the far distant past, was preceded by the uroboric stage of our animal-like origins.

After the patriarchal stage should come the integrative phase when the matriarchal and patriarchal components are reconciled and transcended. In this process pairs of opposites achieve a balance. The male ego recognises its female anima and the female ego recognises its animus. But the key to the process is the archetype of the self, which is now to be clearly distinguished from the ego. The ego is the centre of consciousness and, when well developed, gives a strong conscious sense of identity. But since consciousness is only a part of the psyche the ego cannot be the centre of the psyche. At the centre of the psyche, and circumscribing both the conscious and unconscious areas, is the self, the essential person. What we commonly refer to as an egocentric person is one in whom the ego is trying to usurp the place of the self. For psychic growth 'the ego, once the monarch of totality, is dethroned' (as Jung once said).

The archetype of the self rises up from the collective unconscious where it has existed in a kind of timeless world, constituting the human potential for personhood. The task of the archetype of the self is to embrace all the psychic components and harmonise them into a living whole. The ego must come to terms with the self in much the same way as, in traditional religion, the conscious ego has been encouraged to submit in obedience to God.

There is much more than an analogy involved here. When the ego comes to appreciate the self, or psychic totality of which it forms a part, we may speak of this as growth in self-understanding. In religious tradition it has been referred to, however, as growth in the knowledge of God. Psychologically speaking, the archetype of the self and the archetype of God are one and the same.

This at first sounds quite shocking to many western ears. It is not at all so in the East. The great spiritual insight reached in the Hindu Upanishads was the recognition that brahman (ultimate reality) and atman (human spirit) are really one and it is only the illusion brought on by ignorance which causes us to think otherwise. The religious goal of liberation, *moksha*, sought by the Hindu, is the existential realisation of this truth.

Even in the Christianity of Eastern Orthodoxy the affinity of the self with the reality called God was not entirely foreign, for there the process of Christian salvation has long been referred to in terms of 'deification', i.e. the way in which we humans or sons of God, realise our potential divinity. And the reason for this is that the seeds of it are already there in the New Testament. Note Paul's affirmation in Galatians (2:20): 'I have been crucified with Christ (*identification*); it is no longer I (*ego*) who live but Christ lives in me.' In Jungian terms Paul is saying that his ego no longer reigns supreme but has become reconciled with Christ, who is now his true self.

In a similar way the words placed in the mouth of the Johannine Christ open themselves up to a Jungian interpretation. 'He who has seen me has seen the Father...I am in the Father and the Father in me... I and the Father are one.' Of course this has traditionally been taken to mean how different the divine Christ and the Father are from humans, overlooking the fact that in the same context we read 'In that day you will know that I am in the Father and you in me and I in you.' In other words the God-consciousness or the attainment of true self-hood as manifested in Jesus the Christ is potentially attainable by all.

What has happened in the western religious tradition, much more so than in the East, is that by the psychological mechanism known as projection, our spiritual forebears projected this basic archetype on to an external reality, having no appreciation of their own unconscious depths. Only the medieval mystics thought otherwise. Meister Eckhart, for example could say, 'The eye with which I see God and the eye with which God sees me is one and the same eye.'

The first modern theologian to stumble on some glimmerings of all this was Ludwig Feuerbach who, in his book The *Essence of Christianity*, contended that the real truth about God (the 'true theology' as against the 'false theology' of tradition) is that we have unconsciously objectified into an external reality everything which we inwardly have recognised to be of great value. God is love, justice, goodness, purity etc. magnified to the nth degree. As a result of this projection we humans are left only with the dregs. The more righteous we conceive God to be the more sinful we become. Thus an unbridgeable moral gulf opens up between the wholly righteous God and the wholly sinful human race. Because the very concept of God is a projection of values and aspirations which were originally internal to humankind, this gulf means that the human has become alienated from his true or better self.

Whereas the traditional or 'false' theology expounded the Christian salvation as the means by which sinful humankind is reconciled with God, Feuerbach's 'true theology' expounded Christianity as the way in which the divided human self becomes reintegrated. In other words spiritual salvation consists of achieving personal wholeness. Moreover, by ingeniously standing classical Christian doctrine upside down (or, as he said, 'the right way up'), Feuerbach interpreted Christianity as the religion intended to bring the end to objective theism. He made the doctrine of the incarnation central, claiming that the reason why 'God' could become human was simply because the God image was human in the first place. The death of Jesus on the cross dramatically portrayed the death of 'God' and the end of objective theism. Humans henceforth were liberated from the condition of the divided self into which the projection of their better part into

'God' had led them and they were now free to become whole.

Feuerbach was so ahead of his time that he was largely rejected and later he has rarely been fully appreciated. Even so, because he also preceded the rise of modern psychology, he lacked the psychological explanation of how the projection of 'God' could have taken place initially. Jung's theory of the collective unconscious and the archetypes not only supplies this lack but also preserves a sense of mystery and an awareness of the inner complexity of the human psyche, which seem to be missing in Feuerbach's more mundane analysis.

The recognition that the archetype of God and the archetype of the self (seeking full realisation) are one and the same, is by no means as much at variance with western religious experience as it may first be thought. Indeed it throws new light on many traditional affirmations. When a person says, 'I believe God is telling me to do...', is he or she not referring to a conviction which has risen into consciousness from the unconscious realms of the psyche? The fact that this conviction did not originate in consciousness is shown by the fact that at first the ego may have tried to smother it, being fearful of it, and only after some time become persuaded of the rightness of this inner direction coming from the fuller self (interpreted traditionally as the voice of God).

The inner source of the voice of 'God' was clearly recognised in the early Judeo-Christian tradition. In Acts we read of the Apostles saying, 'It seemed good to us and the Holy Spirit to...' But above all it was built into the symbolic formulation known as the Holy Trinity, the popular understanding of which is a meaningless distortion of what was originally intended. We may say, in Jungian terms, that the symbol of the Holy Trinity was arrived at in this way. Whereas in ancient polytheism it had been customary to project most of the archetypes on to the objective world, it was the genius of the Israelite tradition to deny objective reality to all the gods but One God. This was a very important step in the direction of the integration of the psyche and the realisation of the one true self. In effect the Israelites projected the archetype of their collective self on to the external objective symbol of the Creator and Providential Guide of their people.

The first Christians, being Jews, inherited and continued to embrace this projection. But soon they had problems as they began to reflect on their experience. For the man Jesus of Nazareth made such a spiritual impact on them that the archetype of the self, seeking to be realised within them, was projected also on him. In addition to this, however, they continued to be aware of the voice which spoke to them from within. They called it the Holy Spirit, as Quakers were later to call it the Inner Light. As they wrestled with what at first appeared to be conflicting media of revelation, they eventually tried to resolve it with the formula of the Trinity.

Just as the human psyche, as we have seen above, may have a multiple persona, so the spiritual reality encountered by the conscious ego has been experienced by Christians under three personas — a cosmic persona (Creator Father), an historical persona (Jesus of Nazareth, in whom humanity was fully revealed) and the persona of an inner dynamic power (the Holy Spirit). But these three are in essence also one. They are one because, in Jungian terms, the first two are external projections of the archetype of the self continuing to be active in the third.

Those who take comfort in the conviction that God is an objective reality, a kind of supernatural being wholly external to themselves, are likely to reject this Jungian view of God, overlooking the fact that in doing so they may well be rejecting the Christian doctrine of the Trinity. Much of what has been written and thought in defence of objective theism has been much more consistent with the ancient Greek understanding of God than it ever has been with the classical doctrine of the Trinity. It is ironical that the insights of Jung may come closer to the classical doctrine of the Trinity than has the philosophical theism of the Western intellectual tradition.

To identify the archetype of God with the archetype of the self, i.e. to equate God with the inner voice, does have its dangers. We know only too well how frail and fallible is human thought and judgment, and how ambiguous, as a consequence, the inner voice of the unconscious often turns out to be. For this reason the conscious ego has a very important critical role to play in holding up to careful examination every intimation or message which comes from the unconscious. By this means at least some of the dangers are averted. It is actually the traditional view, however, which is much more dangerous. It is the person who believes implicitly that every intimation from the unconscious is not really from that source at all but from an external objective deity, who is much more to be feared. Such persons become so absolutely sure that they are in possession of the absolute truth that, abandoning all self-criticism, they tend to become fanatics.

The fanatic has taken a blind road deviating from the path of individuation. It is a road on which the ego has surrendered its critical role and usurped the role of the self. In the name of obedience to an objective deity, the ego has unknowingly appointed itself as the deity, often enjoying the self-aggrandisement which supposedly belongs to it.

In the process of individuation, by contrast, the ego and all the other components of a fully-developing psyche are left free to perform their particular functions in ways complementary to one another, the self providing the integrative force. In one sense the goal of complete wholeness is never reached during life in any final or absolute way. It is something we are ever trying to achieve more fully as long as we live. The fact that absolute wholeness is an unattainable ideal is no argument against it. It is striving for the goal which brings zest and meaning to life. The spiritual satisfaction symbolically portrayed in the goal is in fact being experienced in the process leading to it.

This application of Jung's process of individuation to the traditional terminology of religion has drawn chiefly on the Christian tradition. With some adjustment it can be applied to other traditions also. What St. Paul referred to as the Christ dwelling within him, some Buddhists would describe in terms of discovering the Buddha-nature within, and some Hindus would describe in terms of realising their oneness with brahman. Jung believed that all of these could be paths of individuation leading to psychic wholeness. He found this wholeness expressed in the art form known as the mandala, where there is a symmetrical balance of opposites and harmony of diverse colours. The mandala is a visual representation of the archetype of the self seeking wholeness, a symbol of wholeness achieved, a symbol of God.

Bibliography

A. BOOKS BY JUNG

Psychological Types: its Theory and Practice, Kegan Paul, 1923
Modern Man in Search of a Soul, Paul, Trench, Trübner, 1933
The Integration of the Personality, Kegan Paul, 1972
Memories, Dreams and Reflections, Collins, 1963
Man and His Symbols, Dell, 1964 (Only the first ninety-five pages
  are by Jung, but it is one of the last things he wrote.)
Psychological Reflections, anthology ed. by Joland Jacobi & R. F. C.
  Hull, Princeton U.P., 1953

B. BOOKS ABOUT JUNG AS A PERSON

Laurens van der Post, *Jung and the Story of our Time*, Penguin,
  1978
Vincent Broome, *Jung*, Macmillan, 1978

C. BOOKS ABOUT JUNG'S IDEAS

Joland Jacobi, *The Psychology of C. G. Jung*, Routledge and Kegan
  Paul, 1968
E. A. Bennett, *C. G. Jung*, Barrie and Rockliff, 1961
E. A. Bennett, *What Jung Really Said*, Harvill Press, 1966
Marie I. van Franz, *C. G. Jung: his Myth in our Time*, Putnam's
  Sons, 1975
Antonio Moreno, *Jung, Gods & Modern Man*, Sheldon Press, 1974
John Sandford, *Evil — The Shadow Side of Reality*, Crossroad,
  1981
Wallace B. Clift, *Jung and Christianity*, Dove Comm., 1983
Christopher Bryant, *Jung and the Christian*, Darton, Longman and
  Todd, 1983